Worship in the Early Church

Worship in the Early Church

Justo L. González

Catherine Gunsalus González

WESTMINSTER
JOHN KNOX PRESS
LOUISVILLE · KENTUCKY

First English edition
Published by Westminster John Knox Press
Louisville, Kentucky

Spanish edition, *El culto en la iglesia antigua*,
published in 2021 by Editorial Mundo Hispano

22 23 24 25 26 27 28 29 30 31—10 9 8 7 6 5 4 3 2 1

Scripture quotations from the NRSV are from the New Revised Standard Version of the Bible, copyright © 1989 by the Division of Christian Education of the National Council of the Churches of Christ in the U.S.A., and are used by permission.

Book design by Sharon Adams
Cover design by Mary Ann Smith

Library of Congress Cataloging-in-Publication Data

Names: González, Justo L., author. | González, Catherine Gunsalus, author.
Title: Worship in the early church / Justo L. González, Catherine Gunsalus González.
Other titles: El culto en la iglesia Antigua. English
Description: First English edition. | Louisville : Westminster John Knox Press, 2022. | "Justo L. González and Catherine Gunsalus González Spanish edition, El culto en la iglesia Antigua, published in 2021 by Editorial Mundo Hispano." | Summary: "Written for students in introduction to worship and church history classes, this resource will serve as a valuable guide to the historical developments that brought about Christian worship as we know it today"—Provided by publisher.
Identifiers: LCCN 2022027355 (print) | LCCN 2022027356 (ebook) | ISBN 9780664267827 (paperback) | ISBN 9781646982653 (ebook)
Subjects: LCSH: Church history—Primitive and early church, ca. 30–600. | Public worship—History.
Classification: LCC BR162.3 .G6613 2022 (print) | LCC BR162.3 (ebook) | DDC 270.1—dc23/eng/20220725
LC record available at https://lccn.loc.gov/2022027355
LC ebook record available at https://lccn.loc.gov/2022027356

Most Westminster John Knox Press books are available at special quantity discounts when purchased in bulk by corporations, organizations, and special-interest groups. For more information, please e-mail SpecialSales@wjkbooks.com.

Contents

A Word to the Reader

The present book is the outcome of two parallel but different paths that each of its two authors has followed. Originally, Catherine's interest centered on liturgy and worship. which slowly led her to the study of theology and history. While she focused on worship, Justo was particularly interested in theology. That interest led him to the study of history—particularly the history of theology—and to the slow but continuous discovery of the indissoluble relationship between worship and its practices on one hand, and doctrine on another. These two different paths have converged to the point that now we both consider the history of worship as absolutely necessary if we are to understand the development of theology as well as the history of the church.

Given that background, it is important to note that the book has been written jointly; but not in the sense that each of us wrote certain sections and the other the rest, but rather in the sense of a full collaboration in which we have jointly discussed and outlined what the book should include, and conducted the necessary research in ancient writings and other resources available to us.

Although this book deals with the history of Christian worship, it is not a history of worship. The field itself of the history of worship is enormous, and it includes a vast number of questions that specialists are still discussing. While there are many histories of Christian worship, such histories, precisely because they need to deal with so many debatable issues, are not readily available or interesting to the common reader. They certainly are helpful in understanding details as to various practices, or regarding the evolution of a hymn or ancient formula, and this is of great value. Our goal here is both more modest and more urgent. We are not seeking to give our readers a detailed discussion of each of the elements in worship. What we wish is simply to help worship leaders and believers in general relate their worship with that of the ancient church, not because one is better than the other, but rather because that dialogue between generations and centuries will lead to insights that will enrich today's worship—and it is out of its worship that the church lives and has lived over the ages.

This is why in this book we say little or nothing about several ceremonies, practices, and contexts that are certainly important, but are not directly related to the weekly worship in most of our churches today. This includes matters such as the manner in which pastors and leaders were chosen and ordained or commissioned, the history of marriage ceremonies, details about the monastic hours of worship, the origin of various liturgical formulae, and much more. When it has seemed significant, we have referred to some of these issues and practices, but they have not been the focus of this study.

That focus is those elements of worship in the ancient church that are most closely related to worship in most Protestant churches, usually on Sundays. These common essential elements in worship are basically three: preaching, baptism, and Communion. Therefore, in each section of the present book we shall be studying those three subjects—usually in the same order. Our interest is not so much what was done and said, but rather why such things were said and done—in other words, not so much the practice of worship itself as the theology—or theologies—expressed in that practice and shaped by it. Thus we hope to move beyond our present and mostly fruitless debates on worship and into a deeper exploration of the understanding of the church and of the gospel that shapes worship itself. In brief, our purpose is not to let the history of worship be known, but rather to help readers have access to valuable elements of ancient Christian worship that may help us in our reflection and in our present debates about our own worship and our mission as the church. If this book makes a contribution along those lines, we shall be more than amply rewarded.

Abbreviations

ANF   Ante-Nicene Fathers
BAC   Biblioteca de Autores Cristianos
FoC   Fathers of the Church
Mansi   Sacrorum conciliorum amplissima collectio
NPNF1   Nicene and Post-Nicene Fathers, Series 1
NPNF2   Nicene and Post-Nicene Fathers, Series 2
PG   Patrologia Graeca, Migne
PL   Patrologia Latina, Migne

Note: In quotations from ANF, NPNF1, and NPNF2, changes have been introduced to conform with more modern usage.

Introduction

Scope, Limits, and General Parameters of This Study

Before moving into the subject of ancient Christian worship itself, it will be helpful to give the reader a general idea of what is to follow, how it is organized, and to what goal it is directed.

First of all, a word about worship as a general theme. Both authors have devoted long years to the study of the history of doctrine and of Christian thought, as well as of the history of the life and organization of the church, its impact in the world, and several other similar subjects. But another subject has captivated our interest, and is in fact the bond joining these various aspects of Christian history. That subject is worship—meaning by that specifically the time in which a congregation jointly worships God, and the various practices that this entails.

In order to understand any religion, it is not enough to know its doctrines, or to know how it is organized or how it impacts society. The expression of faith in worship must also be taken into account. For instance, in order to understand the religion of ancient Aztecs it is not enough to know what they said about their gods, the origins of things, or the birth of their own people. Nor is it enough to take into account the manner in which those ancient myths were expressed in the social order. One must also take into account Aztec worship—its sacrifices, rites, and prayers. The same is true of Hinduism, Buddhism, Islam, or any other religion. It is through its worship—public, within the household, or in private—that a religion makes its greatest impact on the lives of its followers.

This means that in order to understand Christianity, it is not enough to know its doctrines, or even to know the history of the various ways in which the church has been organized and has related to the surrounding society. One also has to understand Christian worship—worship in its widest sense,

1

meaning all that Christian people do jointly in their devotion to their God. Therefore, while we have both written abundantly on the history of Christian thought and the history of the church itself, we now feel that it is necessary to address Christian worship itself.

This book is limited to the ancient church, by which we understand the church during classical antiquity. Since it is commonly thought that this particular period of history ended with the Germanic invasions, especially beginning in the fifth century, our study closes with those invasions and their most immediate consequences in Western worship. This may seem arbitrary, and in a way it is. But we are also attempting to show throughout the whole of this study that we have much to learn from those first centuries in the life of the church—particularly how that church expressed and shaped its faith through its worship.

If we thus begin our study focusing on the first century—the time during which Jesus and his first disciples lived—and end it with the Germanic invasions and their consequences, we must still divide the time between into a series of periods that allow us to follow the story we are telling.

In reviewing the history of the church, we frequently see the great turning point as the reign of Constantine and its consequences, when persecution ended and the state began supporting the church. This dividing line is important, and we shall use it here. But before doing so, it is important to mention another turning point whose changes were at least as important as those that followed Constantine's policies. This first dividing point, which is often passed over lightly, is the beginning of the church as an institution apart from the synagogue, and of Christianity as a religion apart from Judaism. During a period that lasted more than a generation, the church was seen by Jews and by society at large, as well as by itself, as simply one more sect within a Judaism whose inner vitality was shown in various movements and sects. During that time, most believers in Christ were either people of Jewish descent or Gentiles who for a long time had accepted many of the doctrines and practices of Judaism—the "God-fearers" to whom we shall return later. One could then speak of a "Judeo-Christianity." Such was the state at least until the end of the first century, and in some cases for much longer.

As we study that first period, we must acknowledge that Israel's faith was undergoing a process of deep transformation that led to what today we know as Judaism, and that in many ways differed from the religion of its ancestors. Since it was within that developing faith of Israel that Judeo-Christianity was born and developed, in order to understand the evolution of ancient Christian worship—as well as in order to understand the origins of the church itself— one must take into account the vicissitudes and transformations of the faith of Israel during that first century, and their consequences. Likewise another important matter is that at that time Judaism was not limited to those who descended from Abraham, but was quite attractive to many who, disillusioned by their traditional religions, sought a way to understand the world and to organize their life that was more adequate than the ancient pagan proposals.

Within that evolving Judaism, Judeo-Christians—at that time practically all Christians—sought to remain within the synagogue as long as this was allowed, while at the same time developing their own practices of worship and devotion parallel to those of the synagogue. These practices were profoundly shaped by the traditions of Israel, but also by faith in Jesus Christ as the fulfillment of the ancient promises made to Abraham and his descendants.

Particularly after the end of the first century, the church became increasingly Gentile, and Christianity and Judaism continued diverging. At that point we have to begin taking into account a different worship, still deeply rooted in the faith of Israel and its Scriptures, but also understanding itself as a religion different from Judaism, with which practically all bonds were broken. From the very beginning Judeo-Christians had differed with those who held to a more traditional form of Israel's faith, but now those conflicts increased, and even became actual enmity. Thus, we are now in the second period within our story, which takes us from the beginning of a mostly Gentile form of Christianity to the enormous impact of the new policies established by Constantine and his successors.

During this second period the church developed a form of worship that on the one hand distinguished it from Judaism, but on the other—insisting always on the validity of the history and ancient religion of Israel—gave it a sense of identity vis-à-vis the surrounding society. This was a church marginalized in society, repeatedly threatened by persecution, within a political atmosphere that showed its increasing hostility in ever more severe and cruel persecutions. The documents of that time attest to a double polemic addressed on the one hand against Judaism and on the other against paganism. Within that context, the church found it necessary to develop worship and devotional practices that, while based on the Scriptures of Israel, would also uphold the identity of Christianity as different from Judaism.

This changed radically with the new policies established by Constantine early in the fourth century, so that by the end of that century Christianity had become the official religion of the empire. Now began a third period, a time in which Christian identity was increasingly confused and combined with Greco-Roman identity. It therefore became necessary to teach at least the rudiments of Christian faith to the burgeoning multitudes of followers. Equally necessary was making sure that the people found their identity, not only in their Greco-Roman heritage, but also and above all in the gospel of Jesus Christ and therefore in the Scriptures and faith of the people of

Israel. This resulted in a form of worship that became increasingly elaborate, as seemed to behoove a church that enjoyed imperial support. At the same time, it also resulted in repeated attempts of many church leaders to reaffirm the church's identity within an empire in which the church's interests were increasingly confused with those of the state.

Then the empire itself unraveled. During the fourth and fifth centuries, in a series of successive invasions, various Germanic peoples—as well as others of non-Germanic origin—crossed the frontiers marked by the Rhine and Danube rivers in order to settle in the western reaches of the old Roman Empire. There they established relatively independent kingdoms, even though for some time they theoretically considered themselves subjects of the empire. In the Greek-speaking East, the old Roman Empire now became the Byzantine Empire—which soon would lose much of its territory to Islamic invasions. For these reasons, particularly following the Germanic invasions, Christianity in the West followed a different course than its counterpart in the East.

In the West, these events brought about new circumstances that put an end to classical antiquity and opened the way to the Middle Ages. In the field of worship and devotion, this also led to multiple changes that are briefly mentioned at the end of the present study but are not discussed fully since they would carry us beyond the chronological limits of the present project.

Having said this, several elements and dimensions of worship must be underscored. Possibly the most important is the bidirectional relationship that worship establishes with God. Worship is the praise the people of God render to the sovereign God. But it is also the word that this sovereign God addresses to the people. Worship involves praise, and it also involves listening. In it we not only bring before God our faith, feelings, sinfulness, joy, and hope. We also listen to what God wishes to say to God's people, which is why preaching has a central place in Christian worship. It is there that the church hears the Word of God, both in the Old and in the New Testaments. It is there that this Word of God is heard, interpreted, and applied to present circumstances—which makes it a word from God not only for past times, but also for those who hear it today.

In the pages that follow we also see that the ancient church listened to God not only in preaching and in the reading of Scripture, but also in actions such as baptism and Communion. For that church, baptism and Communion were not foremost actions of the church, but rather divine actions blessing God's people. In those early times there was no emphasis on trying to explain how this was so. Debates on this matter, which eventually led to serious divisions within the church, would come later. But what the church did affirm in those early times was that something did happen in baptism and in Communion, not primarily by human agency, but rather by divine action. Therefore, the people of God were to hear the divine message not only in the reading of Scripture and in preaching, but also in baptism and Communion—as well as in private prayer, mutual love among believers, service to humanity, and so on. In all of this the church is not acting alone, for God is also actively involved, carrying forth the divine design and leading the community of faith to be the people of God as God wishes.

Second, in the pages that follow, we find that the church never believed that it was alone in worshiping God. What the church does in its worship is join the heavenly host that eternally and constantly worships God. And the church does this also as practice and preparation for the day in which it itself will join the eternal choir of angels, archangels, and redeemed saints who lay down their crowns before the throne and the glassy sea.

Finally, in the pages that follow, we shall also see that worship is not merely an individual, private matter. Even though in worship believers address God personally, we do it as part of the people, a people that is also properly called the body of Christ. We address God not as separate individuals but as members grafted into the body of the risen One in whom we also shall rise again. God addresses this community that worships not primarily as a series of isolated individuals, each with their own hopes, problems, and divine calling, but also particularly as a community that God is shaping to be the people of God.

Therefore, in reading these pages and seeking in them inspiration and direction for today's worship, try to think not as separate individuals but rather as a body listening jointly to what God is telling the people of God, to what God expects of this people, and to what God has promised to it.

PART I

Judeo-Christianity

1

The Background

Jewish Worship

JEWISH WORSHIP: THE CRADLE
OF CHRISTIAN WORSHIP

It is astonishing that the people of Israel has survived through the centuries. Israel was a nomadic people that finally found a land to call its own and took possession of it. There it eventually founded a kingdom that had a time of glory, but was soon divided into two. Then the people were conquered, and their leaders taken into exile in Babylon, while others remained in the desolate land. They saw their Temple, the very center of their faith, destroyed. Eventually the exiles returned to the land in order to rebuild both their Temple and their society, only to be conquered again, first by the Macedonians, then by the Egyptians, followed by the Syrians. They were able to rebuild their Temple only to see it destroyed again, now by the Romans. They were a people that rebelled against the Roman invaders and found itself expelled from its own land, with its capital supplanted by a pagan city. Surprisingly, this repeatedly persecuted and exiled people did manage to keep its identity throughout the vicissitudes and tragedies of its history.

What made it possible for this people to retain its unity and identity amid such a turbulent history? Without any doubt, it was its worship. Israel's worship repeatedly recalled and celebrated God's covenant with this particular people. This covenant and its history were one of the main themes of the Scriptures of Israel, and therefore also of its worship. At the heart of this covenant was the Law, which governed all of life—work and leisure, feasts and fasts, family and trade. It was a combination of a daily life ruled by Scripture and the worship of the God who had commanded such a life that enabled Israel to retain its identity through all the changes in its circumstances.

Something similar is true of the church, even though we often do not realize it. The church has lived through times of persecution. It has also known times of outward prosperity, when it enjoyed the support of rulers. It lives scattered throughout the face of the earth, sometimes supported in one area and persecuted in another. It has lived through clashes with political power, conflicts with secular culture, and divisions within itself. It has survived through wars and plagues. And, throughout all of this, it has lived thanks to its worship. In some of its best times, its worship has reflected worship in Israel, which originally shaped it. Like the worship of the Hebrews, Christian worship is based on Scripture, although now including both the sacred books of Israel and others of Christian origin.

Since the church was born within the people of Israel, and its worship was born out of Israel's worship, it is important that Christians understand some elements of that worship in order to understand their own. However, it is not a matter of simply imitating the worship of Israel during the first century. Today many people promote a superficial imitation of first-century Jewish worship, apparently believing that by repeating a particular prayer or words, by imitating certain gestures and actions, by praying in Hebrew, or by other similar means they will bring about a renewal of the power of worship.

However, the truth is that we know little about Israel's worship in the first century. Almost all such details that we know are drawn from much later documents. These may well reflect what was done in the first century, but they probably also include much that reflects later developments. There is no doubt that early Christian worship bears the imprint of Hebrew worship. Later we shall see various elements of that imprint. But it is impossible to reconstruct a detailed description of Israel's worship at the time of Jesus and the apostles.

A further difficulty—and certainly much more significant than the first—is that the easy solution of apparently returning to Hebrew worship misses the core of our problem today. As we write these lines, today's church is deeply divided on how worship is to be conducted. Some prefer a more "traditional" service, while others prefer what they call "contemporary worship." Some prefer to sing the hymns that were popular a hundred years ago, and others insist that all music and songs should reflect the tastes of today's younger generations. Some seem to believe that the only musical instrument acceptable in church is the organ, while others wish to have drum batteries, electric guitars, and tambourines. In the midst of what some call "worship wars," we ignore what really stands between most of our worship and the best of Christian and Jewish worship.

The problem is not what we do in worship as much as what we think worship is. For most of us, no matter on what side of the current worship divide we stand, the purpose of worship is to relate the individual believer with God. Such relationship with God is doubtlessly important and even necessary. But just as important is the need for worship to remind us that, like ancient Israel, we are a *people* of God; that worship is not for me or for you, but for us; that what is important is not that I like worship, or that it expresses my feelings, but that it reminds us that we are God's people. Such worship somehow makes us and remakes us as the people of God.

The great enemy of our worship today is not the repetition of what we deem traditional, or the facile option of what seems to be more up-to-date; it is not one sort of music or another; it is not the tranquil passivity of some or the noisy rejoicing of others. The great enemy of our worship today is a sort of individualism that makes us think that if worship does not satisfy me, it is not true worship; that if I do not like worship, it is not true worship; that if the music is not what I like, worship is not for me. Imbued in this attitude, we forget that when his disciples asked the Lord to teach them to pray he did not tell them to say, "My Father, who art in heaven," but rather, "Our Father, who art in heaven." The individualism permeating much of today's Christian worship, be it "traditional" or "contemporary," is not a recent innovation. It already became common during the Middle Ages, when faith centered on individual salvation, leaving aside other elements of the biblical witness. The great reformers of the sixteenth century offered some alternative insights, but these were soon forgotten—in part because of the growing individualism of modernity, and in part because of the endless debates about the process of salvation itself.

TROUBLED TIMES: THE CONTEXT OF ANCIENT JEWISH WORSHIP

At the time of Jesus and the apostles, life and worship in Judea and the surrounding areas did not take place within a context of peace and tranquility. That land had long been swept by conquest and unrest. It was conquered in 232 BCE by Alexander the Great, whose generals clashed and divided his territories after his death. At first, the ancient land of Israel was ruled from Egypt by General Ptolemy and his successors. But then in 158 BCE the area was conquered by the Seleucids—descendants of Alexander's general Seleucus—who ruled in Syria. Most of these foreign rulers gave Israel a measure of autonomy, even allowing the people to govern their own lives following the Law of Moses. But the political situation also led to a process of Hellenization that the more religious Jews considered an abomination. Such was the case of Joshua ben Sirach, whose *Wisdom* is now included among the deuterocanonical books of the Old Testament, and who was strongly pressured by the authorities to silence his protests. Still, in spite of the resistance of the more devout among the people, some 170 years before Christ the high priests of the people of Israel became champions of the Hellenization of Jewish traditions, and even in several ways agents of Syrian interests.

Eventually, in 167 BCE, the Jews rebelled under the direction of the Hasmonean family. The most distinguished among them, whose name was Judas, was given the title of "Maccabeus," which means "hammer," for he was seen as a hammer beating on the foreign invader. Apparently, while most of the rural population and the impoverished urban masses supported the rebellion, the high classes, being more Hellenized than the rest of the population, saw it as a threat—or at least feared the possible consequences of a failed rebellion. When the Hasmoneans won the nation's independence, at first they opposed all Hellenistic influence, going to the extreme of forcibly circumcising Jews who had not been circumcised. Some members of the family that until then had produced most of the recent high priests fled to Egypt, where in 145 BCE they built a Jewish temple—apparently as a replacement for the one in Jerusalem. That temple continued existing until 73 CE—that is, three years after the destruction of the Temple of Jerusalem—when Emperor Vespasian ordered it closed. Meanwhile, in Palestine the Hasmonean rulers themselves began yielding to the unavoidable Hellenizing pressure, and for that reason began losing the support of many among the people.

While these last events were taking place, the growing power of Rome began to turn its attention eastward. In 63 BCE Roman general Pompey, who was in the region for other reasons, took advantage of the struggle among the Hasmoneans to invade the land, take Jerusalem, and profane the Temple by entering it on horseback. Roman rule was then established over the area.

Roman rule did not bring order immediately, for internecine struggles continued until 39 BCE, when Roman authorities named Herod as king of Judea. Later known as "Herod the Great," this man based his claim to rule in Judea on a distant kinship with the Hasmoneans, but he attained to the throne thanks to Rome's support, with which he was able to conquer the areas of Galilee, Idumaea (Edom), and Samaria, and then march on Jerusalem. There, by promising a pardon for those who had fought against him, he was finally able to become an actual king—a position he held until his death in 4 BCE. In his will, Herod divided his territory among his three children, Archelaus, Antipas, and Philip. Judea fell to the lot of Archelaus, whose cruelties and misdemeanors led Rome to depose him and name a Roman "procurator" in his place. (It is Herod Antipas whom Jesus calls "that fox" [Luke 13:32], and who appears in chapter 14 of Matthew and elsewhere in the Gospels. The "King Herod" in Acts 12 is Herod Agrippa, a grandson of Herod the Great.)

Reacting to Roman rule, Jewish nationalism grew rapidly. Apparently those called "Herodians" even claimed that Herod the Great had been the promised messiah, and on this basis sought to create an independent kingdom under the leadership of his descendants, but this proposal did not go far. Other, more radical groups, generally known as "Zealots," grew rapidly, particularly among the impoverished masses in the countryside. When, in the last decade before Christ, under the direction of Quirinius, governor of Syria, a census was proclaimed that would be the basis for more oppressive taxation, there was a rebellion led by Judas of Gamala, also known as "the Galilean" (Acts 5:37). Its suppression led to increasing bitterness among the people and to the growth of the Zealot party. The history of the Maccabees, now written and presented as a great liberating struggle that had succeeded thanks to the powerful arm of God, prompted many to believe that God would intervene in favor of an armed rebellion, leading to a situation similar to that of the early Hasmoneans. Among the most radical were the "Sicarii," so named after the *sica*, a dagger that they carried as they mixed with the multitudes and killed those supporting Roman rule. (These are the Sicarii with whom the Roman tribune in Jerusalem believed Paul to be connected when he said, "'Then you are not the Egyptian who recently stirred up a revolt and led four thousand assassins out into the wilderness?'" [Acts 21:38, where what the NRSV translates as "assassins" is actually "Sicarii"].)

Finally rebellion broke out in 66 CE, when the Zealots overthrew the government established by Rome and took possession of Jerusalem and much of Judea. Rome was quick to respond. Emperor Nero sent Vespasian to quell the rebellion. Vespasian began by taking possession of the areas around Jerusalem before attacking it. This strategy, and disorder in Rome, took place in the same year there were three successive emperors, which encouraged the rebels and gave them a chance to gain strength. In 69, when Vespasian left the campaign to become emperor in Rome, he put his son Titus in charge of military operations in Judea. Titus, who would later become emperor, was able to take part of the city of Jerusalem and besieged the rest, so that eventually the city surrendered. In the Temple itself there was a massacre, and much of the city was sacked and burned. In another memorable siege, the Zealots defending the fortress in Masada chose suicide over surrender to the Romans. This put an end to the rebellion, whose cost was enormous. All of Judea was impoverished, and the Temple disappeared. As we shall see, this had enormous consequences for both Judaism and Christianity.

Even this bloodbath was not enough to put an end to the people's dream to become once again an independent nation where they could fully obey the laws that God had given. The spirit of rebellion finally exploded in 115, and then again in 132. In a way, the first of these two rebellions was the most dangerous for Roman rule, for Jews also rebelled in the Roman territories of North Africa and Egypt, as well as in Mesopotamia and Judea. The rebels were crushed by the Roman army under the leadership of Quietus, and therefore that episode is commonly known as "the war of Quietus." Responding to the continued unrest in Judea, Emperor Hadrian based an entire legion at Caesarea, the seaport serving Jerusalem. When the Romans began building on the ruins of Jerusalem a new city, which they called Aelia Capitolina, and building a temple to Jupiter on the mound where the Jewish Temple once stood, the Jews rebelled again and were able to expel the Romans from much of Judea. Emperor Hadrian responded by sending six legions and several auxiliary units to retake the area and punish the rebels severely. Many of those who did not die in the war or in the ensuing famine were sold into slavery. Furthermore, with very few exceptions, Jews were forbidden access to Jerusalem.

These events and their consequences were the context of the parting of ways between Jews and Christians, and therefore also the context within which each of the two groups developed its own identity and worship.

THE TEMPLE

At the time of Jesus, the Temple of Jerusalem, at the highest point in the city, was the center of Jewish religious life, and to a certain degree also a center of political power in Judea. At that point the Temple was the one built by Zerubbabel (Ezra 3), but this had been restored and amplified to such a degree by Herod the Great that it is usually known as Herod's Temple. That restoration began some twenty years BCE, and continued for long after Herod's death. In John 2:20, when Jesus has been speaking about the destruction of the Temple, those who hear him say, "'This temple has been under construction for forty-six years, and will you raise it up in three days?'" The work on the Temple continued until about the year 63—that is, only some seven years before the Temple itself was destroyed by the Romans.

It is possible to know something about the construction of the Temple, as well as its physical appearance, thanks to the writings of Flavius Josephus, who lived in the first century. One also finds some data in later Hebrew literature—particularly in the Mishnah. As frequently happens in such cases, these sources do not agree on all the details. Scholars generally seem to accept the data of Josephus above the rest, although also acknowledging it is quite possible that Josephus may have exaggerated both the splendor and the dimensions of the Temple. There is no doubt that Josephus himself knew the Temple well, for he was part of an elite within the Jewish priesthood. During the rebellion that eventually led to the Temple's destruction, he served as a general of the rebels defending Galilee, and in the year 67 surrendered to the troops of Vespasian. After serving Vespasian for some time as a slave, he was granted freedom. At that time Josephus took the name of "Flavius," which was the name of Vespasian's family. He eventually became a Roman citizen and served Titus as a translator at the siege of Jerusalem in the year 70. For these reasons, many Jews considered him a traitor. His works, apparently written partly in order to regain the goodwill of the Jewish people, and partly so that the Romans could understand the greatness and wisdom of his own people, are one of the main sources we have for the story of the rebellion itself and for our knowledge of the Temple.

When Herod began the process of rebuilding the Temple he had to be careful not to offend the Jewish people, who did not trust him and feared that he would destroy the existing Temple and not build another. Therefore, before beginning to demolish the sections that had to be rebuilt, he had most of the material needed for the entire project brought to Jerusalem and stored near the Temple. Only then did construction actually begin. Also, since the project required some laborers to enter parts of the Temple that were reserved for priests, Herod collected a core of a thousand priests who were also stonemasons or carpenters, for the specific purpose of working in those sections of the building. The project itself occupied some ten thousand other workers. Thanks to this enormous number of builders, it took only a year and a half to finish most of the work, although minor projects occupied another eighty years.

The main building was surrounded by a wall around a yard that was slightly under two hundred meters wide and four hundred in length. Inside that wall was a roofed walkway held by two rows of columns on three of its sides, and three rows on the fourth side. This space within this outer wall was the "court of the Gentiles," for they were admitted into it. Inside this wall was another surrounding a smaller court. Part of this court—separated from the rest by another wall—was the "women's court." The rest was the "court of the men of Israel." Still further in was a smaller court for the priests. It was within this court that the actual Temple stood, with an altar for burnt offerings in front of it. To the north of this altar there was a space where animals to be sacrificed were killed, skinned, and prepared for burning. The Temple itself had a porch some fifteen meters wide and ten meters deep. Its eastern façade was covered with gold and would shine at sunrise. Beyond this area one finally came to the "holy place," a space of some twenty meters by ten meters. This is where the breads of propitiation were kept and renewed every Sabbath. In the same room were the menorah and an altar for burning incense. Finally one would come to the "holy of holies," which was empty and where only the high priest was allowed to enter once a year for the Day of Atonement. (The Ark of the Covenant had disappeared when Solomon's Temple was destroyed.)

This was the annual day of fasting and sacrifices prescribed in Leviticus 16. Besides the sacrifices offered on that day, there was also a ceremony in which two rams played a special role. One was sacrificed and the other was cast out into the desert, taking with itself all the guilt and sins of the people. As this ram was led to the desert, people would spit at it as a sign of rejection. (Hence our word "scapegoat.") After the destruction of the Temple, when it was no longer possible to offer sacrifices, the Day of Atonement took the form of Yom Kippur, which the Jewish people still observe. The Day of Atonement was influential in Christian interpretations of the sacrifice of Jesus, as may be seen in several books of the New Testament, particularly Hebrews. Other feast days are discussed later in this chapter.

An establishment as large as the Temple required a vast number of people to care for it. Among them was the Temple guard, whose chief was one of the most important priests. It was he who managed all physical and administrative matters having to do with the Temple. Under his leadership, the Temple guard kept order and made sure that each person remained in the proper court or area within the Temple compound. We have an example of their work in Acts 4:1.

In brief, Israel's religion until the time of the Temple's destruction in the year 70 was essentially a religion of sacrifice. In the strict sense, sacrifices could only be offered in the Temple at Jerusalem, and the manner in which they were to be performed was under strict regulation, as prescribed by the Law. What was to be sacrificed must be of top quality, for sacrificing an imperfect animal was an abomination. If the person offering the sacrifice had a physical defect, or if it was a slave or a woman, they were not allowed to place their hands on their own sacrifices as a sign of dedication. There was also a careful classification of various sorts and motives for sacrifice, for while some of them were offered in expiation, others were simply offerings of gratitude in which one returned to God part of what God had given.

Despite its enormous size, the Temple and its courts were not enough to hold all the population of Jerusalem—and even less all the Jewish people. The Temple was not, as we would think today, a place where all the faithful gathered to worship, but rather the center of a worship life that reached not only throughout Judea but wherever the people of Israel found themselves. Wherever they were, be it in Jerusalem itself or in faraway lands, Jews should turn toward the Temple when they prayed. If at all possible, their hours of prayer should be the same as those at the Temple. Every male Jew over twenty years of age, no matter where they lived, must send every year half a shekel—approximately a fourth of an ounce of silver—as a substitute for the sacrifices that he could not present personally.

Even though the Temple was dear to Jews throughout the world, and even though they considered it the center of their worship, the place where most Jews gathered regularly to worship God and study Scripture was the synagogue, to which we shall return later.

SCRIPTURE

While the Temple was the heart of Jewish religion, Scripture was the means by which most Jews were able to relate more directly to God and to the worship that took place in the Temple. Except for those who lived in Jerusalem or nearby, the Temple was a venerated but distant reality. Although all sought to visit it whenever this was possible and to offer there the sacrifices that the Law required, and although many dreamed of such visits, the majority of the Jewish people, scattered as they were throughout the Roman Empire, could only visit the Temple in their imagination. But Scripture was at hand, not only in its original Hebrew, but also in translations into Aramaic, the language of most Jews in the Holy Land, in Syria, and further east—translations known as "Targums"—and also into Greek, the lingua franca of a large part of the Roman Empire—a translation known as the "Septuagint." However, exactly which books were to be considered Scripture had not yet been decided among Jews. There was general agreement regarding "the Law and the Prophets" (see, for instance, Matt. 7:12; 11:13; 22:40; Luke 16:16). The books that came to be known as "the Writings" (Job, Proverbs, etc.) were usually held in high regard but were not normally included among the inspired books of Scripture. The main exception to this was the book of Psalms, which—particularly since they were often employed in worship—were also believed to be divinely inspired. This may be seen in the manner the New Testament presents Jesus as well as others citing the Psalms and using them to support their views and arguments. It was somewhat later, in the city of Jamnia, that Jewish authorities set the exact limits of the canon, including the Law, the Prophets, and the Writings. Even then, however, some Jews who preferred Greek and therefore used the Septuagint still employed the books that today are called "deutero-canonical" (that is, books of a second canon) or, less precisely, "apocryphal"—Maccabees, Judith, Tobias, and so on.

Scripture was at the very heart of Jewish religion, built on the Law of God that had been delivered to Moses. This Law was both the foundation and the highest expression of the covenant that God had made with the people on Sinai. Therefore, it was not just a set of instructions regarding what God had commanded the people to do, but also the very foundation of Israel's identity as a people. To study and obey it was part of the covenant. Thus, the study of the Law served not only to tell Israel how to behave, but also to remind it of its own identity. The Law, and worship around it, reminded Israel of who they were as God's people.

This dimension of the Law as a reminder was of paramount importance, for the covenant was based on the great acts of God for God's people, and therefore following the Law was a statement of who they were and of their dependence on God's will and grace. This is why the Law itself repeatedly shows that its foundation is the memory of what God has done for Israel. A few examples should suffice. In the introduction to the Decalogue, before giving the Commandments, God reminds Israel: "I am the LORD your God, who brought you out of the land of Egypt, out of the house of slavery" (Exod. 20:2; see also Deut. 5, where the introduction regarding God's actions is much more detailed).

A similar example refers to the commandment regarding the Sabbath:

> Observe the sabbath day and keep it holy, as the LORD your God commanded you. Six days you shall labor and do all your work. But the seventh day is a Sabbath to the LORD your God; you shall not do any work—you, or your son or your daughter, or your male or female slave, or your ox or your donkey, or any of your livestock, or the resident alien in your towns, so that your male and female slave may rest as well as you. Remember that you were a slave in the land of Egypt, and the LORD your God brought you out from there with a mighty hand and an outstretched arm; therefore, the LORD your God commanded you to keep the sabbath day. (Deut. 5:12–15)

Later in the same book, now referring to the Feast of Weeks, God declares,

> Rejoice before the LORD your God—you and your sons and your daughters, your male and female slaves, the Levites resident in your towns, as well as the strangers, the orphans, and the widows who are among you—at the place that the LORD your God will choose as a dwelling for his name. Remember that you were a slave in Egypt, and diligently observe these statutes. (Deut. 16:11–12)

As a final example, further in the same book God commands,

> You shall not deprive a resident alien or an orphan of justice; you shall not take a widow's garment in pledge. Remember that you were a slave in Egypt and the LORD your God redeemed you from there; therefore I command you to do this. (Deut. 24:17–18)

In summary, the Law, rather than a series of precepts, was an instrument for the people of Israel to remember its own history and how God had acted in it.

In studying it, each generation saw in it not only a guide and direction for life, but also a witness to their own identity as part of the people of God.

As to its content, the Law included instructions about sacrifices and the worship that the people should render to God, about how Israel was to remain pure and free of all that was unclean, and about the social order that God demanded among the people. Much later, a distinction would be made between laws having to do with rites and purity on the one hand, and those having to do with moral, social, and justice issues on the other. On the basis of this distinction, Ephesians 2:15 says about Jesus, "He has abolished the law with its commandments and ordinances, that he might create in himself one new humanity."

Soon, when speaking of Scripture as "the Law and the Prophets," the latter were given an authority similar to the Law itself. Those prophets had repeatedly spoken of justice among the people and insisted on the need to obey the Law not only in matters referring to worship, sacrifice, and religious festivals, but also in those having to do with justice—particularly justice for those whom no one protected, such as widows, orphans, the poor, and strangers.

The prophets had also spoken about God's promises. These included on the one hand a new order of peace and justice (see, for instance, Isa. 11 and Mic. 4:1–4), and on the other the advent of an anointed One or God's Messiah, who would bring about that new order. That messianic expectation and what it should imply for present life were understood in various ways, but they were always part of the faith of any good Jew.

DIVERSITY AMONG THE JEWISH PEOPLE

Despite their unity around the Temple, Scripture, and to a certain degree messianic expectations, in Judea itself Jews did not agree as to the place of each of these in the life of the people. Frequently the various groups resulting from such differences are called "sects," for this is the name given them by the main ancient source dealing with them. That source is the writings of Flavius Josephus, who has already been mentioned. Josephus refers to these "sects" in various places, but the passage in which he most clearly discusses and compares them is in his *Jewish Antiquities*:

> For some time, the Jews have had three philosophical sects of their own: the Essenes, the Sadducees, and a third set of opinions belonging to the Pharisees. . . . The Pharisees live in austerity, rejecting pleasures in their diet. They follow the path of reason, and whatever it tells them to do, this they do. They are convinced that they should follow this path. They also pay special respect to the elderly, and will

not contradict them. . . . They believe that souls have an inherent immortal force, and that there will be rewards below the earth as well as punishment. They think that those who are to be rewarded will rise to live again. These views make them popular among the masses. Whatever they do in divine worship, in prayers and in sacrifices, follows the same foundation. As a result, urban people speak highly of them for their clearly virtuous conduct in all that they do as well as in what they say.

But the doctrine of the Sadducees is that souls die with their bodies. They also hold that it suffices to do whatever the Law commands. . . . But few follow their teachings, and those are only people of high status. They cannot achieve what they intend, since when they attain to power and could attempt somehow to lead others, they have to follow what the Pharisees say, for otherwise the people would reject them.

What the Essenes teach is that everything should be ascribed to God. They believe in the immortality of souls and therefore they also hold that the rewards of virtue are to be sought above anything else. . . . They do not offer sacrifice in the Temple, for they have their own ritual washings. For that reason they are excluded from the common court of the Temple. But they perform their own sacrifices. Their style of life is better than the rest. . . . They are to be highly admired because they excel all others in virtue. In this they surpass whatever others have done, be they Greeks or barbarians. (*Antiquities* 18.1.2–5)

When these Jewish sects are discussed, the impression is often given that the Jewish people were distributed among these three—and perhaps others. However, Josephus himself seems to imply that actually it was only the Essenes who constituted a sect in the sense that they withdrew from the rest of the population. As to the Sadducees, Josephus shows clearly that there were a minority of aristocratic tendencies staunchly opposing what they took to be innovations, such as belief in life after death and other similar matters.

It is clear from both Josephus and other sources that the high levels of the priesthood were held by the Sadducees, who represented the higher classes of society and collaborated openly with Roman authorities. The high priesthood, which had been traditionally hereditary and lifelong, had ceased to be such at the time of the Maccabees, and ever since had lost much of its prestige among the general population. Herod as well as later Roman authorities would name and depose high priests at their whim. This is why Josephus claims that no matter what the Sadducees believed and preferred, they frequently found that they were not able to impose their views on the people, who sympathized mostly with the Pharisees.

The Pharisees deserve some attention and clarification, for they are frequently said to have been hypocrites—this, to such an extent that in common parlance to call somebody "pharisaic" is an insult, an accusation of hypocrisy.

Naturally, this is due to the conflicts between Jesus and the Pharisees that appear repeatedly in the Gospels—even though in the Gospels themselves there are also cases of Pharisees who listened respectfully to what Jesus said. In order to understand the true nature of the Pharisees, it is crucial to understand that the reason why Jesus attacked them repeatedly, and practically ignored the Sadducees, was not that he preferred the latter, but rather that it was the Pharisees who were closer to his own teachings. The Pharisees were not content with merely obeying the letter of the Law, but rather sought to understand what the Law implied for daily life. In contrast, the Sadducees were content with their power and the control they had over Temple worship. At the same time, while the Sadducees collaborated with the Roman government, and even represented it on occasion, the Pharisees, without openly opposing that government, kept their distance from it.

This last point leads us to bring up another group that Josephus does not mention in the above-quoted passage—although he goes on to speak of Judas the Galilean—but which was also of enormous significance for the history of Palestine in the times immediately following Jesus' death and resurrection. These are the Zealots, already introduced when discussing the process leading to the Jewish rebellions and eventual destruction first of the Temple and then of Jerusalem itself.

THE SYNAGOGUES AND THE DIASPORA

The origins of the synagogue are lost in the shadows of history. While it is impossible to determine when the synagogues emerged, there is no doubt about their purpose. The people of Israel, first taken into exile in Babylon and then scattered throughout the Mediterranean world, still looked to Jerusalem and its Temple as the center of their faith; there they found their own identity. However, they could not limit their worship of God and their religious formation to the rare occasions when some of them could visit the Temple. Even in Palestine itself, most people were able to visit the Temple only occasionally, for such visits often had to overcome long distances and many difficulties.

Thus, at a time that is impossible to determine, the people of Israel began the custom of gathering periodically—particularly on the seventh day of the week, the Sabbath—to study Scripture, to pray, and to affirm their identity as God's people. The word "synagogue," which is Greek in origin, simply means "gathering" or "assembly"—and thus it is very similar to the word "church," whose original meaning was precisely that of an assembly or gathering. "Synagogue" was the Greek word by which the Septuagint translated Hebrew Bible references to the assembly of the people. Actually it is quite possible that before the term "synagogue" came to have its present meaning, the name that was most commonly given to the meetings that the Jews held in order to pray and study Scripture was *proseuchē*, which simply meant "prayer." This is the word that the NRSV translates as "a place of prayer" in Acts 16:13. At any rate, although both words were employed in antiquity to refer to the group that gathered in order to pray and study Scripture, eventually these terms were also used to designate the place in which those groups gathered—just as today we speak of a "church" referring sometimes to the congregation itself, and at other times to the building where it meets. From the first century on, the word "synagogue" became the most commonly used both for those meeting and for the place where the gathering took place. This change may be seen both in the writings of Jewish philosopher Philo of Alexandria—a contemporary of Jesus—and in the New Testament. Another name that sometimes was given to the synagogue during the first century is *sabbateion*, for the synagogues usually gathered on the Sabbath. The synagogue was both a center of study and teaching and a place of worship. It was led by a rabbi or teacher—a man who was a careful student of Scripture and who therefore could both teach and interpret it in study as well as in worship.

Leaving aside the still-ongoing controversy regarding the origins of the synagogue, one can at least affirm that at the time of Jesus, the synagogue was an important element in the religious life of the Jewish people. In the Temple itself there was a space devoted to the reading and study of the Law. Some suggest that Luke 2:46 refers to this when telling the story of Mary and Joseph finding Jesus "in the temple, sitting among the teachers, listening to them and asking them questions." Acts 6:9 also has a reference to other synagogues in Jerusalem, although the text itself is not clear as to the number of synagogues listed: "some of those who belonged to the synagogue of the Freedmen (as it was called), Cyrenians, Alexandrians, and others of those from Cilicia and Asia." Furthermore, according to an ancient rabbinic tradition, when the Temple was destroyed in 70 CE, there were 480 synagogues in Jerusalem. Synagogues have a very important place in the Gospels, which reference them frequently. For instance, in Luke 4:15 we are told that Jesus "began to teach in their synagogues." Unfortunately, although excavations in Judea have unearthed ruins of several synagogues, it is impossible to affirm with absolute certainty that any of them date from the first century. (The famous synagogue in Capernaum, which pilgrims often visit because of its place in the stories of the life of Jesus, probably dates from the third century—although it is quite possible that under it may be the ruins of the synagogue at the time of Jesus.)

The buildings themselves varied in their size and architecture. Some ancient texts declare that a synagogue should be built so that, while praying, people would be facing the Temple in Jerusalem. Frequently in the ruins of ancient synagogues one finds stone benches built against some of the walls. Perhaps other seats made out of wood were also within the room itself, but if they existed, archaeology has not been able to find any sign of them. We know there was a special area for women, apart from men, and that women were not strictly considered members of the synagogue, nor could they be counted in order to attain the necessary number to hold a service. Yet some texts say that women could be among the seven people who were to read Scripture aloud—although the reading of the Law was reserved to men.

The most important place in the building was the niche where the scrolls of Scripture—made out of leather—were kept. This niche was protected by a cloth or veil behind which the scrolls were rewound after being read. The reading itself was done from a platform. After the reading of the sacred text there was an opportunity for a teacher or distinguished visitor to comment on it. This was sometimes done sitting and sometimes standing. Thus we must understand the episode described in Luke where we are told that Jesus "rolled up the scroll, gave it back to the attendant, and sat down. The eyes of all in the synagogue were fixed on him" (Luke 4:20). This does not mean, as we might think today, that he went back and sat in his place amid the congregation, but rather that he sat before it, in a seat of authority from which he would comment on what he had just read. Apparently in other cases the teacher invited to comment on what had been read did so standing. Such is the case in the episode in Antioch of Pisidia, where "after the reading of the law and the prophets," Paul and Barnabas are invited to speak, and "Paul stood up and with a gesture began to speak" (Acts 13:15–16).

Just as when discussing the Temple we did not attempt to describe in detail what took place in it, we do not offer much here about worship in the synagogue. Whatever may be said has to be carefully nuanced because—as in the case of the Temple—little is known about synagogue worship in the first century. All existing documents are the product of a much later date, and it is impossible to know to what extent they describe synagogue worship in the first century or to what extent they reflect later conditions—perhaps even in some cases practices resulting from the conflict between Judaism and Christianity, or local practices that should not be taken as general.

We do know that the reading of the Law was divided into 155 sections, each to be read on a Sabbath, so that the entire Law would be heard and studied in a cycle of three years. We also know that certain prayers and blessings were repeated at particular moments in worship. In Palestine and other areas where Aramaic was spoken, it was customary to read the text in Hebrew first and then translate what had been read into Aramaic. Although professional translators specialized on this task, occasionally someone else was invited to perform it—sometimes even a child, who was to take this opportunity to show their own knowledge of Hebrew. This latter detail fits with the traditional function of synagogues as the place where children learned the traditions, history, and identity of Israel.

We also know that there was singing, sometimes antiphonal, although it is impossible to say much about the music that was used. Most probably there was a single melodic line, and when the singing took place antiphonally a cantor or a choir would do most of the singing, with the congregation responding periodically by singing a simple line. Apparently in some other cases the cantor sang the psalm itself while the choir responded with a brief word or phrase. Quite possibly other music and texts were employed besides the Psalms of the Bible. According to Philo of Alexandria, the Jewish sect that he calls the "Therapeutae," whose base was in Egypt, "only spend their time in meditation, but they also compose songs and hymns to God. These are done in every variety of meter and melody, but they divide them into measures of more than common solemnity" (quoted by Eusebius of Caesarea, *Church History* 2.17.13; NPNF2 1:118). Some scholars also suggest that quite probably in Jewish worship, both at the Temple and in the synagogues, there were several brief melodic formulae for benedictions, hallelujahs, and so on. But, once again, one must remember that the most ancient samples we have that say much about music in the synagogues are no earlier than the seventh century CE.

It is clear that, although the synagogues claimed to follow the same religion that was practiced in the Temple, differences and tensions soon emerged between the two institutions. Some complained that there were synagogues whose building seemed to imitate the Temple and declared this to be a usurpation. Some criticized an invitation in which people were not told to "come and pray" but rather to "come and offer." According to these critics, the only place where sacrifices were to be offered to God was the Temple, and by inviting the people with a formula that should be reserved for sacrifice, the synagogue was usurping the Temple's function. Some refuted such views by quoting Psalm 141:2—"Let my prayer be counted as incense before you, / and the lifting up of my hands as an evening sacrifice"—where prayer itself is a sacrifice.

But there were other reasons for the conflict between the Temple and the synagogues. The Temple was mostly in the hands of the Sadducees, and synagogues generally leaned toward the more popular religion, which was more like that of the Pharisees. These tensions were made worse because most of the Jewish people did not live in Judea, but in the Diaspora. In such places, the distance between them and the Temple led the majority of Jews to center their faith in the practices and teachings of the synagogue and to relate to the Temple only in an ideal manner, and by sending their annual offering.

THE JEWS OF THE DIASPORA

The Diaspora or dispersion of the Jews had begun long before the time of Jesus, back at least to the Babylonian exile, in the sixth century BCE. One consequence of that period of exile was the presence of a vast number of Jews in Mesopotamia, Babylonia, and Media. Later, as first the Macedonians, then the Syrians, the Egyptians, and finally the Romans conquered the ancient lands of Israel, Jews were scattered throughout the Mediterranean basin. At the time of Jesus, there were Jews and synagogues in almost all the provinces of the Roman Empire and beyond. Particularly in the areas of Mesopotamia, Syria, Egypt, Asia Minor, and Rome itself, the Jewish population was most numerous. Although knowing their exact numbers is impossible, some data may help us understand the magnitude of that dispersion.

Josephus claims that during the time of the Jewish wars there was a massacre of Jews in the city of Damascus in Syria in which between ten thousand and eighteen thousand Jews were killed. (Josephus himself offers these two different numbers in different places.) In the great city of Alexandria, which was the second largest in the Roman Empire, there were five sections, two of them occupied by Jews, according to Philo of Alexandria. There were also more Jews in the interior of Egypt, such that Philo claims a million Jews inhabited the land. In the region of Cyrene, in North Africa, Josephus says that the population was divided into four groups, one of which was the Jews. In the same area, when the great Jewish rebellion to which we have already referred took place early in the second century, the rebels were so many that they were able to kill more than two hundred thousand Gentiles. On the island of Cyprus, during the same rebellion, the number of the dead was almost a quarter of a million. In Syria there were almost a million Jews. Rome itself considered them a bad influence, and repeatedly thousands of Jews were expelled or deported to other areas, although quite likely many of them eventually returned to the capital. During the reign of Emperor Tiberius (14–37 CE), the Jewish population in the capital approached 7 percent of the total population. In summary, even the most conservative numbers would seem to suggest that about 7 percent of the entire population in the empire were Jews—and others suggest higher percentages.

The impact of this Jewish presence on the rest of society and its customs was significant. Josephus, probably exaggerating, declared,

> For quite some time Gentiles have become very interested in our religious customs, to such a point that there is no longer even a single city among the Greeks, nor a people among the barbarians, where our name is not known or where they do not follow our custom of resting once a week, our fasts, the festivals of lights, and many other things

having to do with our diet. Just as God is to be found everywhere, so has the Law traveled among humans. Let each one look at their own land and in their own family and they will corroborate the truth of my words. (*Ag. Apion* 2.39.282)

The impact of Judaism on the surrounding society was partly due to the efforts of the Jews themselves. Several of them wrote in defense of their faith, trying to show that it agreed with the best of Greek philosophy. The best known among these Jewish apologists is Philo of Alexandria, but there were many others. Such seems to be the clear purpose of the fourth book of Maccabees, as well as of the *Sibylline Oracles*, written to show that the ancient Sybil announced the truth of Judaism—and later interpolated by Christians with a similar aim. One of those oracles makes a claim similar to that of Josephus: "You have filled the sea and the land" (*Sibylline Oracles*, 3.27).

The expansion and impact of Judaism were such that Strabo, who had traveled far and wide, said that in the first century BCE the Jews "are to be found in every city, and it is difficult to find a corner of the world where they have not entered and of which they have not taken possession" (quoted by Josephus, *Antiquities* 14.7.2). And much later, Augustine quoted what Seneca wrote in the first century about Jews: "The style of life of these horrible people, however, has gained such impulse that it is now accepted everywhere. The conquered have given their laws to the conquerors" (*City of God* 6.11).

Notably, in most of these testimonies one sees at once suspicion and hatred toward Jews and an admiration for their style of life and their perseverance.

THE CALENDAR, THE TIMES, AND JEWISH IDENTITY

One of the main elements binding Jews together even as they were scattered throughout the Roman Empire and beyond was the calendar. From one extreme to the other of their vast dispersion, Jews could express and experience their unity by sharing a single calendar with similar activities.

The center of this calendar was the seven-day week, culminating on the Sabbath with its observances and celebrations. Each day began at sundown and ended at the next sundown. Much has been said about the endless discussions regarding what was legitimate to do on the seventh day of the week. There certainly were cases in which Hebrew piety carried its obedience to Sabbath laws to such a point that the Sabbath ceased to be a day of joy celebrating the love of the Creator God. We find in the Gospels frequent cases in which Jesus collided with synagogue leaders on matters related to Sabbath observance. But such cases should not eclipse the reality of the Sabbath as a day of celebrating the providential gifts of God, and therefore also as a time of love and sharing among the people of God. Furthermore, the Jews themselves disagreed on what was legal to do on the Sabbath. The two great rabbinic schools of the first century BCE, usually called the schools of Hillel and of Shammai, differed on such matters. The followers of Hillel were more liberal in their understanding of the Sabbath, while Shammai's were more conservative and stricter. It was actually in the time of Jesus that Rabbi Akiba decided—and gaining wide agreement among the people—that all that could be done any other day must not be done on the Sabbath, but that what could not be done at another time and was necessary could licitly be done even on a Sabbath. That seems also to be Jesus' lesson, as we see in the Gospels. As a result, the sixth day of the week came to be known the "day of preparation," for on this day one was to prepare food and do all that was necessary to be able to keep the Sabbath.

The Sabbath was celebrated in the Temple with special sacrifices, and also by renewing the loaves of propitiation. Both the beginning and the end of the Sabbath were signaled by the sound of a trumpet—one at sunset of the sixth day, and the other on the next sunset. Also, at least from a time five centuries BCE, synagogues throughout the world gathered on the Sabbath. It is impossible to know the details of the Sabbath worship that took place in the synagogues in Jesus' time. Most probably, before the destruction of the Temple, what was done in the synagogue would reflect the opinions and inclinations of various schools, groups, or "sects" into which the people were divided. But after the destruction of the Temple there seems to have been a movement toward unity, so that worship became increasingly uniform. Even though the details are not known, from the New Testament and from the witness of Josephus there were clearly readings of the Law as well as of the Prophets. When there was a distinguished visitor, he was invited to comment on the passages that had been read—or if not, a member of the synagogue would offer the commentary. Certain prayers were also included, some of them prescribed. There was also reading—or more likely singing—of some selected psalms. We also know that, for reasons not entirely understood, it was customary to fast on the second and fifth days of the week. At any rate, Sabbath observance became such a marked characteristic of Judaism that, as Josephus says, the Gentile population in various areas soon imitated it.

Besides the weekly calendar that formed the base of the Hebrew calendar, there was also an annual calendar including several important dates. Beyond that was a calendar lasting several years that, like the week, was based on the number seven. Each seventh year was a sabbatical year, and after seven sabbatical years there was a year of Jubilee or "pentecostal year"—the fiftieth year. During each year itself there were particular feasts and observances. Some of them, such as the Feast of Dedication (Hanukkah) and that of Purim, celebrated relatively recent episodes in the history of Israel. The first of these two commemorated the deeds of Judas Maccabeus and his victories over the Syrians, culminating in the dedication of the Temple. Purim celebrated the story of Esther and Mordecai against the machinations of Israel's enemies. The Feast of Tabernacles and the Feast of Weeks celebrated the completion of the harvest. We have already spoken of the Day of Atonement. However, the most important among all the feasts of Israel was Passover, which celebrated the liberation of Israel from the yoke of Egypt when the people received instructions to mark their doors with the blood of a lamb, and the angel of destruction passed over the houses that bore that sign, but entered those of the Egyptians and slew their firstborn. Among all Jewish festivities, Passover was not only the most important but also the one that most influenced Christian worship.

According to the book of Exodus, the celebration of Passover was ordered by God even before the liberation that it celebrates had taken place:

> Then Moses called all the elders of Israel and said to them, "Go, select lambs for your families, and slaughter the passover lamb. Take a bunch of hyssop, dip it in the blood that is in the basin, and touch the lintel and the two doorposts with the blood in the basin. None of you shall go outside the door of your house until morning. For the LORD will pass through to strike down the Egyptians; when he sees the blood on the lintel and on the two doorposts, the LORD will pass over that door and will not allow the destroyer to enter your houses to strike you down. You shall observe this rite as a perpetual ordinance for you and your children. When you come to the land that the LORD will give you, as he has promised, you shall keep this observance. And when your children ask you, 'What do you mean by this observance?' you shall say, 'It is the passover sacrifice to the LORD, for he passed over the houses of the Israelites in Egypt, when he struck down the Egyptians but spared our houses.'" (Exod. 12:21–27)

The word "paschal" is an adjective derived from "pascha," which in turn comes from the Hebrew word meaning to go by or to leave aside—therefore, "pass over." Although Passover originally referred specifically to the commemoration of the sacrifice of the lamb and the ensuing liberation, beginning in the second century its meaning widened, now to include the various services surrounding that date. In that sense, Passover became practically synonymous with the Feast of Unleavened Bread. But in the first century the distinction was still made between that feast and Passover. Passover was specifically the celebration that took place on the fourteenth day of Nisan, and it signaled the opening of the seven days of the Feast of the Unleavened Bread.

According to Josephus, each year some one hundred thousand pilgrims went to Jerusalem to celebrate Passover.

Much of what is known today about that celebration in Jerusalem during the first century is based on what the New Testament says, as well as on the witness of the Mishnah. The celebration began by disposing of old leaven, in remembrance of the day when, fleeing Egypt, the children of Israel ate unleavened bread. Then, at the ninth hour (approximately 3 p.m.), the sacrifice began of the many lambs to be used for the feast. All Jews should partake of the paschal feast jointly with others, because the paschal lamb had to be consumed in its entirety. Therefore, those who were not part of a large family would plan to join others for the feast. The Levites sang Psalms 113 to 118 while the lambs were killed and bled. Their blood was collected and later poured over the altar, where part of the fat was also burned. The lamb was then returned to those who had brought it to take home and roast it. As all the generations of a particular family gathered for this special celebration, one of the youngest was to ask, "How is this night different from all others?" The answer was given in songs and narratives regarding the day in which God freed Israel from slavery in Egypt, and then went on to speak of God's other great redeeming acts. Usually, the last petition was that God would free the land from Roman occupation. (Later, this last prayer was substituted by another asking God to allow Israel to return to Jerusalem.) This celebration clearly served to cement Israel's identity as the people of God, and to raise new generations to see themselves as heirs of the great feats of God that were commemorated in the feast itself.

Notably, the Passover celebration did not take place mostly at the Temple or the synagogue, but rather in the homes—although in Jerusalem the Temple was assigned the task of preparing the lambs, and in the synagogues there were particular Passover observations. The Law, in commanding that Passover be celebrated annually and giving instructions for that celebration, commanded that the lamb had to be entirely eaten. This meant that a small family would have to join others. It also implied that any Jew who was living alone or for some reason did not have a family with whom to celebrate must join others for the celebration, so that no Jew was to spend Passover alone. This was a great festival of the people, not an individual matter or even a purely family matter—even though the family itself had an important place in the celebration. Since the celebration took place in the home, the strict separation between men and women that existed in the Temple and in the synagogue did not apply in the same manner. It was normally the women who prepared the food for the celebration, but besides this traditional role they also had a part in the religious rites that took place around the paschal supper.

At the time of Jesus, Passover and the Feast of the Unleavened Bread were practically a single public celebration attracting numerous pilgrims from foreign lands. After the destruction of the Temple, this was no longer possible, and the paschal feast became a rite celebrated mostly within the family. Without the Temple, there was no place to sacrifice the fat of the lamb, but the supper continued following the earlier practices. This paschal supper became known as the "Seder," a word meaning "order." Since this way of referring to the Passover meal appears only in documents after 70 CE—that is, just after the destruction of the Temple—this is an indication that the supper itself was being more tightly regulated. Now that the Passover could no longer be observed by means of pilgrimage to the Temple and ceremonies in it, the family's role in the celebration became even more prominent.

The rules that were set late in the first century and afterward certainly kept intact many of the ancient traditions of Israel regarding the paschal feast. However, some scholars argue that this meal was now influenced by the Hellenistic tradition of a "symposium," which was a banquet often devoted to discussing matters of philosophy. One detail pointing in this direction was the custom of lying prone when eating the meal, as was done in Greek symposia. But even so, the center of the meal was—and still is—the narrative of the great saving acts of God that are the foundation of Jewish identity. Thus, while in a traditional Greek symposium there would be a discussion on philosophy or ethics, what was discussed and told in the Seder was the story of the liberation of Israel when it was enslaved in Egypt—and then other similar divine interventions. Another difference between a Greek symposium and the Seder meal is that, while the former was elitist, limited to those who were able to discuss certain profound questions, the Hebrew Seder was an intergenerational celebration, including all present, from the oldest to youngest, in which one of those very young participants was to open the path of the narrative by asking, "How is this night different from all others?"

As its name implies, the Seder meal was to follow a detailed and clearly structured order, all of which need not be discussed here. However, it is important to point out some elements that would be significant for the development of Christian worship. Possibly the most important of these is the central place of bread and wine in the Seder meal. The bread is to be unleavened, commemorating the hasty flight from Egypt, when the Hebrews were not able to take leaven with them. One of the prayers to be said over the bread is an act of thanksgiving: "We bless you, Lord, spirit of the universe, who makes the earth give us bread; we bless you, Lord, spirit of the universe, who commanded that we eat this bread." There was also a special blessing for each cup of wine. Over the first of these, called the cup of blessing, the prayer should be, "We bless you, Lord, spirit of the universe, who has created the fruit of the vine; we bless you, Lord, spirit of the universe, who has raised us up, raised us and brought us to this blessed time." Upon blessing the last cup of wine the door was to be open in order to invite the prophet Elijah to join the meal. A cup of wine was placed for him at the middle of the table. The meal would then end with a proclamation of the constant hope of meeting again in Jerusalem.

As we shall see later on, the Synoptic Gospels place the last meal of Jesus with his disciples before his arrest on the day of Passover, while John (19:14) implies that the death of Jesus took place as the paschal meal was being prepared.

The other celebration within Israel that later became important for Christians was Pentecost. The name of this feast, "Pentecost," means "fiftieth," for it came after a week of weeks following Passover—therefore on the fiftieth day. It seems that originally Pentecost was the celebration of a completed harvest, and its observance included the sacrifice of two loaves of bread resulting from that harvest, as well as some animals (see Lev. 23:15–21). Slowly, and particularly after the destruction of the first Temple, the feast also came to be a celebration of the giving of the Law to Moses on Mount Sinai—and this was its most important meaning at the time of the New Testament.

Finally, still on the subject of the calendar and the management of time, one must mention the times set aside for prayer. Naturally, any moment was good for prayer. But there were three particular hours each day in which prayers were celebrated in the Temple, and all Jews—wherever they were— were to stop other activities in order to pray, be it at the Temple, at the synagogue, or in private. These were the third, sixth, and ninth hours—that is, approximately at nine in the morning, at noon, and in midafternoon, at about 3 p.m. Note that, even though these prayers may be said in private, they were not private prayer in the sense that their intention was to establish a bond between the individual and God, but rather a common prayer the entire people jointly addressed to God. As we shall see later, these hours of prayer also influenced Christian devotional practice.

PROSELYTES AND GOD-FEARERS

Much of the numerical growth of Judaism during the first centuries after Christ was due to proselytism. (Although today the word "proselytism" has a negative connotation, often referring to undue means of gaining disciples and followers, in this context it means simply the desire to let other people know one's faith and invite them to follow it. It is thus that ancient texts speak of Jewish "proselytes.") It may be difficult for us today to think of Judaism as a proselytizing religion, for our most common experience is that almost all the Jews we know are such by birth. But when Christianity entered the scene, Judaism was a proselytizing religion, seeking followers throughout the world. In some cases, its proselytizing success was remarkable. A good example is the conversion of the entire kingdom of Adiabene, in the valley of the Tigris, at the border between the Roman and Parthian empires. This took place while Claudius reigned in Rome (41–54 CE)—the same Claudius who expelled the Jews from Rome, apparently because of the disturbances caused among Jews by teachings and conflicts about Jesus. Shortly before that time, Herod had forced the Edomites—the people of Idumaea—to become Jews, and they remained such even after Herod's death. Even earlier, in 129 BCE, the proselytizing zeal of Jews in Rome was such that they were expelled both from the capital and from other cities in Italy. As is common in such cases, those who rejected the teachings of the Jews claimed that the latter were enemies of humankind, that they followed a barbaric superstition, that they had no visible God, and that instead of the gods they worshiped the sky and the clouds. All of this led to repeated massacres of Jews as well as to Jewish rebellions that caused numerous deaths, among Jews and Gentiles. But despite such events Judaism continued making headway among the pagan population.

One reason for the proselytizing success of Judaism was the decline of most ancient religions, whose validity many doubted. In their disillusionment with such religions, people sought after a new "philosophy" that would be more useful for life itself. (One must remember that at this time the ancient philosophies of Plato's Academy and Aristotle's Peripatos had receded in the face of the growth of philosophical currents whose interests dealt more with practical life than with metaphysics and epistemology—philosophical currents such as Stoicism, Epicureanism, and Middle Platonism. Within that context, Judaism could present itself as a philosophy competing with these other alternatives. The same would soon be true of Christianity, which many of its followers defined and announced as the "true philosophy.")

Those pagans who approached Judaism came to be known as "God-fearers" or "proselytes." Although there was some confusion in the use of these two names, they eventually became distinct. A "proselyte" was someone who not only accepted the faith of Israel and its Law, but also committed to follow that Law in doctrinal, moral, and dietary matters. Also, as a sign of conversion and commitment, as well as of cleansing, the proselyte was baptized. Such baptism took place no matter the gender of the convert. As to whether circumcision was necessary, the rabbis did not agree. The more traditional demanded that the entire Law be obeyed, including matters such as food, ritual cleanness, and the circumcision of every male. But others—apparently the minority—did not require more than obedience to the moral principles of the Law and belief in a single God, Creator of all things. For most Jews, Gentiles who followed the moral commandment of the Law and believed in Israel's God but did not follow the dietary commandments and were not circumcised were not proselytes, but only "God-fearers." Thus, when Paul and others began to admit God-fearers into the church, leading to polemics among Jewish Christians as to whether they should be circumcised, Paul and those who agreed with him could appeal to a certain rabbinic tradition.

Conversion to Judaism was not a light matter. According to the rabbis, if within a Gentile marriage only one of the two became a convert, the marriage itself was dissolved, and the children became illegitimate. In theory at least, being a proselyte did not make one less Jewish than those who were such by birth. Indeed, some of the most famous Rabbis were either proselytes or descendants of proselytes.

Jesus criticized the proselytizing zeal of the Jews of his time, not because of their desire to share their faith, but apparently because while sharing that faith they also placed on the proselytes a burden that would become a new form of oppression: "'But woe to you, scribes and Pharisees, hypocrites! For you lock people out of the kingdom of heaven. For you do not go in yourselves, and when others are going in, you stop them. Woe to you, scribes and Pharisees, hypocrites! For you cross sea and land to make a single convert, and you make the new convert twice as much a child of hell as yourselves'" (Matt. 23:14–15). (At this point, some ancient manuscripts seem to imply that the reason Jesus criticized Jewish proselytizing was that it was not sufficiently interested in matters of justice. According to these manuscripts, what Jesus says is, "'Woe to you, scribes and Pharisees, hypocrites! For you devour widows' houses and for the sake of appearance you make long prayers; therefore you will receive the greater condemnation.'")

No matter how many the proselytes were, the number of God-fearers was much greater. They were ready to accept Jewish monotheism and the moral principles of the Law, and they attended worship in the synagogue; but for one reason or another they did not become proselytes, and thus were not committed to obeying the entire Law. It was among such God-fearers that much of the Pauline mission had its greatest success, as we shall see in the next chapter.

THE DESTRUCTION OF THE TEMPLE
AND THE EXPULSION FROM THE SYNAGOGUES

As a consequence of Jewish rebellion, the Temple in Jerusalem was destroyed in 70 CE. This obviously had enormous consequences for the faith of Israel. From then on, it was no longer possible to obey the laws relating to sacrifices owed to God—except in places such as the already mentioned rival Temple in Egypt, closed shortly after the destruction of the Temple in Jerusalem. Now deprived of their centers of worship and of power, the Sadducees practically disappeared. The Pharisees, whose base had always been in the synagogues, were able to shape the Judaism resulting from that catastrophe, now called rabbinic Judaism. This was more interested in the love of God and in justice than in the sacrifices that had been made in the Temple. In support of this emphasis, the words of the prophets were repeatedly quoted—for instance, Hosea 6:6, "For I desire steadfast love and not sacrifice, / the knowledge of God rather than burnt offerings." Judaism as we know it today is the heir of that tradition of the Pharisees and the rabbis, and of their careful study and application of the Law.

Now being unable to gather in Jerusalem, the Sanhedrin was reorganized—with the approval of Emperor Vespasian—in the city of Jamnia, near the northern end of Judea. It was this Sanhedrin that at some point around 90 CE determined what would henceforth be the Hebrew canon of Scripture, comprising the Law, the Prophets, and the Writings. This canon based on the Hebrew text is commonly called "the Jerusalem canon," and most Protestant Bibles follow it today, while Catholic Bibles follow the "Alexandrian canon," which includes the deuterocanonical books and therefore reflects the Greek translation that early Christians used—the Septuagint.

The Sanhedrin in Jamnia was headed by Gamaliel II, who took the title of "nasi" or "prince" at some point around the year 80—that is, some ten years after the fall of Jerusalem. Gamaliel had great success in reorganizing and unifying Judaism. Part of this project was defining the list of sacred books resulting in the Jerusalem canon. Also as part of his project of unity and uniformity, he codified the prayers and rites that should be followed in the synagogue. Finally, he also decreed the expulsion from the synagogues of various groups that he considered heretical or sectarian—Christians among them. This took place toward the end of his rule, around 100 CE, and therefore that date may serve as a watershed marking the decline of Judeo-Christianity and the beginning of a church composed mostly of Gentiles.

2

Jewish and Judeo-Christian Worship

SOURCES AND LIMITS

Before discussing Judeo-Christian worship, it is necessary to understand what we mean by "Judeo-Christianity." In a way, practically all Christianity is Judeo-Christian—with the possible exception of people such as Marcion and his followers, who claimed that the God of Israel was not the same as the God of Jesus Christ. Throughout the centuries, Christians have affirmed that their God is the same as the God of Abraham and of Israel, and that Hebrew Scripture is the Word of God. Therefore, in the widest sense, "Judeo-Christian" would be the same as "Christian," because all Christianity—even its anti-Semitic strains—has Jewish roots. At the other end of the spectrum, it is possible to limit the name of "Judeo-Christian" to the many teachers and movements in ancient times that, while following Jesus, insisted on the need to obey all the Law of Israel, including in matters such as diet, circumcision, and ritual purity. Between these two extremes, when here we speak of "Judeo-Christianity," we refer to the time in the early church when most of its membership was still Jewish, and the church had not been completely and officially expelled from the synagogue and cut off from Judaism. Since, as we have seen in the last chapter, the definitive breach between church and synagogue took place when Gamaliel II led the Sanhedrin, at the very end of the first century, we shall employ that dividing date in order to distinguish between this section of our study and the next. However, it suffices to read the New Testament to see the degree to which the distance between church and synagogue was already growing in the first century. Therefore, when speaking of a "breach" around the end of the first century, two caveats must be raised. First, the decree by which Gamaliel II expelled Christians from the synagogues was not merely an anti-Christian action, for it was actually part of his wider project of bringing together a new form of Judaism that could no longer center on the Temple, which had been destroyed. Second, according to the witness of the New Testament, the process of distancing between Judeo-Christians and other Jews began much earlier. This may be seen in the story of the martyrdom of Stephen and in Paul's early enmity toward those following "the Way." Somewhat later, it is repeatedly seen in the reaction of many in the synagogues where Paul preached. It may also be seen in the Epistles and other New Testament books, where the matter of relations between Judeo-Christians and more traditional Jews is a frequent theme.

For these reasons, the significance of year 100 or of Gamaliel's decree as a dividing line should not be exaggerated. In some areas Judeo-Christianity persisted for several generations. The documents from those generations allow us a glimpse into how those Jews who converted to Christianity and still remained Jews understood their faith.

Along these lines, one must point out that, even though common opinion has usually held the contrary, most probably the evolution of Christianity and its worship was not a process leading from an original uniformity to later differences, but rather one moving from a wide diversity of practices and traditions toward a measure of unity and uniformity. This may be seen in the history of the New Testament itself and the origin of a canon that includes several Gospels that originally circulated independently, each of them mostly in a particular area and with its own perspectives, and then all joined in a single canon that also includes several other books of different origins. Christian worship seems to have followed a similar course, so that originally each church or community had its own practices and customs, and the interchange among believers slowly gave rise to common practices and a measure of uniformity. Thus, we should not be surprised that, just as we find differences among the Gospels, when we study the history of Judeo-Christian worship, we would also find different practices in various documents.

As to the documents that serve as sources for our knowledge of the church and its worship during its early years, none are as significant as those that are now part of the New Testament. There we see hints of the process through which Judeo-Christianity was making way for Gentile Christianity. We can see this in the Gospels themselves, for while Matthew and Mark—and also John to a certain degree—mention Jewish festivities and customs without explaining them, Luke seems to feel the need to give such explanations, implying that his intended audience was no longer as familiar with Judaism and its customs.

Beyond the New Testament itself, very few Christian documents could be dated as early as the first century. One that has the support of many scholars for an early date is the *Didache* or *Teaching of the Twelve Apostles*. Originally written in Greek, the *Didache* seems to be the product of Christians in the dry desert areas of Syria late in the first century. This document is important for our study, for it includes some of the earliest instructions we have for the administration of baptism and for the celebration of the Lord's Supper. Furthermore, the emphasis of the *Didache* on these two rites shows that they were at the very center of Judeo-Christian worship and devotion. At approximately the same time, the church in Rome wrote to its counterpart in Corinth, where apparently divisions remained similar to those that we find in Paul's correspondence with that church. Since Clement was bishop of Rome at the time, this document is usually called Clement's *Epistle to the Corinthians*. Whether Clement himself was originally a Jew is not clear. Some point to the influence of Stoicism in the letter as a sign that Clement was a Gentile. However, this is not a strong enough argument to settle the matter, for within first-century Judaism some currents were profoundly influenced by Stoicism. At any rate, the epistle itself abounds in references to the history of Israel.

Then there are other documents, some of them surviving only in fragmentary form, that seem to be the product of Judeo-Christians, if not in the first century, at least in the second. According to historian Eusebius of Caesarea, who wrote in the fourth century, shortly before the fall of Jerusalem Christians living in the city received a revelation ordering them to flee and find refuge in the city of Pella, in the region of Perea, south of the Sea of Galilee. He then adds,

> After James was martyred and Jerusalem was conquered, which followed immediately, it is said that the apostles and disciples of the Lord who were still alive came together with the relatives of the Lord according to the flesh (for the majority of them also were still alive). They took counsel as to who was worthy to succeed James. With one voice they pronounced Symeon, the son of Clopas, whom the Gospel mentions, to be worthy of the episcopal throne of that parish. He was a cousin, as they say, of the Savior, for Hegesippus records that Clopas was a brother of Joseph. (*Church History* 3.11; NPNF2 1:146)

Several ancient authors speak of a *Gospel according to the Hebrews* that expresses the views of that group, and may have been written before the year 100—although this is doubtful. Unfortunately, all that remains of this Gospel is a few fragments quoted by Origen, Eusebius, Jerome, and others. Several of these authors claim that this particular Gospel came from the region of Perea, and therefore it may have reflected the opinions and practices of Jewish Christians who had fled from Judea to that area. Somewhat later one still finds echoes of that ancient form of Judeo-Christianity in some other documents coming out of Syria. One of these is the so-called *Gospel of Peter*, which seems to have been written toward the end of the second century, and which later writers mention. Since Theodoret of Cyrus referenced it in the fifth century as being used by those whom he calls "Nazarenes," it would seem that even at that late date there were still some Judeo-Christians in the area of Syria. According to Theodoret, "The Nazarenes are Jews who revere Christ as a just man and who employ the Gospel said to be according to Peter" (*Fables of the Heretics* 2.2). Apparently the influence of this Judeo-Christian tradition lasted for some time, for late in the eighth century or early in the ninth someone in southern Egypt took the trouble of copying the *Gospel of Peter*—and more than a millennium later, in 1887, archaeologists would rediscover it. At any rate, this particular document is not of use for our study, for what remains of it is only a narrative of the passion and resurrection of Jesus, mostly drawn from the Synoptic Gospels and redacted so that Pontius Pilate and the Romans have nothing to do with the death of Jesus. The Jews alone are now blamed. In a word, what we find here is one of many efforts on the part of those ancient Judeo-Christians to show their independence from Judaism and their fidelity to Roman authorities after the great rebellions of the first and second centuries—possibly hoping to avoid persecution by the Roman government. If Jesus was not killed by imperial authorities but only by the Jews, this implies that he was not executed for sedition, but simply out of Jewish injustice, and that therefore his followers are not seditious people whom Romans should persecute.

Other documents dating from the second century, but still with strong Judeo-Christian characteristics, are the *Ascension of Isaiah*, the *Testaments of the Twelve Patriarchs*, and the *Second Book of Enoch*. However, it is quite likely that at least some of these are originally Jewish writings to which Christians later added some interpolations. These also say very little regarding early Christian worship.

In summary, the best sources that we have for first-century Judeo-Christian worship are the books that today we know as the New Testament—with the addition of the *Didache*.

THE TEMPLE AND ITS WORSHIP

The very first Christians did not reject the Temple or its worship. On the contrary, immediately after Pentecost we are told that the followers of Jesus "spent much time together in the temple" (Acts 2:46). The very next chapter in the book of Acts begins by informing us, "One day Peter and John were going up to the temple at the hour of prayer, at three o'clock in the after-noon." It is there in Solomon's portico that Peter makes his first speech after

Pentecost. Later, when an angel frees them from prison, the apostles "entered the temple at daybreak and went on with their teaching" (5:21). Many other passages mention Christians attending the Temple in each of the three traditional hours of prayer: third, sixth, and ninth. Some interpreters suggest that the place where the disciples were gathered on the morning of Pentecost (Acts 2:1, 15) was the Temple, which would clearly be the place where the various people mentioned in verses 9–11 would be gathered. Later, in Joppa, Peter is said to have gone up to the roof to pray at noon, or the sixth hour (Acts 10:9)—by which he was simply following the Jewish custom of praying at the same times as prayer was held in the Temple. As to the ninth hour, we have already mentioned the visit of Peter and John to the Temple at three o'clock in the afternoon. There are echoes of this practice in the *Didache*, which—after presenting its slightly different version of the Lord's Prayer than we find in either Matthew or Luke—ends by saying, "Pray in this way three times a day" (*Didache* 8.3). Although the *Didache* does not say explicitly that these were the same hours as those in the Temple, there is no reason to think that they would not be. This would seem to agree with what has already been said about the hours of prayer among Jews: that they were not primarily a time of private devotion, but rather a time in which the people as a whole approached God jointly and simultaneously.

Just as early Christians continued gathering at the Temple and following the traditional Jewish hours of prayer, they also followed the traditional Jewish calendar. There are abundant references to Paul's Sabbath visits to the synagogues in the cities he visited. There he took part in worship, and when invited to speak, he announced the message of the death and resurrection of Jesus as the fulfillment of ancient prophecies and of the promises made to Israel. Frequently this would provoke adverse reactions from the more traditional Jews; but Paul's purpose was not to criticize Jews or their synagogues, but rather to let them know that the great promise for which they had awaited for centuries had now been fulfilled in the person of Jesus.

As to other special festivities, Christians continued observing them following the traditional Jewish calendar. Acts tells us that Paul "was eager to be in Jerusalem, if possible, on the day of Pentecost" (20:16). As is well known, due to what Acts 2 says about events on a day of Pentecost, that date has long had great importance for Christians. Furthermore, in the pages that follow, we have ample opportunity to discuss the significance of the Jewish Passover for Christians.

In summary, those first Judeo-Christians did not believe that they belonged to a new religion, but rather saw themselves as a particular group within the people of Israel—a particular group because they knew that the Anointed of God, the Messiah, had already come in the person of Jesus. For them, other

Jews—those who had not accepted the message regarding Jesus—were still followers of the same religion, although they had not yet heard or accepted what God had done in Jesus.

However, not all Jews had the same positive attitude toward the Temple and its religious festivals. Controlled as it was by the aristocratic Sadducees and by high priests who were often agents of the Roman government, the Temple itself was not always seen in a positive light. Such was the general attitude of the Pharisees, who still declared that they respected the Temple and continued worshiping in it, but criticized or ignored the aristocratic Sadducees. As to Judeo-Christianity, it also often included criticism of what took place in the Temple. We have an example in Stephen's speech before the Sanhedrin, where he looks back to a better time when God was worshiped at a tabernacle that moved around with the people, and does not seem very enthusiastic about the Temple: "'But it was Solomon who built a house for him [God]. Yet the Most High does not dwell in houses made with human hands'" (Acts 7:47–48). Furthermore, according to the narrative, Stephen's attitude regarding the Temple was already somewhat known or suspected, for the witnesses bribed to accuse him say, "'This man never stops saying things against this holy place and the law'" (Acts 6:13).

Judeo-Christians were also critical of at least some religious festivals. This may be seen in Paul's Epistles, for he tells the Galatians, "Now, however, that you have come to know God, or rather to be known by God, how can you turn back again to the weak and beggarly elemental spirits? How can you want to be enslaved to them again? You are observing special days, and months, and seasons, and years" (Gal. 4:9–11). Paul's opinion regarding the power of the Law to justify is well known. While he was convinced that the Law was given by God, and that the way of life that it teaches is correct, he was also convinced that justification cannot be attained by obeying the Law, "For 'no human being will be justified in his sight' by deeds prescribed by the law, for through the law comes the knowledge of sin" (Rom. 3:20). And earlier in the same Epistle, while showing respect for the Law, he points out that what is important is not the text of the Law itself, but rather its moral teaching: "When Gentiles, who do not possess the law, do instinctively what the law requires, these, though not having the law, are a law to themselves. They show that what the law requires is written on their hearts" (Rom. 2:14–15).

This is not the place to discuss Paul's theology regarding the Law. It should suffice to point out that both Paul and later Christian theology affirm that the entire Law was given by God, but then they also affirm that it is mostly its monotheism, and its teachings regarding morality and justice, that are still valid. This was based on a distinction between ceremonial commandments and those that express the unique and just nature of God. Colossians 2, having to do with food, drink, and feast days, goes on to say, "These are only a shadow of what is to come, but the substance belongs to Christ" (Col. 2:17). A similar distinction appears also in Ephesians, where, after claiming that the apparent differences between those of Jewish blood and those of Gentile origin are not such, the author closes the subject by declaring that Christ "abolished the law with its commandments and ordinances, that he might create in himself one new humanity in place of the two, thus making peace" (Eph. 2:15).

What we read in Colossians, that the ancient ceremonial was only a "shadow" of what was to come, is fundamental if one is to understand the manner in which Judeo-Christians, and then most ancient Christian theologians, understood God's revelation in the ancient laws having to do with sacrifices, rites, circumcision, diet, festivities such as Passover, and other similar means. All of this was a "shadow" or "figure" that has been fulfilled in Christ. This exegetical method is commonly known as "typology," and is discussed further in chapter 3.

THE BREACH

As we saw in the previous chapter, Judaism toward the end of the first century was taking a new shape due mostly to the debacle of the destruction of the Temple, and it was at that time that Gamaliel II decreed the expulsion of Christians from the synagogues. However, we must not think that animosity between Judeo-Christians and other Jews moved only in one direction. It was not only the more traditional Jews who suspected Judeo-Christians, but also the latter who were constantly distancing themselves from the former. This had to do partly with political and social issues, and partly with strictly religious or theological matters.

Regarding the political and social motivations behind the growing enmity between traditional Jews and Judeo-Christians, one must mention that most Judeo-Christians, following the emphasis of Jesus on the love of neighbor and on pacific attitudes, apparently did not support the rebellion in the decade of the 60s as other Jews expected. When they heard Judeo-Christians speak of the fulfillment of the promises, and of Jesus as the Messiah, other Jews would expect them to support the rebellion. But it was not so. We have already quoted Eusebius referring to the flight of Judeo-Christians from Jerusalem to Pella. Whether this was due to a particular revelation, as Eusebius claims, or to some other reason, the fact is that Christians abandoned the city of Jerusalem when it was threatened by Roman conquest and reprisal. From the point of view of Jews remaining in Jerusalem—no matter what their attitude might have been regarding the rebellion—this came very close to treason, or at least to a lack of patriotism.

The enmity between the two groups continued growing, since both claimed for themselves the same inheritance and the same Scripture—although interpreting them differently. According to Roman historian Suetonius, around 52 CE Emperor Claudius expelled the Jews from Rome "for they were causing constant disturbances because of a certain *Chrestus*" (*Life of Claudius* 25.4). Most scholars are inclined to think that this *Chrestus* is none other than *Christus*, Christ. There are echoes of this event in the story of Priscilla and Aquila, whom Paul met in Corinth and who soon joined his work: "Paul left Athens and went to Corinth. There he found a Jew named Aquila, a native of Pontus, who had recently come from Italy with his wife Priscilla, because Claudius had ordered all Jews to leave Rome" (Acts 18:1–2). Later, when Nero persecuted Christians, blaming them for a fire in Rome, and clearly distinguishing between them and Jews, Judeo-Christians saw this as an injustice not only on the part of Nero, but also on the part of other Jews, who did not suffer the same punishments.

When finally the Jews were able to convince Emperor Vespasian to allow them to organize themselves under the rule of a Sanhedrin, and his project of building Jewish unity and uniformity led Gamaliel II to the official expulsion of Judeo-Christians from the synagogues, practically all Christians—even though still mostly Jewish by birth, or at least converts among the God-fearers who had been attending the synagogue before hearing the Christian message—had broken with the synagogue and taken a path independent of Judaism.

Throughout that process, Christian accusations against Jews became ever more extreme. Late in the first century, the *Didache* instructed its readers to fast on the days that today we would call Wednesday and Friday: "Do not let your fasts be at the same time as the hypocrites. They fast on the second and fifth day of the week. You should fast on the fourth day [Wednesday] and the Day of Preparation [Friday]" (*Didache* 8.1; ANF 7:379). This is one of many cases in which Christians took a traditional Jewish practice and changed it in such a way that it came to be distinctively theirs. What Jews called the "day of preparation" was the day preceding the Sabbath, which was so named because during it one was to prepare all that was necessary for the proper Sabbath observation. Therefore, it could not be a day of fasting. But Christians, remembering that the sixth day of the week was also the day of the crucifixion of Jesus, turned it into a day of fasting, with the result that they kept the basic structure of the Jewish week, but changed its specific observances. Although neither this text nor any other from the first century explain why Wednesday became a day of fasting, a later explanation was that this was the day of the betrayal by Judas, and that it was therefore a day of sorrow for all Christians. At any rate, the sign of the growing distance between the two groups is not so much that they chose to fast on different days, but rather that in this text Jews who follow the traditional pattern of fasting are called "hypocrites." At approximately the same time, the book of Revelation refers to "'those who say that they are Jews and are not, but are a synagogue of Satan'" (2:9). In other words, the true Jews are now said to be the Judeo-Christians whom Revelation addresses, and not those who belong to the Jewish synagogue in Smyrna. It is rather tragic to note that the persecution that seems to have been the context for the book of Revelation was addressed not only against Christians, but also against Jews, and that Revelation completely ignores this.

That growing enmity was eventually enhanced by an anachronistic reading of the New Testament. When the Gospels refer to the "Jews," or when on the day of Pentecost Peter says that it was the Jews who crucified Jesus, those who are speaking are also Jews. Thus, it is not a case of racial anti-Semitism. It is rather the way one Jew is depicted as criticizing the actions of other Jews. The New Testament is mostly a Jewish document—Judeo-Christian certainly, but precisely for that reason also Jewish. To use it for the mass condemnation of the Jewish people is to betray what those Judeo-Christians were saying and writing.

All these social and political factors played an important role in the growing enmity between Judeo-Christians and those Jews who did not accept Jesus of Nazareth as the Christ or the Anointed One. This also found expression in various elements of worship, which is our main concern here. Although these elements are so intertwined that it is impossible to discuss one of them apart from the rest, in the following pages we devote separate chapters to each of the following: first, Judeo-Christian preaching and how that preaching made use of the Scriptures of Israel (chapter 3); second, the development of a new calendar that no longer revolved around the Sabbath or seventh day of the week, but rather around the first day—which we now call Sunday (chapter 4); third, the practice of baptism and how it was interpreted (chapter 5); and finally, Communion (chapter 6). Once again, discussing any of these subjects while ignoring the rest is impossible, for they all arise at the same time and each affects the others. Even so, for reasons of clarity, we need to look at each of them separately and in turn.

3

The Judeo-Christian Message

The book of Acts includes a number of speeches—some of them rather extensive—that provide a window through which one may look into the preaching of early Christian generations. Very few of them address a gathering of the church. The main exception seems to be Peter's speech in Acts 1:15–22 in which he proposes naming someone to take the vacancy left by Judas. Many of the speeches in Acts address Jewish audiences. Such is the case of Peter's speech on Pentecost (2:14–20), his speech after healing the lame man at the Temple (3:12–26), his defense before the Sanhedrin (4:8–12), and Stephen's defense in similar circumstances (7:2–53). As to Paul, the first mention of his preaching simply tells us that he proclaimed Jesus in the synagogues, saying, "'He is the Son of God'" (9:20). The same seems to have been his practice from the beginning of his missionary travels, for "When they arrived at Salamis, they proclaimed the word of God in the synagogues of the Jews" (13:5). And at the very end of his career, we are told that Paul, now a prisoner in Rome, "called together the local leaders of the Jews"—on which follows the last of his speeches in Acts (28:17–28). Acts does not tell us what Paul preached or said on each of these occasions, but it seems to indicate that it was something similar to the rather extensive speech in Acts 13:15–41—to which we shall return shortly. Acts also includes other speeches by Paul, although not addressing a worshiping audience. One of these is his defense before Felix (24:10–21), and another is his famous speech at the Areopagus (17:22–31). In brief, the book of Acts summarizes many speeches addressed to pagans, but the majority of its speeches are addressed to Jews, to God-fearers—as in the case of Peter at the home of Cornelius (10:34–43)—or to both. The most extensive example of Paul's preaching in the synagogues is set in Antioch of Pisidia (13:14–52).

45

The common thread running through most of these speeches in Acts is that Jesus is the promised Messiah, God's Anointed—or, in the Greek translation of "the anointed," the Christ—in whom the promises made to Abraham and his descendants and announced by the prophets and the Psalms are fulfilled. A clear example of this is Peter's speech on Pentecost. Peter begins by rejecting the notion that the disciples are drunk, but immediately moves to a passage from the prophet Joel (Acts 2:17–21; Joel 2:28–32, quoted from the Septuagint). After that quote, Peter tells the story of the death and resurrection of Jesus and then relates it to several verses from Psalm 16 (again, quoting from the Septuagint), in order to conclude that "'God has made him both Lord and Messiah [Christ], this Jesus whom you crucified'" (Acts 2:36). He is not telling them simply that they are sinners and that there is salvation in Jesus Christ. He is telling them that their sin is enormous, for they have rejected the promised Messiah. In order to grasp the significance of what is being said, remember that for centuries Israel had been awaiting the promised Messiah. Now Peter tells them that the Messiah did come, but that instead of accepting and following him they rejected him and had him crucified! When his listeners ask Peter and his companions what they are to do, Peter responds by inviting them to be baptized "'in the name of Jesus Christ so that your sins may be forgiven; and you will receive the gift of the Holy Spirit'" (Acts 2:38). Later (in chapter 5) we shall return to the subject of baptism. Of present note is that Peter's message before his Jewish audience is that Jesus is the Christ or Messiah promised by God for the people of Israel, and that this gift is also for others: "'For the promise is for you, for your children, and for all who are far away, everyone whom the Lord our God calls to him'" (Acts 2:39).

In Acts 10, Peter is called to the home of the centurion Cornelius. There his message is similar. Apparently what Peter says is not new for Cornelius and those gathered there, for Peter says, "'You know the message he sent to the people of Israel, preaching peace by Jesus Christ—he is Lord of all.'" Then follows the story of the death and resurrection of Jesus, leading to the conclusion that "'he is the one ordained by God as judge of the living and the dead. All the prophets testify about him that everyone who believes in him receives forgiveness of sins through his name'" (Acts 10:36, 42–43). We usually think that Peter is simply preaching to a pagan audience—which leaves us wondering how they could understand what Peter was saying. There is no doubt that Cornelius and those with him are Gentiles, not Jews. But they are not really pagans. Acts 10 says that he was "a devout man who feared God with all his household; he gave alms generously to the people and prayed constantly to God" (10:2). Later on we are told that Cornelius was "'an upright and God-fearing man, who [was] well spoken of by the whole Jewish nation'" (10:22). In other words, Cornelius and those in his household were among the God-fearers to whom we have already referred. They were not Jews by birth. Nor had they become Jewish proselytes. But they performed acts of mercy and raised their prayers to the only true God, the God of Israel. Peter's message to them is that Jesus Christ is the fulfillment of the promises, the Anointed, God's Messiah. Then the Holy Spirit intervenes directly to lead Peter to baptize Cornelius and his household.

Something similar had already happened in the story of the Ethiopian eunuch in Acts 8, although there Philip does not give a speech but rather helps the Ethiopian understand the Scripture he is reading. We are not told in so many words that the Ethiopian himself was a God-fearer, but this is implied in that he had gone all the way from Ethiopia to Jerusalem in order to worship there. The long distance that he traveled shows that this certainly was not a pagan who worshiped the traditional gods of Ethiopia. Furthermore, when Luke says that the Ethiopian was a eunuch, he may be mentioning the reason he had not become a Jewish proselyte, for the Law would not allow a eunuch to join the congregation of God (Deut. 23:1). According to Acts, the eunuch was reading Isaiah 53—although we are not given the number of the chapter, for at that time the Bible was not divided as it is today into chapters and verses, and therefore the only way to provide a reference was to quote the beginning of the passage. The eunuch wonders whether this passage in Isaiah refers to the prophet himself or to someone else. Beginning with that passage, Philip tells him "the good news about Jesus" (Acts 8:35). Although Luke tells the story in a few lines, it is not clear that this was a very brief conversation. Philip and the Ethiopian are riding in the latter's chariot, and their conversation may have lasted several hours, or even days. In the end, when they reach a place where there is water, the Ethiopian asks Philip if there is any reason why he is not to be baptized. Philip could well have responded by quoting the words in Deuteronomy. Certainly the eunuch, who knew enough about the religion of Israel to travel all the way to Jerusalem to worship, would be aware of that prohibition affecting him directly. But the same prophet Isaiah, when speaking about what would happen when the promises were finally fulfilled, had said that in that blessed time the curse over eunuchs would be abrogated (Isa. 56:3–5). In other words, what the eunuch is asking Philip is whether, since the promises of God are being fulfilled in Christ, he can now be added to the people of God. Philip's answer is brave and radical: he goes down to the water with the eunuch and baptizes him. The message of those early Christians, all of them Jews, addressed both to Jews and to Gentile God-fearers, was that now, since the promises of God have been fulfilled in Christ, the way is open for God-fearing Gentiles to become part of the people of God. (See further in chapter 5.)

Both in Peter's speech on Pentecost and in the story about the Ethiopian, the issue is not so much a matter of individual salvation as fulfillment of what

God has promised regarding the people of God. Peter speaks of what God had promised to the people of Israel. In the case of the Ethiopian, it is the promise that people such as he would be brought into the people of God. Once again, but still at the center of early Christian faith, worship was not so much about an individual relationship between the believer and God as about that believer's participation in the worship of God with the people of God.

THE CASE OF ANTIOCH OF PISIDIA

All of this, and the consequences it would have for the Christian community, may be seen in the episode in Antioch of Pisidia. Paul's visit and speech in that city, of which we read in Acts 13:14–52, are typical of what would take place in many other cities that Paul visited. Luke does not repeat in every city what Paul said, but simply lets us understand that Paul's speeches and the ensuing events were usually replicated in other cities and synagogues that he visited.

Upon arriving at Antioch of Pisidia on what is commonly known as his first missionary voyage, Paul along with Barnabas followed the practice that according to Acts was their custom: "on the sabbath day they went into the synagogue and sat down" (13:14). After the reading of Scripture, they were invited to give "'any word of exhortation.'" In response to that invitation, Paul stood and made a speech in which he addressed his audience first as "'you Israelites, and others who fear God,'" and then as "'you descendants of Abraham's family, and others who fear God'" (13:16, 26). These references to those who fear God are not just a redundant repetition of "you Israelites" or "you descendants of Abraham's family," which clearly means the Jews listening to him. Those who "fear God" are the God-fearers already mentioned—Gentiles who believe the faith of Israel but have not actually joined the synagogue as proselytes. After recounting the history of Israel and then speaking of the death and resurrection of Jesus, Paul declares, "'And we bring you the good news that what God promised to our ancestors he has fulfilled for us, their children, by raising Jesus, as it is written'" (13:32–33). It is by virtue of that resurrection of Jesus, God's Anointed, that Paul announces, "'Let it be known to you therefore, my brothers, that through this man forgiveness of sins is proclaimed to you; by this Jesus everyone who believes is set free from all those sins from which you could not be freed by the law of Moses'" (13:38–39). In other words, not only those who are Jews by birth, but also the God-fearers who are present, are justified by Jesus Christ.

What then follows is what would normally happen when such preaching came to the synagogues. Many of those who heard Paul invited him and Barnabas to tell them more about this. The impact of what they said was such that "the next Sabbath almost the whole city gathered to hear the word of the Lord" (13:44). Although Luke is probably exaggerating, this is an indication of the attraction that Judaism had among Gentiles, many of whom were ready to follow the doctrinal teachings and ethical principles of Judaism, but not all its other laws—particularly those regarding unclean foods and circumcision. As a result of the interest that the Gentiles show for what Paul and Barnabas teach, which is tantamount to telling all these Gentiles that they can now become children of Abraham, "when the Jews saw the crowds, they were filled with jealousy; and blaspheming, they contradicted what was spoken by Paul" (13:45). This is not surprising. Up to that time those who were Jews by blood and the proselytes among the Gentiles who were ready to subject themselves to the entire Law had a position of privilege in the synagogue over those who were mere God-fearers—although there are also indications that proselytes were not considered equal to the descendants of Abraham. But now this Christian message threatens to destroy the privileges of the descendants of Abraham, and there is an immediate reaction. Luke tells us, "When the Gentiles heard this, they were glad and praised the word of the Lord. . . . But the Jews incited the devout women of high standing and the leading men of the city, and stirred up persecution against Paul and Barnabas, and drove them out of their region" (13:48, 50–51). In the midst of these events, Acts tells us that Paul and Barnabas declared, "'We are now turning to the Gentiles.'" This last phrase, however, does not mean that they would now cease preaching in the synagogues and speak only to pagans. On the contrary, in the very next city, Iconium, the events in Antioch are repeated. Throughout the entire book of Acts, whenever Paul arrives at a new city, he goes to the synagogue and preaches his message there. In short, the Pauline mission is not so much among pagan polytheists as it is among God-fearers in the synagogues.

This is of crucial importance if we are to understand Paul's preaching and the nature of the Christian community in those early generations. Early Christian preaching was most often addressed to God-fearers, and was most successful among them. Apparently, its main attraction was that now they could share in the promises made to the children of Abraham without being subject to the ceremonial and ritual strictures of the Law of Moses. These God-fearers who accepted Christian preaching would continue attending synagogue on the Sabbath days for as long as they were allowed to do so; but at the same time, as we shall see, they would also hold their own Christian meetings. Since at that time, shortly before the destruction of the Temple and the formation of the new Sanhedrin in Jamnia, there was no universal authority within Judaism, these Christian groups—which included some Jews by birth, but mostly God-fearers—were able to continue attending synagogue in some places, and not in others.

PREACHING IN CHRISTIAN CHURCHES

When discussing early Christian preaching, it is customary to fix attention primarily on the speeches that appear in the New Testament, mostly in the book of Acts. This does not yield much regarding early Christian preaching, for the speeches in Acts, besides being summaries rather than speeches, are usually not delivered within a church that has gathered for worship, but are rather addressing a Jewish audience letting them know that the promises of God have been fulfilled in Jesus—as we have seen in Peter's sermon in Pentecost and in Paul's sermons in the synagogues. Others are speeches in which Christians defend their faith before Jewish authorities—as in the speeches before the Sanhedrin. Still others address pagans who may or may not be interested—as in Paul's speech at the Areopagus and his other speeches before Roman authorities. Thus, if we only take into account the speeches that appear in Acts, we can say little about preaching within the Christian community of faith, for we have no text of a sermon or speech addressing such a community during the first century. Perhaps what comes closest to meeting this standard is Paul's farewell speech in Ephesus (Acts 20:17–35); but even in that case Paul is not speaking to the church, only to the elders.

However, this does not mean that there was no preaching in Christian gatherings. In his Corinthian correspondence, Paul set some principles for preaching in church, which was usually known as "prophesying." The prophet was a person who, after the reading of Scripture, would explain it, not primarily in its historical sense but rather showing what Scripture was saying to this particular church in its concrete situation. Some of what Paul says in his Corinthian correspondence may be confusing and difficult to understand, for on the one hand he gives rules for when men and women prophesy—that is, preach—and on the other he forbids women to speak. Thus, in 1 Corinthians 11:4–5 he says, "Any man who prays or prophesies with something on his head disgraces his head, but any woman who prays or prophesies with her head unveiled disgraces her head." Shortly thereafter he seems to contradict himself, for he writes, "Women should be silent in the churches. For they are not permitted to speak" (1 Cor. 14:34). This is not the place to discuss the matter in any detail, but the NRSV correctly points out that "other ancient authorities put verses 34–35 after verse 40." What we have here is commonly called a "floating text"—one that appears in different places within a larger text. Normally such floating texts are the result of someone writing a marginal note that then the various later copyists placed within the text, each choosing what seemed to be the most appropriate place. Apparently, these lines are taken from similar words in 1 Timothy 2:12. This does not solve the problem, for it would still be necessary to deal with 1 Timothy, but it does make clear that Paul was telling the Corinthians that women were allowed to prophesy—as long as they covered their heads.

Having women remain silent in the congregation was not an originally Christian idea, for it was already the general practice in the synagogue. The church also adopted another practice from the synagogue that is very important when it comes to considering women's role within the church. This is what could well be called the "order of widows." Israel's Law repeatedly commands care and protection for widows, orphans, the poor, and strangers. Widows are included in this list of people lacking protection because frequently, when a woman's husband died, she was left without any means of support. Obviously, as we see in Acts 6, the church continued this practice of offering support to needy widows—as the synagogues also did. One may well imagine that in the particular case of the church, which most Jews considered a heretical group, there would be women who not only had lost their husbands but were also rejected by their families because they had embraced Christianity. Such women would have no other support than what the church could give them, and therefore the church did help them with offerings brought by the faithful. As time went by and these widows became more numerous, they not only had a place reserved for them in worship but also were given special tasks. With that society's customs, it was very difficult for a man to serve as a teacher or spiritual guide to women. Therefore, these widows—as well as other women—were charged with those and other similar tasks. There are echoes of this not only in the above-quoted passage in Acts, but also in 1 Timothy 5:3–8. Later some single women would join this group of women who taught and provided spiritual direction within the church. (Since we are dealing with the subject of leadership roles for women, it is important to point out that, even amid all the prejudice of that society, in the New Testament there is at least one woman who is a deacon: Phoebe, in Romans 16:1. We say "a deacon," and not "a deaconess," because today this latter word refers to women whose tasks and authority are different from those of deacons, while in antiquity it was simply the feminine form of the same word. Another woman, Priscilla, apparently teaches theology to a famous preacher. Another is called an "apostle"—Junia, in Romans 16:7. And Lydia seems to be the economic mainstay of the church in Philippi.)

Paul's Epistles provide other indications as to what took place in Christian worship. Some people spoke in various tongues. Paul affirms that this is a gift of the Spirit and therefore is not to be demeaned. However, he also says that it is much more valuable to "prophesy"—which simply means to speak in a manner that the congregation understands, and thus receives a word from God. This is seen clearly in his first Epistle to the Corinthians, where, immediately after the famous eulogy to love in chapter 13, he writes,

Pursue love and strive for the spiritual gifts, and especially that you may prophesy. For those who speak in a tongue do not speak to other people but to God; for nobody understands them, since they are speaking mysteries in the Spirit. On the other hand, those who prophesy speak to other people for their upbuilding and encouragement and consolation. Those who speak in a tongue build up themselves, but those who prophesy build up the church. Now I would like all of you to speak in tongues, but even more to prophesy. One who prophesies is greater than one who speaks in tongues, unless someone interprets, so that the church may be built up. (1 Cor. 14:1–5)

Having said this, we may now return to the center of our discussion, whose purpose is to remind us that, although we do not have texts of sermons or speeches that Christians gave in churches during the first century, we do know that such preaching took place. This should not surprise us, for Judeo-Christians would not find in the biblical interpretation offered in the synagogue an affirmation and application of their own faith, or an exhortation as to how to follow it. Therefore, when they met as a separate group—usually to celebrate Communion, as we shall see in chapter 6—they would soon begin to provide opportunity for preaching or prophesying within a clearly Christian context.

This practice of having "prophets" or preachers speak, while providing for the edification of the community, also had its own difficulties and dangers, for apparently some people preached doctrines that were not acceptable to the rest of the church, and some preached for their own financial profit. On this subject, a passage in the *Didache* is quite instructive:

Therefore, receive whoever comes and teaches you all these things that have been said. But if the teacher changes and begins to teach something that destroys this, then do not listen to him. But if he teaches that which increases righteousness and the knowledge of the Lord, receive him as you would the Lord. This is what the Gospel decrees concerning apostles and prophets: Let every apostle that comes to you be received as the Lord. But he shall only remain one day, although it might be necessary to stay until the next day. But only a false prophet would stay three days. And an apostle should take nothing away with him except bread to last until his next lodging. Only a false prophet asks for money. Every prophet who speaks in the Spirit you shall not try or judge, for every sin shall be forgiven, but this one shall not be forgiven. However, not everyone who speaks in the Spirit is a prophet, but only if he follows the ways of the Lord. Therefore, you can tell the true prophet from the false by their ways. Every prophet who orders a meal in the Spirit does not eat from it, unless he is a false prophet. Every prophet who teaches the truth but does not do what he teaches is a false prophet. And every prophet proved a true one, who works toward the mystery of the church in the world and yet does not teach others to do what he does, shall not be judged by you, for his judgment is with God, for the ancient prophets also did this. But whoever in the Spirit says, "give me money" or something else, do not listen to him. But if he asks you to give him something for the sake of others who are in need, let no one judge him. (*Didache* 11; ANF 7:380–81)

EPISTLES AS A FORM OF DISTANCE PREACHING

When discussing early Christian preaching, we frequently forget that the Epistles and several other books of the New Testament are also, in a way, an example of Christian preaching. One may well imagine the church in one of the cities where Paul had preached—Corinth, for instance. We do not know how long Judeo-Christians in Corinth were allowed to continue attending synagogue, but we may well assume it was not long. At any rate, when Scripture was taught and discussed in those synagogues, nothing would be said about Jesus of Nazareth as the Messiah or the Anointed of God. We also know that from an early date Judeo-Christians gathered, among other things, to break bread (see chapter 6). In those gatherings, the custom would soon develop of commenting on Scripture, not as was done in the synagogues, but rather reading it as a promise fulfilled in Christ. This would be the beginning of Judeo-Christian preaching, no longer in the synagogues, but now in Christian assemblies that came to be called "churches." Unfortunately, we do not have a single text representing that sort of commentary on Scripture that would take place in the gathering of the church for the breaking of the bread. But what we do have is a collection of letters and other documents that circulated among the churches with the purpose of being read out loud to the entire assembly—which would normally take place just before the breaking of bread.

One may well imagine what would happen in Corinth when a letter arrived from Paul. Paul did not write that letter so that each recipient would read it alone at home, as we often do today, but rather so that the entire letter would be read out loud as a message from Paul to the whole church. Paul did not usually write to individuals, but rather to churches. This is true not only of letters such as those to the Romans, Corinthians, and Thessalonians, but even of letters that seem to be more personal, like the one that we now call the Epistle to Philemon. That letter is not addressed only to Philemon, but rather "to Philemon our dear friend and co-worker, to Apphia our sister, to Archippus our fellow soldier, and to the church in your house" (Phlm. 1b–3). Thus, even this letter, addressed to a particular believer regarding how he would relate with a former slave, was not written to be read in private, but rather so that the entire church would receive it as a message from Paul, primarily to Philemon, but also to all the rest. The same is true, even more clearly, of Paul's correspondence with the Corinthians, which is largely dedicated to answer questions they had, and to draw their attention to some of their own problems.

Paul was not the only author of such "epistolar sermons." The very short Epistle of Jude was directed to Judeo-Christian congregations that apparently had not been greatly influenced by Gentile Christians. Here there are allusions to Jewish writings that are not now part of the Bible, which would only be known to those who had been raised within a Jewish context. The Epistle seems to have been written because of rumors that some itinerant preachers were visiting congregations and corrupting their behavior. Such people are showing that they hold another faith, which leads to a different morality. What they teach must be rejected, and steps must be taken to correct the damage they have done (Jude 3–4, 19–23).

The same is true of one of the most clearly Jewish books of the entire New Testament, the Revelation of John. We say that it is "clearly Jewish" because it contains so many allusions to Scripture and other Hebrew literature that scholars tell us that there is hardly a verse in the entire book that does not contain at least one such reference. There is no doubt that John, who addresses this book to the churches in Asia, is a Judeo-Christian who is writing mostly to other Judeo-Christians, for the book itself would make little sense to someone who did not know the Scriptures of Israel, as well as other Jewish traditions. Revelation was definitely written in order to be read out loud within the church, for at the very beginning it says, "Blessed is the one who reads aloud the words of the prophecy" (1:3). The entire book ends with the words "Come, Lord Jesus!" (22:20), just before a final benediction. This was an invocation commonly used at the beginning of Communion. Therefore, it is clear that in writing this book John proposed that it be circulated at least among the seven churches to which specific letters are written, that each of them would hear also the reading of the messages to the other six, and that all of them would hear the reading of the entire book immediately before Communion. Also, whatever may have been the purpose of the Epistle to the Hebrews, there is no doubt that it also circulated widely, for although it seems to have originated in or near Egypt, very soon Clement's *Epistle to the Corinthians*, written in Rome, drew inspiration from Hebrews.

As to the Gospels, they were intended to be read within the context of worship. The earliest of them, Mark, seems to have been written shortly before the fall of Jerusalem. It circulated so widely that scarcely two decades later both Matthew and Luke used it as one of their sources. The history of the

Gospel of John is still much debated among scholars, but consensus seems to indicate that it was already circulating in Asia Minor by the end of the first century. At any rate, even though each of the four Gospels was more known and read in a different area, and each understood the message of Christ from its own perspective, the churches in an area would share with other churches the particular Gospel they had. In consequence, by the end of the first century the three Synoptic Gospels were generally admitted by all churches. John, long preferred in Asia Minor, was also beginning to make headway in the West, so that by the end of the second century the entire church shared the four Gospels that we now find in our New Testament. What is interesting in this context is that, just as the development of worship does not lead from an original uniformity to a growing diversity—but rather from an original variety to growing uniformity—something similar happened regarding these books that, originally read in a particular church or region, eventually were joined together in the New Testament.

THE INTERPRETATION OF SCRIPTURE

This is not the place for a detailed examination of all the preaching and teaching appearing in the New Testament. But it is necessary to point to the significance of an interpretive method that Judeo-Christians and Gentile Christians both learned, at least in part, from Judaism. While in Greece philosophers sought eternal and unchanging truths, far beyond time and its vicissitudes, Hebrew tradition found its truth in its own relationship to God's actions in history and within God's people. In this tradition, what is most important is, rather than knowing that God is immutable, omniscient, and omnipresent, knowing and experiencing that this God is present in today's life in a manner similar to how God was present in yesterday's events, and will also be present on the morrow. The God of Israel, who says, "I AM WHO I AM," shows this divine being by calling Moses, by freeing Israel from the yoke of Egypt, by restraining its enemies, and by always being present among the people.

The Judeo-Christians of the New Testament follow the same pattern. They were not interested in declaring how God is in Godself or in defining the divine eternal attributes—beyond being merciful—but rather in pointing to what God is doing now, and what God will do in the future, on the basis of what God has done in the past and has promised to do. This is why the reading of Scripture was followed by a sermon or commentary that established the link between the past history of the people of God and their present condition.

This is what is commonly called "typology," for it presupposes that God acts following certain "types" or patterns of action that, without ever repeating in an identical fashion, are still recognizable. Typological theory would develop later, beginning in the second century. But one can already see it at work in the New Testament. This is what Paul means in Colossians when declaring that "matters of food and drink or of observing festivals, new moons, or sabbaths" are "only a shadow of what is to come, but the substance belongs to Christ" (2:16–17). These matters of food and drink are what the Epistle to the Ephesians calls "commandments and ordinances" that God has abolished in Christ (2:15). This does not mean that such "commandments and ordinances" were bad, or that they were not given by God. What it means is that they were a "shadow" or announcement of what would become true in Jesus—and once the reality has come, the shadow is no longer necessary.

Typological interpretations appear everywhere in the New Testament. One may take as an example what Paul says 1 Corinthians 10, where he tells his readers, apparently most of them still Judeo-Christians, "I do not want you to be unaware, brothers and sisters, that our ancestors were all under the cloud, and all passed through the sea, and all were baptized into Moses in the cloud and in the sea, and all ate the same spiritual food, and all drank the same spiritual drink. For they drank from the spiritual rock that followed them, and the rock was Christ" (10:1–4). Likewise, in Romans 4:18–25, Paul relates the promises made to Abraham with their fulfillment in Jesus Christ, so that the promises were a shadow or figure of Christ:

> Hoping against hope, he believed that he would become "the father of many nations," according to what was said, "So numerous shall your descendants be." He did not weaken in faith when he considered his own body, which was already as good as dead (for he was about a hundred years old), or when he considered the barrenness of Sarah's womb. No distrust made him waver concerning the promise of God, but he grew strong in his faith as he gave glory to God, being fully convinced that God was able to do what he had promised. Therefore his faith "was reckoned to him as righteousness." Now the words, "it was reckoned to him," were written not for his sake alone, but for ours also. It will be reckoned to us who believe in him who raised Jesus our Lord from the dead, who was handed over to death for our trespasses and was raised for our justification.

In conclusion, besides the summaries that appear in Acts, we have no Christian sermons that can be dated back to the first century. If by "preaching" we mean the oral delivery of a message to a congregation of believers, little can be said about Christian preaching during that first century. But if by "preaching" we mean the exposition of the message of the Bible within the church, what we have is even better than written sermons: we have abundant examples of how some highly respected leaders within the churches, but for some reason absent from them, let the churches know their thoughts and instructions. This approach also implies that a careful study of first-century Christian preaching, rather than centering mostly on the outlines and summaries of sermons that one finds in Acts, must take into account as an example the entire New Testament.

4

The Christian Calendar

CONTINUATION OF THE JEWISH CALENDAR

Early Judeo-Christians clearly continued following the same Jewish calendar that had long ruled their lives. The seven-day week, the center of the Jewish calendar, remained the center of the Christian calendar. Within each of those days, Judeo-Christians continued observing the same main three hours of prayer they had learned from their youth. Although in recent centuries the matter of how and when the Sabbath is to be observed has been a subject of discussion and disagreement among Christians, that does not seem to have been the case among the first Judeo-Christians. In the Gospels we do find frequent cases in which Jesus disagreed with the leaders of a synagogue on what could or could not be done on the Sabbath. However, although today we might think this was a radical view or an innovation on Jesus' part, some distinguished rabbis taught that the law of Sabbath rest should never be placed above love of neighbor.

Furthermore, surprising as it may seem to some, apart from those episodes in the Gospels, very little in the New Testament may be seen as a repudiation or criticism of Sabbath observances. The harshest passage along those lines is the one quoted earlier from Colossians: "do not let anyone condemn you in matters of food and drink or of observing festivals, new moons, or sabbaths" (2:16). But even that comment regarding the Sabbath was not as harsh as many of the sayings of the ancient prophets of Israel. What is new in Colossians is the claim that such things "are only a shadow of what is to come, but the substance belongs to Christ" (2:17). As already stated, this was a way of interpreting Scripture in which the commandments regarding ritual purity were understood as pointing to Christ, and therefore no longer binding. Apparently the Sabbath itself was one of those practices that pointed toward the future and whose promise was fulfilled in Jesus. Even so, as is clear throughout the book of Acts, Paul and other Christians were faithful participants in Sabbath synagogue worship.

Leaving aside Jesus' conflicts with some synagogue leaders regarding whether healing and other works of love should be conducted on the Sabbath, the rest of the New Testament does not seem that concerned about the Sabbath. This is particularly notable in Acts 15, which tells the story of the so-called Council of Jerusalem. First in Antioch, and then elsewhere through Paul's mission, quite a number of Gentiles—most of them God-fearers—had joined the church. A more conservative Judeo-Christian group centered in Jerusalem—according to Acts, Pharisees who had accepted the message of Christ—insisted that such people should keep all the Law of Moses and be circumcised. The debate is summarized in Acts, so there is no need to review it here. What is remarkable is that neither circumcision nor the Sabbath are mentioned in the final decision. Instead, Gentile believers are now told that "it has seemed good to the Holy Spirit and to us to impose on you no further burden than these essentials: that you abstain from what has been sacrificed to idols and from blood and from what is strangled and from fornication" (Acts 15:28–29).

This list of forbidden things has a long and complicated history. Shortly after the gathering in Jerusalem, the Corinthians asked Paul whether believers should be allowed to eat meat that had been sacrificed to the idols—meat that was sometimes made available to the needy or sold at low cost. Paul's answer is that in truth the idols are nothing, and that therefore eating meat sacrificed to them is not in itself evil: "We are no worse off if we do not eat, and no better off if we do" (1 Cor. 8:8). However, believers who understand this must take care that "this liberty of yours does not somehow become a stumbling block to the weak" (8:9). Apparently, what had been decided in Jerusalem was not a final word, but rather a guide for believers. Still later, the *Didache* would command, "Concerning food, be as careful as you can. As to food that has been sacrificed to idols, be strongly on your guard, because it is in the service of dead gods" (*Didache* 6.3; ANF 7:379).

A further problem with the supposed "decree" of Jerusalem is that ancient manuscripts do not entirely agree among themselves. A papyrus that may well be the most ancient surviving text of this particular passage lists three things from which Gentiles added to the church must abstain: idolatry, that which is drowned, and blood. Most scholars agree that the original text is more accurately transcribed in other ancient manuscripts. These other manuscripts reflect what is called the "common text." Their list includes, besides the three mentioned in that papyrus, fornication—and instead of "drowned," the common text has "strangled." Other generally less trustworthy manuscripts, known as the "Western text," list idolatry, fornication, and blood. These differences are important, since this latter list obscures the meaning of the decision. The Western text and its list were long considered in the Latin church to refer to the three great sins from which Christians should abstain. By interpreting this passage without taking into account its background in the Law of Israel, "blood" was understood to mean homicide, and therefore there were three great sins: idolatry (which included apostasy in times of persecution), fornication, and homicide. On the basis of the common text, one may see that the background of the Jerusalem decree is in Leviticus 17 and 18, which list what a stranger living within the bounds of Israel must do in order to be allowed to eat with the children of Abraham. Thus, what was under discussion in Acts 15 were not the moral laws that were to be followed, but simply what Gentile converts must do in order to eat with the children of Israel. This was particularly important since, as we shall see in chapter 6, a meal was at the very heart of Christian worship. How, then, could good Jews who accepted Jesus as the Messiah eat with Gentiles who had been God-fearers and who now had joined the church? What is to be required of these Gentile Christians so that Jewish Christians will be able to eat with them?

Clearly, the instructions of that gathering in Jerusalem were not always followed. As already mentioned, Paul himself would declare that there is no evil in eating meat sacrificed to the idols, while the *Didache* held the opposite opinion. Furthermore, Paul also says that both Peter and Barnabas hesitated on eating with Gentile believers:

> But when Cephas [Peter] came to Antioch, I opposed him to his face, because he stood self-condemned; for until certain people came from James, he used to eat with the Gentiles. But after they came, he drew back and kept himself separate for fear of the circumcision faction. And the other Jews joined him in this hypocrisy, so that even Barnabas was led astray by their hypocrisy. But when I saw that they were not acting consistently with the truth of the gospel, I said to Cephas before them all, "If you, though a Jew, live like a Gentile and not like a Jew, how can you compel the Gentiles to live like Jews?" (Gal. 2:11–14)

This shows the difficulties in the transition from being a Christian community composed almost exclusively of descendants of Abraham to another that was mostly Gentile in origin. The passage also shows that this transition was not always easy or uniform. If it were, the conversion of Cornelius and the response of the church in Jerusalem accepting it (told in Acts 10 and 11) should have sufficed. Or, if not, the decree of Jerusalem would have settled the matter. But debate and diverse practices continued for quite some time, to which the New Testament itself is a witness. Once again, the process was long and complicated, with a variety of practices and different ideas that slowly made way for more uniformity.

Back to the matter of the weekly calendar: significantly, the Judeo-Christian community originally kept not only the seven-day week but also its emphasis on a day of rest or Sabbath. Moreover, questions as to how this particular day was to be observed do not seem to have been at the forefront of Christian debate or disagreement. Although we know that some demanded that every-one keep the Sabbath, their number rapidly dwindled, and the most common opinion by the second century was that it was licit both to keep the Sabbath (which was preferable) and not to keep it—but that no one should demand that others keep it. In short, in most cases Christians who were able to do so seem-ingly kept the Sabbath, and others did not. Those who, like Paul and Barnabas, had kept the Sabbath throughout their lives would have no difficulty continu-ing after they accepted Jesus of Nazareth as the Messiah. But this would not be as easy—or even possible—for Gentiles who became Christians. One cannot well imagine a centurion such as Cornelius telling his superior officer, "For-give me, sir, but today is a day of rest and therefore I cannot drill the troops."

A NEW FOCUS IN THE WEEKLY CALENDAR

A change in the calendar that is noticeable from the very beginning is a new emphasis on different days of the week. The most notable among these changes is the first day of the week, which today we call "Sunday." The name that this day is given in most Romance languages—domingo, dominica, and so on—derives from the Latin *dominus*, Lord, and thus means the "Lord's day." Since all surviving Christian texts from the first century that we have are in Greek rather than Latin, what we find there is the word *kyriaka*, which also means "Lord's day" or "day of the *Kyrios*."

Following the Jewish way of reckoning the beginning and ending of days—from sunset to sunset—this particular day, the first of the week or *kyriaka*, began with the sunset of the Sabbath and ended at the next sunset. This would make it easier for those believers—either Jewish or previous God-fearers—who had kept the Sabbath before becoming Christians to join with other believers immediately after the end of the Sabbath—that is, on what today we would call Saturday evening, but for them it was already the first day of the week. Even while they might still be allowed to join the synagogue in worship, they would find it necessary to gather to break bread with other Christians, and to interpret Scripture in such a way that it pointed to Jesus. However, as the number of Gentiles in the church grew, and particularly after Christians were expelled from the synagogues, meeting in the evening, after the Sabbath sunset, became increasingly difficult. Eventually, as Christianity gained more followers among Gentiles and became less Judeo-Christian, it became more convenient to continue meeting on the first day of the week, but now before sunrise rather than on the previous evening.

The New Testament is clear about the significance of the first day of the week. There are numerous references to the resurrection of Jesus on that first day of the week. On that day the women went to the sepulcher. It was on that day that the Lord met some disciples on the way to Emmaus. The clearest reference that we have to Christian worship on the first day of the week appears in Acts 20: "On the first day of the week, when we met to break bread, Paul was holding a discussion with them; since he intended to leave the next day, he continued speaking until midnight." The narrative continues with the episode of the young man who falls from a window and the resumption of the gathering "until dawn" (Acts 20:7, 11). In other words, Paul is preaching on the first day of the week—that is, after the sunset of the Sabbath. This is why lamps are necessary, and why the young man falls asleep. The gathering continues for several hours, until dawn.

Clearly the main reason the first day of the week was of particular significance for Christianity was that this was the day of the Lord's resurrection. No matter whether they gathered earlier in the synagogue or not, Judeo-Christians felt an impulse to gather on this particular day in order to celebrate the resurrection of Jesus. Christians felt that the first day of the week was of particular significance for two other reasons, but since these only appear in later texts, we return to them in the second part of this study (chapter 11).

Besides the first day of the week, Christians also attached particular significance to the sixth day. This day—what we now call "Friday," but was traditionally known as the "sixth day of the week" or the "day of preparation [for the Sabbath]"—was the day of the crucifixion. While every first day of the week the Lord's resurrection was celebrated, every sixth day his death was remembered. It was therefore a day of sorrow, introspection, and fasting.

THE YEARLY CALENDAR

As we have seen, Jews had not only a weekly calendar but also an annual one setting aside particular dates. The most important of these was Passover, in which Israel's liberation from the yoke of Egypt was both commemorated and relived. The Gospels show a chronological relationship between the death and resurrection of Jesus and Passover—although on the exact chronology there are differences between the Synoptic Gospels on the one hand and the Fourth Gospel on the other. Despite such differences, the clear connection between

Passover and the events that the church commemorated and celebrated every sixth and first day of the week—Friday and Sunday—led to the custom of setting aside one particular week every year, generally at the same time when the Jews celebrated the Passover, to pay particular attention to the crucifixion and resurrection of Jesus. Every Sunday was for them a day of resurrection, of celebrating the victory of Jesus over death. But there was also one great Sunday of resurrection—what today we call Easter Sunday. Although no first-century text refers to this custom, it was so common and deeply rooted by the second century that one may surmise that Christians began celebrating this particular Sunday before the end of the first century. As we shall see later, in the second century the difference between John and the Synoptic Gospels regarding the connection between the last days of Jesus and the Jewish Passover led to serious controversies among Christians—the "Quartodeciman" controversy. However, that controversy should not obscure the connection that Christians soon established between the sacrifice of Jesus and the sacrifice of the Passover lamb—on which all agreed. Paul's words are well known: "our paschal lamb, Christ, has been sacrificed" (1 Cor. 5:7). And Jesus as the Lamb of God is a theme that permeates the book of Revelation.

The other Jewish feast that plays an important role first in the New Testament and then among Christians is Pentecost. The process by which Christians took possession of this date in the Jewish calendar and reinterpreted it is not clear. There is no doubt that in Acts 2 Pentecost is given a particular significance that is well known, for it was on this day that the Holy Spirit descended on the disciples. However, Pentecost is not mentioned again in the entire New Testament as a day of particular significance for Christians, even though there are many other references to various outpourings of the Spirit. Still, for reasons and in a manner that cannot be explained, Pentecost clearly became a day of particular significance for Christians. Witness to this is what we shall see later: when those who were ready to receive baptism on Easter Sunday were unable to receive it for some reason, they would be baptized on Pentecost. But even so, that in the entire New Testament there is no indication of how Christians celebrated this particular day is still surprising.

In summary, just as it developed its worship out of what was done in the synagogues, so did the Judeo-Christian community adopt the Jewish calendar and, while retaining its basic structure, give new meaning to certain days of the week as well as to some of its annual observances.

5

From Conversion to Baptism

CONVERSION AND WORSHIP

The book of Acts records large numbers of people accepting Jesus as the Messiah as a result of Christian witness. Acts tells us that on the day of Pentecost, after Peter's sermon and invitation to his hearers to repent and be baptized, "about three thousand persons were added" (Acts 2:41). Similarly, after Paul's preaching in Antioch of Pisidia, numerous God-fearers accept his message—which results in the opposition of the more traditional Jews and the expulsion of Paul and Barnabas from the city.

Events following those two episodes help us understand why after those early occasions there were fewer conversions both in the Temple and in the synagogues. When Peter and John are found preaching in the Temple, the Sanhedrin first demands an explanation and eventually forbid their preaching. When Paul preaches in a synagogue in Antioch, his very success provokes the opposition of other Jews. Although the book of Acts does not explicitly retell the entire story, it is clear that in most cities where Paul and his companions arrived and began preaching in the synagogue they had an initial success, but there was soon strong and often violent resistance from the more traditional Jews.

In short, as Judaism was becoming increasingly aware of the contrast between its beliefs and those of Judeo-Christians, it became more difficult to preach Jesus as the Messiah at the Temple or in most synagogues. After that time, very few conversions would take place in the context of synagogue worship. Even fewer—if any—conversions would take place in Judeo-Christian worship. Before the final breach between Christianity and Judaism, Judeo-Christians attending synagogue might have an opportunity to witness to their faith. However, when they gathered for Christian worship, this centered on Communion. Since only those who had been baptized could participate, there would be no attempt to evangelize them. In that context, preaching was not seen as an invitation for people to accept Jesus as the Messiah and Savior, but rather as a process whereby believers came to know Scripture and to relate it to their daily living—and those who had not received baptism prepared for it.

From an early date that is impossible to determine, Christian worship consisted of two main parts. The first eventually came to be known as the "service of the Word," and the second as the "service of the Table"—that is, Communion. Those who were not baptized could attend the service of the Word, but they were dismissed before the service of the Table. Even though those who were not baptized were allowed to attend the first part of the service, it was unlikely that someone who did not have other connections with the church and had not heard the gospel would attend even that part. Jews considered Christianity a heresy. Rumors circulated among pagans that Christian worship was both immoral and uncouth. The authorities frowned on Christianity and often persecuted its followers. Given such circumstances, someone who attended the service of the Word would have already heard the gospel and at least been attracted to it.

For these reasons, conversion was most often not the result of a sermon, but rather of the witness of neighbors, relatives, clients, or visitors. By the second century we do learn of cases where someone was converted to Christianity after an intellectual quest for the "true philosophy." Such cases are better known than the process of conversion of common folk, for people who followed such an intellectual quest wrote about its result—which most others could not do. In short, most conversions took place as a result of the witness of believers whose names are unknown. Although they date from the second century, the following words of a pagan regarding Christian propaganda would already be true toward the end of the first century. That pagan, whose name was Celsus, says,

> We see those who work in wool and leather, persons who are uneducated and uncultured, who would not dare to utter a word in the presence of their elders and wiser masters. They go into private homes, and there they get hold of the children privately and some women who are as ignorant as they are, and they pour forth wonderful statements. They say that these children and women ought not to pay attention to their fathers and teachers, but should obey them. Their parents and teachers are foolish and stupid and know nothing and cannot do anything that is really good, because they are preoccupied with empty trifles. But these Christians alone know how people ought to live, and that if the children obey them, they will be happy

themselves, and they will also make their home happy. (Quoted by Origen in *Ag. Celsus* 3.55; ANF 4:486)

When today we speak of ancient Christian worship, we must keep this situation in mind, for if we think of worship as primarily an evangelistic occasion, it would be very difficult for us to understand what took place in it. Furthermore, one must also realize that the very idea of evangelization was not primarily focused on convincing an individual to accept Jesus as a personal Savior or as the promised Messiah—which certainly was important—but rather on leading the individual to become part of this Christian community, this church, this body of believers that, as the New Testament affirms, is also the body of Christ.

The manner in which a person was joined to this body of Christ was baptism, whose significance was such that it deserves careful attention.

JEWISH ANTECEDENTS

A rapid reading of Hebrew Scripture clearly shows that water was used in various rites to purify people as well as things. In most cases, such as hand washing or ritual bathing, the person being purified also performed the rite. There is no doubt that such rituals are part of the background of Christian baptism, but it is difficult, and even impossible, to determine which of these influenced Christian baptism and how. Besides the ablutions that the Law required before certain activities and rituals, or to cleanse a person or an object that had become unclean, there is no doubt that the baptism of proselytes practiced by Judaism has left its imprint on Christian baptism.

As we have seen, a proselyte was a Gentile who, after participating for some time in the life of the synagogue as a God-fearer, decided to join the people of Israel. This required first of all a moral purification, leaving aside any practice contrary to justice and to God's love. It was then followed by a ritual purification. The rabbis did not agree on whether it was necessary for every male proselyte to be circumcised in order to join the people of Israel—although the majority held that such was the case. This was then followed by the baptism of the proselyte—which if the person had been circumcised was postponed until he had healed. Such baptism was neither public nor private. It was not public, because the person to be baptized had to be naked. But it was also not private, for it was necessary for two witnesses of the same gender to be present. Also, normally this baptism was not conferred by another person; rather, it was the proselyte who entered the water alone and submerged himself or herself. The task of the witnesses was not to baptize, but rather to certify that the baptism had taken place.

As to the place where the person was to be baptized, there were several rules, although apparently not excessively rigid. For reasons that are not quite clear, many believed that the Jordan should not be used for these purifying baths, for its waters were "mixed"—which may be interpreted in different ways. The same tradition also speaks of baptismal pools, which were necessary not only for proselyte baptism but also for other ritual ablutions. Although archaeological excavations in Jerusalem have been limited, they have yielded such a number of these pools that they suggest that in the first century the city contained hundreds of baptismal pools. The reason would be that ritual bathing was necessary under many different circumstances, so only a few pools would not suffice for the city. Signs of other such pools have also been found in nearby towns. Ritual baptism in these pools required the entire body to be washed, and therefore total immersion was expected. However, the Talmud allows the possibility of pouring water repeatedly over a person's head instead of total submersion—of which we will find a Christian parallel in the *Didache*. Finally, the Essenes also practiced a series of ablutions. One interesting point about these ablutions that may relate them to Christian practices was that there was among the Essenes a baptism that a person underwent after a period of preparing to join the community, and which signaled that the baptized was now a member of the community—as was also the case among Christians.

The most significant Jewish antecedent for Christian baptism—and also the most controversial—is John the Baptist, or "the baptizer." That title and the Gospel narratives show that, differently from the usual self-baptism that a proselyte and others underwent, John baptized those who came to him. Just as proselyte baptism required a period of ritual and moral purification, so did John's require repentance. Thus, following the example of many earlier prophets in Israel, John was reminding the children of Israel that they were not as pure as they should be, and that they were in need of purification much as a proselyte was. Another characteristic of John's baptism, at least as presented in the Gospels, was its eschatological emphasis. The reason John calls for repentance is not just that those who hear him have sinned, but also that the end approaches, that the promise of a Messiah is about to be fulfilled, and that all must prepare for it.

The history of John the Baptist, who goes out into the desert and there baptizes people in the Jordan, appears in all four Gospels. All of them quote the words of the prophet Isaiah: "voice of one crying out in the wilderness" (Matt. 3:3; Mark 1:3; Luke 3:4; John 1:23). Although our common understanding of those words is that John is speaking and no one listens, in their original use in Isaiah this voice was calling in the desert announcing a new exodus, a new delivery from captivity—in this particular case, captivity in Babylon—and once again a return through a desert, although not the same desert as in the time of Moses. Isaiah clearly connects the path that God is about to make in the desert with the earlier action of the same God making a way for the people to leave Egypt through the waters. In the Gospels, Jesus will be the guide in a new exodus, as was Moses before. This new exodus is one of liberation from sin, and is announced by the voice of John calling in the desert for the people to repent. This typology of the exodus is one of the important links connecting the actions of God in the Hebrew Scriptures and those in the New Testament.

Finally, John's going out to the desert to baptize in the Jordan deserves some consideration. It is not clear that in John's time the notion already circulated that the waters of the Jordan were not sufficiently pure to be used for the baptism of proselytes. If that were the case, this would seem to indicate that John's action was part of a movement of protest against the manner in which religious leaders understood and demanded purity—a movement of protest that Jesus would later embody. At any rate, going to the desert to be baptized is an allusion to the pilgrimage of the tribes of Israel in the desert for forty years. Later we shall see that early Christians understood what was taking place in Jesus as a new Passover and a new exodus. Therefore, John's going out to the desert may be seen as a call to cross the waters in a new exodus.

JESUS AND BAPTISM

In the Gospel narratives, Jesus goes out to the desert to be baptized by John in the Jordan. Even before Jesus' baptism, John had already been announcing another who would come after him whose sandals he would not be worthy of untying. When he sees Jesus, John immediately connects him with the paschal lamb in Exodus: "'Here is the Lamb of God who takes away the sin of the world!'" (John 1:29). Although some scholars believe that John's movement was independent from that of Jesus, and that for some time there was some rivalry between the two, the picture that the Gospels present is different. In the Gospel of John, the Baptist declares,

> "I saw the Spirit descending from heaven like a dove, and it remained on him. I myself did not know him, but the one who sent me to baptize with water said to me, 'He on whom you see the Spirit descend and remain is the one who baptizes with the Holy Spirit.' And I myself have seen and have testified that this is the Son of God." (John 1:32–34)

Something similar is said in the Synoptic Gospels. In Matthew, for instance, the story is as follows:

> Then Jesus came from Galilee to John at the Jordan, to be baptized by him. John would have prevented him, saying, "I need to be baptized by you, and do you come to me?" But Jesus answered him, "Let it be so now; for it is proper for us in this way to fulfill all righteousness." Then he consented. And when Jesus had been baptized, just as he came up from the water, suddenly the heavens were opened to him and he saw the Spirit of God descending like a dove and alighting on him. And a voice from heaven said, "This is my Son, the Beloved, with whom I am well pleased." (Matt. 3:13–17)

There has been much discussion among Christians about why Jesus had to be baptized. If John's baptism was based on repentance, and Jesus had no sin, why did he need to be baptized? The only possible answer that the Gospels offer is the explanation by Jesus himself that he must "'fulfill all righteous-ness'" (Matt. 3:15). The question regarding the reason why Jesus was baptized was asked by believers, if not already in the first century, certainly by the beginning of the second in the so-called *Gospel of the Hebrews*, now lost. One of the few surviving fragments of this document is quoted by Jerome as follows:

> Behold, the Lord's mother and his brother said: John the Baptist bap-tizes to forgive sins. Let us go also and be baptized by him. But he said to them: "What sins have I committed that I need to be baptized? Or perhaps my asking this is a case of ignorance." (Jerome, *Against the Pelagians* 3.2)

Although this document does not appear to have circulated widely, in the early second century some provided an answer to this question that may sur-prise us, and will be discussed later (chapter 9).

As to whether John baptized any of the disciples of Jesus, there can be no definitive answer. Some quote the words of Peter in Acts 1:22 when he suggests that the one to be chosen to take the place of Judas among the dis-ciples should be one who had been with them "'beginning from the baptism of John.'" However, this does not prove that the disciples themselves were baptized by John, for Peter may simply be referring to Jesus' baptism in the Jordan. In any case, according to the Gospel of John, Jesus himself baptized: "He spent some time there [in the Judean countryside] with them and bap-tized" (John 3:22). This is also what John's disciples told him somewhat later: "'He is baptizing, and all are going to him'" (John 3:26). But soon thereaf-ter the same Gospel declares, "It was not Jesus himself but his disciples who baptized" (John 4:2). Therefore, all that can be said about baptism by Jesus is that the Synoptic Gospels do not even mention it, and the Gospel of John seems to imply that sometimes it was Jesus himself who baptized, and in other cases it was his disciples.

The passage that most closely connects Jesus with the practice and commandment to baptize others is part of the "Great Commission" that Jesus gives his disciples after his resurrection, telling them that they should go "'and make disciples of all nations, baptizing them in the name of the Father and of the Son and of the Holy Spirit'" (Matt. 28:19). An element that is often forgotten when quoting this Great Commission is that it is based on the universal power or authority that Jesus has received by virtue of his death and resurrection. Jesus himself begins his words sending the disciples by telling them, "'All authority in heaven and on earth has been given to me. Go therefore . . .'" (Matt. 28:18–19).

In virtue of that supreme authority that Jesus has been given, his disciples are to go. The significance of this is, among other things, that the people whom the disciples were to baptize would not become their disciples, but would be disciples of Jesus. In other words, in affirming his supreme and universal authority, Jesus is declaring that he is not only the only Lord, but also the only true Teacher of all.

BAPTISM IN PAUL AND IN ACTS

Baptism has always held an important place in the life of the church. However, this is a baptism different than John's. The Gospels themselves already point to the difference, for in Mark 1:7–8 John the Baptist says, "'The one who is more powerful than I is coming after me; I am not worthy to stoop down and untie the thong of his sandals. I have baptized you with water; but he will baptize you with the Holy Spirit.'" And in John 1:33 the Baptist again distinguishes between his own baptism, which is with water, and that of Jesus, who ""'"baptizes with the Holy Spirit."'""

The book of Acts has a similar emphasis on baptism, and on its significance and power. Peter's suggestion, that Judas's successor must be one of the disciples from the time of the baptism of John, shows the significance that he attaches to that event. On the day of Pentecost, Peter explains what is taking place as a result of the outpouring of the Holy Spirit by inviting his listeners to share the experience of that outpouring by means of baptism: "'Repent, and be baptized every one of you in the name of Jesus Christ so that your sins may be forgiven; and you will receive the gift of the Holy Spirit'" (Acts 2:38). The result is that "those who welcomed his message were baptized, and that day about three thousand persons were added" (Acts 2:41). Thereafter, there are many other cases in which baptism is seen to be at the very center of the church's life. In Acts 8, first the Samaritans and then the Ethiopian are baptized. Two chapters later, upon seeing that Cornelius and his household receive the Holy Spirit, Peter has them baptized. When asked by the church in Jerusalem to explain what he has done in his visit to Cornelius, Peter tells them that he remembered what the Lord had said: "'"John baptized with water, but you will be baptized with the Holy Spirit"'" (Acts 11:16). And the story continues along similar lines throughout the entire book—with the difference that, while in the case of Cornelius the outpouring of the Spirit precedes baptism, in other cases this order is reversed.

If we then turn to Paul himself, it immediately becomes clear that baptism has an important place both in his teaching and his own life. According to Acts 9:18, as soon as Ananias restored his vision, Paul "got up and was baptized." Then, throughout his ministry, there are repeated references to baptism. One of them, to which we return later, occurs in Ephesus, where Acts presents Paul echoing the Gospels by saying, "'John baptized with the baptism of repentance, telling the people to believe in the one who was to come after him, that is, in Jesus.'" The result is that "on hearing this, they were baptized in the name of the Lord Jesus. When Paul had laid his hands on them, the Holy Spirit came upon them, and they spoke in tongues and prophesied" (Acts 19:4–6). These are only a few of the many passages in Acts that refer to baptism. On the whole, two elements appear repeatedly: The first is the relationship between the baptism of John and that of Jesus through the church. It is a relationship affirming a certain continuity, but at the same time there is a clear declaration that Jesus' baptism is unique. The second element worthy of mention is the constant yet varied relationship between baptism and the outpouring of the Holy Spirit.

There is no doubt that baptism is of fundamental importance for Paul, as may be seen in his Epistles—which mostly antecede the writing of the Gospels. The well-known passage in 1 Corinthians 12, where Paul speaks of the diversity of gifts as parallel to the diversity of the members in the body, each with a particular function, is not a mere illustration taken from common human experience, but much more. Paul grounds this relationship among the members of the body on baptism:

> For just as the body is one and has many members, and all the members of the body, though many, are one body, so it is with Christ. For in the one Spirit we were all baptized into one body—Jews or Greeks, slaves or free—and we were all made to drink of one Spirit.
> Indeed, the body does not consist of one member but of many.
> (1 Cor. 12.12–14)

This passage in Corinthians is one of many that could be quoted in order to show that the Epistles of Paul reflect what we have already seen in Acts, that is, that there is a close connection between baptism and the Holy Spirit. Furthermore, in Paul we find a theme that appears repeatedly in later discussions regarding baptism: through baptism, believers become members of the body of Christ. The various members are one body because "in the one Spirit we were all baptized into the body." Paul says something similar referring to the manner in which the Gentiles have been grafted into the olive tree that is the people of Israel:

> But if some of the branches were broken off, and you, a wild olive shoot, were grafted in their place to share the rich root of the olive tree, do not boast over the branches. If you do boast, remember that it is not you that support the root, but the root that supports you. (Rom. 11:17–18)

We do not always notice the relationship that Paul frequently establishes between baptism and death. For the apostle, baptism is a dying with Christ in order then also to live with him. The lengthy passage (Rom. 8–9) regarding baptism and its relationship to Christian life and with the Holy Spirit is announced in chapter 6 with radical words regarding baptism:

> Should we continue in sin in order that grace may abound? By no means! How can we who died to sin go on living in it? Do you not know that all of us who have been baptized into Christ Jesus were baptized into his death? Therefore we have been buried with him by baptism into death, so that, just as Christ was raised from the dead by the glory of the Father, so we too might walk in newness of life.
> For if we have been united with him in a death like his, we will certainly be united with him in a resurrection like his. (Rom. 6:2–5)

The same idea appears in Colossians:

> If with Christ you died to the elemental spirits of the universe, why do you live as if you still belonged to the world? Why do you submit to regulations, "Do not handle, Do not taste, Do not touch"? . . .
> So if you have been raised with Christ, seek the things that are above, where Christ is, seated at the right hand of God. Set your minds on things that are above, not on things that are on earth, for you have died, and your life is hidden with Christ in God. When Christ who is your life is revealed, then you also will be revealed with him in glory. (Col. 2:20–21; 3:1–4)

Furthermore, it is thus that the often-misinterpreted passage in Galatians where Paul speaks of being crucified jointly with Christ should be understood.

In that passage, Paul is not claiming a particular virtue or a particular close-ness with Christ, so that he has now come to the point of being crucified jointly with Christ. What he saying is rather that, by virtue of baptism, which is a dying in Christ, all Christians have been crucified jointly with Christ. Paul is telling the Galatians that all of them, precisely because they have been baptized, have been crucified with Christ. It is to stress this point that he says,

> I have been crucified with Christ; and it is no longer I who live, but it is Christ who lives in me. And the life I now live in the flesh I live by faith in the Son of God, who loved me and gave himself for me. I do not nullify the grace of God; for if justification comes through the law, then Christ died for nothing.
> You foolish Galatians! Who has bewitched you? (Gal. 2:19–3:1)

In brief, Paul takes baptism very seriously. It is a matter of death and life—of death with Christ and of new life with Christ. This he expresses in various ways, all of them interconnected. In the already mentioned long pas-sage in Romans regarding baptism, Paul uses several images. First, baptism is similar to the manumission of a slave. For Paul, sin is much more than an error, a fault, or an evil action; it is above all a subjection, a form of slavery. This is why he tells the Romans that "you, having once been slaves of sin, have become obedient from the heart to the form of teaching to which you were entrusted, and that you, having been set free from sin, have become slaves of righteousness" (Rom 6:17–18). In other words, humans are always servants, but they may be either servants of sin or servants of the justice of God. Through baptism, their bond in slavery to sin is dissolved. Later in the same passage Paul compares baptism and the death it entails with the situa-tion of a woman who is widowed. As long as her husband lived, were she to join to another man, she would be committing adultery; but once her husband dies, she may join another without committing adultery. This is what happens when, by virtue of baptism, the slavery to sin is undone:

> We have been buried with him by baptism into death, so that, just as Christ was raised from the dead by the glory of the Father, so we too might walk in newness of life.
> For if we have been united with him in a death like his, we will certainly be united with him in a resurrection like his. We know that our old self was crucified with him so that the body of sin might be destroyed, and we might no longer be enslaved to sin. For whoever has died is freed from sin. (Rom. 6:4–7)

Another image relates baptism to a new birth, on which the third chapter of John is often quoted. When Nicodemus approaches Jesus, this leads to a conversation about the new birth in the Spirit, which is different from birth in the flesh. Paul seems to be referring to the same idea when speaking of the adoption as children of God that takes place for the benefit of the believer and by work of the Spirit. Regarding baptism, the apostle tells the Romans, "If you live according to the flesh, you will die; but if by the Spirit you put to death the deeds of the body, you will live. . . . For you did not receive a spirit of slavery to fall back into fear, but you have received a spirit of adoption. When we cry, 'Abba! Father!' it is that very spirit bearing witness with our spirit that we are children of God" (Rom 8:13–16).

In all this, it is interesting to note that, despite what would later become the common view in many churches, Paul does not say that baptism is a manner of witnessing to the faith, but rather that it is the life following baptism that witnesses to baptism itself and to the manner in which the believer has died with Christ. Also—another interesting detail—in the Pauline Epistles the subject of baptism as a washing, which later became one of the main metaphors to understand baptism, does not seem to play an important role. The main passage that may be interpreted in that manner is 1 Corinthians 6:11, where, after referring to the evil deeds of others, Paul says, "And this is what some of you used to be. But you were washed, you were sanctified, you were justified in the name of the Lord Jesus Christ and in the Spirit of our God."

OTHER BOOKS OF THE NEW TESTAMENT

Little is said about baptism in the rest of the New Testament. Apart from the Gospels and the Pauline corpus, it is mentioned explicitly only in 1 Peter and in Hebrews. These two books seem to be sermons, or at least messages addressing a church that has begun to lose something of its original enthusiasm. Peter relates baptism to the story of Noah and the ark, offering a typological interpretation in which the ark and the water become a type, shadow, or announcement of baptism:

> God waited patiently in the days of Noah, during the building of the ark, in which a few, that is, eight persons, were saved through water. And baptism, which this prefigured, now saves you—not as a removal of dirt from the body, but as an appeal to God for a good conscience, through the resurrection of Jesus Christ. (1 Pet. 3:20–21)

Hebrews mentions baptism explicitly only once, and even then, only in passing (Heb. 6:2). But—as with the rest of the New Testament—Hebrews is addressing the church, and therefore what it says is grounded on the baptism that all in its audience share.

THE ADMINISTRATION OF BAPTISM

Although matters having to do with the administration of baptism have long been debated, the New Testament says very little about it. Certainly, the image of baptism as death and resurrection implies that there was a total immersion. This followed the pattern of the Jewish baptism of proselytes, which required that the person be completely covered with water. The most ancient text that we have mentioning another form of baptism is the *Didache*, which directs that baptism should be in running water—"living water"—and, although taking for granted that baptism will normally be by immersion, allows for other possibilities, apparently because water was scarce in the area where the book was written. The same passage also adds that both the person to receive baptism and the person who will administer it must be fasting. The passage itself is fairly brief:

> As to baptism, follow this way: after having said all these things, bap-
> tize into the name of the Father, and of the Son, and of the Holy
> Spirit, in living [running] water. If you do not have running water,
> baptize in other water. If you do not have cold water, use warm. But
> if you do not have either, pour water on the head three times in the
> name of the Father and Son and Holy Spirit. But before the baptism
> let the one baptizing fast, and the one being baptized, and whoever
> else can. But you shall order the one being baptized to fast one or two
> days before. (*Didache* 7; ANF 7:379)

The words "having said all these things" refer to the preceding six chapters of the book, which spell out some of what people preparing for baptism should know and do. That earlier material is framed within the contrast
between a wide path leading to death and a narrow one leading to life. Thus,
those first chapters of the *Didache* are probably the most ancient document
we have regarding the preparation for baptism—what came to be known as
"catechesis." Although here all that is required before baptism is this previous
instruction and fasting, other later Judeo-Christian documents do refer to the
duration of initial instruction and trial before baptism. The so-called *Clementine Recognitions*—a document that seems to have come out of Syrian Judeo-
Christian circles during the third or fourth centuries—set a period of three
months of preparation for baptism (*Clem. Recognitions* 3.67). Also the *Manual
of Discipline* found among the Dead Sea Scrolls requires a year of preparation
and instruction before the baptismal rite of initiation into the community of
the Essenes.

An ancient Coptic manuscript of the *Didache* also contains a reference to
the "oil of anointment." Later we shall see that during the second century it

was customary to anoint the neophyte upon leaving the waters of baptism, as a sign that this person was now part of the royal priesthood that is the church. The prayer over the "oil of anointment" that is found in this manuscript possibly refers to this anointing after baptism, even though the text itself does not say so. As a matter of interest, the text is as follows:

> Over the oil of anointing, you shall thus give thanks:
> We thank you, our Father,
> for the oil of anointing,
> which you have revealed
> through Jesus Christ, your servant.
> To you be glory through the ages.

There is no reference to infant baptism in any of the ancient Judeo-Christian documents. Although it is not explicitly forbidden, the numerous references connecting repentance and baptism would seem to imply that it was expected that the person receiving baptism should have the ability to repent. In the next section of our narrative we see the first references to infant baptism.

Nor do we find in these documents any directive as to who has the authority to baptize. In the Gospel of John, the disciples of Jesus baptized. Later there are references to baptisms by Philip and Paul. But there is no rule regarding the matter.

Finally comes the question of whether Judeo-Christian baptism was in the name of the Trinity or in the name of Jesus alone. There are four places in which the book of Acts is relevant to this discussion. The first follows Peter's speech on Pentecost. When those who hear Peter ask what they should do, Peter tells them, "'Repent, and be baptized every one of you in the name of Jesus Christ so that your sins may be forgiven; and you will receive the gift of the Holy Spirit'" (Acts 2:38). The second refers to the visit of Peter and John to Samaria, where Philip had been preaching, and the apostles pray with them "that they might receive the Holy Spirit (for as yet the Spirit had not come upon any of them; they had only been baptized in the name of the Lord Jesus)" (Acts 8:15–16). The third is part of the narrative regarding Cornelius, when after Cornelius and those who were with him receive the Holy Spirit, Peter "ordered them to be baptized in the name of Jesus Christ" (Acts 10:48). Finally, we come across an interesting story in which the disciples in Ephesus had not even heard about the Holy Spirit, but had only been baptized "'into John's baptism.'" Then they were baptized "in the name of the Lord Jesus" (Acts 19:1–6).

On the other hand, there is the Great Commission, in which Jesus tells his disciples that they are to baptize "'in the name of the Father and of the

Son and of the Holy Spirit" (Matt. 28:19). There are also a number of passages, particularly in the Pauline corpus, that clearly affirm a Trinitarian perspective. Most of these appear in benedictions such as the one at the end of 2 Corinthians: "The grace of the Lord Jesus Christ, the love of God, and the communion of the Holy Spirit be with all of you" (13:13). Likewise, there is a Trinitarian formula in 1 Peter 1:2, where the Epistle is addressed to those "who have been chosen and destined by God the Father and sanctified by the Spirit to be obedient to Jesus Christ and to be sprinkled with his blood."

We cannot settle this matter here. Some churches today insist on baptizing only "in the name of Jesus," basing their arguments on Acts, and usually rejecting the doctrine of the Trinity. Most churches today and throughout history baptize and have baptized in the name of the Trinity, following the instructions in the Great Commission. Over the years, theologians have dealt with these issues in different ways. Some suggest, for instance, that there is only one "name," for the name is the very substance of the named, and Father, Son, and Holy Spirit share in the same divine substance. On this basis, one may claim that the name of Jesus is the same as the name of the Trinity. In any case, it is important to note that wherever Acts speaks of baptism in the name of Jesus there is an immediate reference to the Holy Spirit—sometimes before and sometimes after baptism.

Within the context of our interest here, the apparently conflicting witness as to what baptismal formula was used in the early church confirms the view that early liturgical development did not move from an original uniformity in the direction of diversity, but the contrary: an original diversity moved in the direction of uniformity. Quite possibly, some Christian communities used one formula, and others used another. At any rate, by the end of the first century there is almost unanimous consensus on baptism in the name of the Trinity.

BAPTISM AND THE PEOPLE OF GOD

As we come to the close of this chapter, we can see clearly that baptism in the New Testament is not a private matter of the relationship between the believer and God, nor is it limited to a witness that the person being baptized gives. Baptism is rather the sign that makes a believer part of the people of God—of this body of Christ that is the church. In a way, in the church baptism comes to have a significance similar to circumcision for the people of Israel, where an individual was not circumcised as a sign of personal faith, but above all as a sign that he was part of the people of God. By the power of the Holy Spirit, those who are baptized become part of the people of God in a manner similar to that in which those circumcised were marked as part of the people of Israel—with the all-important difference that baptism is not limited to males, for, as Paul says to the Galatians, "In Christ Jesus you are all children of God through faith. As many of you as were baptized into Christ have clothed yourselves with Christ. There is no longer Jew or Greek, there is no longer slave or free, there is no longer male and female; for all of you are one in Christ Jesus" (Gal. 3:26–28).

6

Communion

SOME BASIC FACTS

From a very early date, Christian worship centered on Communion or the Lord's Supper. According to the narrative in Acts, immediately after Pentecost, "Day by day, as they spent much time together in the temple, they [the followers of Jesus] broke bread at home and ate their food with glad and generous hearts" (Acts 2:46). Notice that this refers to a time when the disciples were still able to worship in the Temple. Even so, they were already gathering in the homes to break bread. Further on, in Acts 20, one finds the episode at Troas, when "on the first day of the week" believers "met to break bread" (v. 7). And near the end of the book, when Paul and his companions are about to be shipwrecked, there is a narrative that has overtones of Communion. After promising all those who were aboard that they would survive, Paul "took bread; and giving thanks to God in the presence of all, he broke it and began to eat" (Acts 27:35). What is clear in this passage is that the verbs are practically the same as appear in other texts referring to the Lord's Supper: he *took* bread, he *gave* thanks, he *broke* it, he *ate*. The only verb missing in the traditional formula is "he gave." This is understandable, for those who were with him were mostly pagan. In any case, the important point is that from its very birth the church gathered to break bread.

This is clearly connected with the narrative that appears in the Synoptic Gospels regarding the Last Supper of Jesus with his disciples before his arrest and crucifixion. The most ancient of the Gospels, Mark, written before the destruction of the Temple, tells of these events:

> While they were eating, he took a loaf of bread, and after blessing
> it he broke it, gave it to them, and said, "Take; this is my body."
> Then he took a cup, and after giving thanks he gave it to them, and
> all of them drank from it. He said to them, "This is my blood of the
> covenant, which is poured out for many. Truly I tell you, I will never
> again drink of the fruit of the vine until that day when I drink it new
> in the kingdom of God." (Mark 14:22–25)

Moving from the Synoptic Gospels to the Pauline corpus—parts of it earlier than the Gospel of Mark—we find that Paul also stresses the importance
and significance of the Lord's Supper. Later we consider other pertinent passages, but his narrative of the institution of the Supper itself is well known:

> For I received from the Lord what I also handed on to you, that the
> Lord Jesus on the night when he was betrayed took a loaf of bread,
> and when he had given thanks, he broke it and said, "This is my body
> that is for you. Do this in remembrance of me." In the same way he
> took the cup also, after supper, saying, "This cup is the new covenant
> in my blood. Do this, as often as you drink it, in remembrance of me."
> For as often as you eat this bread and drink the cup, you proclaim the
> Lord's death until he comes. (1 Cor. 11:23–26)

The unanimous witness of the New Testament places these events on or
near the day of Passover. Clearly, in the Gospel narratives, Communion,
while still reflecting the Hebrew Passover, had a further significance in connection with Jesus himself. However, there is a difference between the Synoptic Gospels and John, for the latter does not tell the story of the institution of
the Supper; it also places the crucifixion not on the day of Passover, but rather
a day earlier, when it was customary to sacrifice the lamb that would be eaten
at Passover. John says that, after the death of Jesus,

> Since it was the day of Preparation, the Jews did not want the bodies
> left on the cross during the sabbath, especially because that sabbath
> was a day of great solemnity. So they asked Pilate to have the legs of
> the crucified men broken and the bodies removed. Then the soldiers
> came and broke the legs of the first and of the other who had been
> crucified with him. But when they came to Jesus and saw that he was
> already dead, they did not break his legs. Instead, one of the soldiers
> pierced his side with a spear, and at once blood and water came out.
> (John 19:31–34)

As already explained, the "day of preparation" was the sixth day of the
week, when people prepared for the observance of the Sabbath. Thus, all four
Gospels agree that Jesus was crucified on the sixth day of the week (Friday).
A somewhat surprising difference is that, while all three Synoptics tell the

story of the Last Supper of Jesus with his disciples before his crucifixion, and therefore of the institution of the Lord's Supper, John does not. This does not mean, however, that John did not consider Communion to be central to the Christian faith. On the contrary, John more than any other Gospel alludes to Communion in many different ways—speaking, for instance, of Jesus as the bread of life. His Gospel was intended to be read in church in connection with worship, which entailed Communion. This is why so many passages in John point to Communion. Apparently, precisely because the story of the institution of the Supper as told by the Synoptics and by Paul would be repeated when Communion was to be celebrated, John was more interested in helping his readers look at Communion from a wider perspective.

What is clear, and cannot be sufficiently underscored, is that throughout the New Testament there is a link between the Jewish Passover and Jesus' death and resurrection. In the Synoptics this appears in the narrative itself, while both in Paul's writings and in the Fourth Gospel it appears more clearly in the theological expressions that show the convergence—as well as the contrast—between the Jewish Passover and the culmination of the Gospel in the death and resurrection of Jesus. In order to explain this more fully, it is helpful to look first at what the Pauline corpus says about Communion, and then look at the Johannine corpus in similar fashion.

PASSOVER AND COMMUNION IN PAULINE THEOLOGY

Although when we think about Paul and Communion, what first comes to mind is the already quoted passage in Corinthians where he tells of the institution of the Supper in a fashion very similar to the Synoptics, in truth the Supper and its significance have a much more important place in Pauline theology. Much of the significance of the Supper and the events around it has to do with the relationship between the sacrifice of Jesus, Passover, and the Lord's Supper. One must not forget that what was being celebrated on Passover was the day in which God liberated the children of Israel from their Egyptian yoke by bringing about the death of the firstborn of Egypt, while the avenging angel passed over the houses of the Hebrews, whose doors bore the mark of the blood of a lamb. Throughout the centuries, whenever Israel celebrated Passover it was remembering and reliving that great liberation that had taken place by means of the blood of the paschal lamb. It is also helpful to remember that the paschal season included the Feast of Unleavened Bread, in remembrance of the people's hasty flight from Egypt, which did not allow them to eat leavened bread. Combining all of this, Paul tells the Corinthians,

"Clean out the old yeast so that you may be a new batch, as you really are unleavened. For our paschal lamb, Christ, has been sacrificed" (1 Cor. 5:7). Joining this to what we have already learned regarding typology and the manner in which Paul refers to the commandments of the Law as a shadow or announcement of what was to come, we see that what is being said here is that the first Passover, the lamb sacrificed in it, and every other Passover since, as well as all the lambs sacrificed in them, were a shadow or announcement of the Lamb that was to come. Just as the blood of that first Passover lamb saved the Israelites from death, so does the blood of this new and final paschal lamb, who takes away the sins of the world, save those who follow him. The Pauline corpus includes the statement that God has reconciled "to himself all things, whether on earth or in heaven, by making peace through the blood of his cross" (Col. 1:20). "In him we have redemption through his blood, the forgiveness of our trespasses, according to the riches of his grace" (Eph. 1:7). And Gentiles may be told that "now in Christ Jesus you who once were far off have been brought near by the blood of Christ" (Eph. 2:13). In a word, the events of that first Holy Week are the fulfillment of what until then was a shadow announcing the great salvation through the sacrifice of Jesus.

Furthermore, this Supper that Jesus' followers now celebrate as the fulfillment of all the previous Passover meals and of the very original Passover in Egypt is also a guideline for how those who partake of it are to understand themselves and their mutual relationship. Paul says it clearly: those who partake of the bread are to be like unleavened bread precisely because Christ, the paschal lamb, has been sacrificed. And this must give rise to a particular unity among those who eat this bread and drink this cup: "The cup of blessing that we bless, is it not a sharing in the blood of Christ? The bread that we break, is it not a sharing in the body of Christ? Because there is one bread, we who are many are one body, for we all partake of the one bread" (1 Cor. 10:16–17). This unity is not just a sort of friendship, for it implies a new social order. In the same letter to the Corinthians, Paul warns them, "Whoever, therefore, eats the bread or drinks the cup of the Lord in an unworthy manner will be answerable for the body and blood of the Lord" (1 Cor. 11:27). Throughout the history of the church, this passage has been interpreted as referring to the bread and wine as somehow being the body and blood of Jesus. In consequence, eating "unworthily" has been understood in terms of not seeing in the bread and wine the body and blood of Jesus. But as one reads the entire passage it becomes clear that this is not what Paul is warning against. The problem in Corinth is not a mistaken doctrine regarding the presence of Christ in Communion. It is rather that some attend the Supper bringing much food that they will not share; therefore while some are overfed and even inebriated, others are hungry and thirsty. The problem in Corinth is that those who are behaving in this manner do not take into account that those who are present with them there are, as Paul repeatedly says, the body of Christ. "Not discerning the body of Christ" is not to realize that all believers are members of a single body and that, therefore, they must be treated with respect, love, equity, and justice.

In short, in Pauline theology the Lord's Supper or Communion is both the fulfillment of what was announced in the first Passover in Egypt and a sign that is to mark the behavior of this new people to whom Jesus has given freedom and newness of life through his sacrifice on the cross and his victory in the resurrection.

PASSOVER AND COMMUNION IN JOHANNINE THEOLOGY

Under this heading we discuss mostly two very disparate books, both connected with the name of John: the Fourth Gospel and Revelation—although we shall also look at the Johannine Epistles. Even though traditionally all of this literature has been attributed to the same author, the scholarly consensus is that they are not the work of a single author. This does not contradict the places where the text says "John," for this was a fairly common name in the early church. The reason scholars do not believe that all of this literature comes from the same hand is that the style and vocabulary of Revelation are radically different from those of the rest of the Johannine corpus. Even so, there are reasons to include all of this material under the same heading. While the literary style of Revelation is markedly different from that of the Gospel of John, points of contact show the influence of a particular theological school. An example of this is that it is only in these books that Jesus is called the "Word" or "Logos" (John 1:1, 14; 1 John 1:1; 5:7; Rev. 19:13).

Communion has an important role both in the Fourth Gospel and in Revelation. The image of Jesus as the Lamb of God, which runs throughout Revelation, also appears in the Gospel of John, and not in any of the others. When we read these books, we note that, while reference to Jesus as the "Lamb of God" appears only in Johannine literature, this is parallel to the manner in which the Pauline corpus connects the work of Jesus with the first Passover.

While quite different from one another, the Fourth Gospel and Revelation have another common characteristic that we often do not see because we do not take into account that these books were not written to be read in private, but rather to be read out loud before the congregation—that is, in worship. These books give us a glimpse into a time when, although not yet officially expelled from all synagogues, believers in Jesus—besides gathering to break bread, as they had done from the beginning—also had to gather to study

Scripture from a different perspective than in the synagogues. As the congregation gathers to break bread, it also listens to the reading and interpretation of the ancient Scripture of Israel in the light of what has happened in Jesus. Furthermore, just as distinguished visitors were invited to speak in the synagogue, now when the congregation of believers in Jesus gathers to study Scripture and to break bread, there is an opportunity to hear the reading of messages for the edification of believers written by distinguished leaders of the church. This is clearly the case in Revelation, which presents a picture of John exiled on the Isle of Patmos writing to the churches in Asia Minor a long message that is to be circulated among those churches and read out loud. Similarly, the Fourth Gospel consists mostly of a series of stories about Jesus, many of them related in various ways to the breaking of the bread that would take place after reading and commenting on the stories. For this reason, John's Gospel does not include the story itself of the Last Supper, which in any case would commonly be retold at the beginning of Communion.

From its early chapters, this Gospel speaks of Jesus as the Lamb of God. In chapter 2, the first miracle of Jesus, at a wedding feast, is transforming water into good wine. In Revelation, the future announced is the wedding feast of the Lamb:

> "Let us rejoice and exult
>   and give him the glory,
> for the marriage of the Lamb has come,
>   and his bride has made herself ready;
> to her it has been granted to be clothed
>   with fine linen, bright and pure"—
> for the fine linen is the righteous deeds of the saints.
>   And the angel said to me, "Write this: Blessed are those who are
> invited to the marriage supper of the Lamb."
>
> > Rev. 19:7–9

Those Christians in Asia Minor who, late in the first century, would hear the reading of these words would also be preparing to celebrate a foretaste of the marriage feast of the Lamb: Communion. Or, if the reading was from the Fourth Gospel, upon hearing the story of the wedding at Cana, where common water becomes excellent wine, they would understand that, despised by the world as they were and disenfranchised by the synagogue, they were now celebrating a meal that was a sign of the great feast of the marriage of the Lamb, and that they themselves, like the water in Cana, would be transformed in that final day.

However, the message that was heard was not always one of pure joy, but also of warning, for "nothing unclean will enter it [the holy city of God], nor anyone who practices abomination or falsehood, but only those who are written in the Lamb's book of life" (Rev. 21:27).

When we read Revelation not as a book written to be read for our private edification but rather as a call to faithfulness addressed to the church as a whole—a call made immediately before Communion—we find in its words clear messages that we would not see otherwise. An example is the well-known words of Revelation 3:20: "'Listen! I am standing at the door, knocking; if you hear my voice and open the door, I will come in to you and eat with you, and you with me.'" Today we usually interpret these words in light of the famous image depicting Jesus knocking at the door of the heart and asking to be let in. There is no doubt that Jesus demands entrance into the human heart. But this passage itself gains deeper significance when we understand that when hearing these words the church in Laodicea would be gathered to celebrate a meal. The Laodiceans would understand that, for the reasons John tells them, Jesus himself is left outside knocking at the door of a meal at which he should be both the host and the guest of honor.

In summary, much of the New Testament gains new meaning as we realize that what we now read in private was actually written to be read out loud before a congregation preparing to celebrate the Lord's Supper.

But this does not suffice. To understand how that early church approached Communion, we have to stress the relationship between Communion and the paschal feast of Hebrew tradition. It is not simply, as we are often told, that according to the Synoptic Gospels Jesus instituted the Lord's Supper at a paschal dinner. It is also that this very context gives a deeper significance to the Communion that we celebrate in our churches today.

Although this is not the place to review the entirety of New Testament theology regarding Communion, we must at least look at one of the most controversial and difficult passages, so as to show how an understanding of Passover and of its context helps us understand what Communion meant for those early Christians. The passage itself is found in the Gospel of John. The subject is introduced with what seems to be a passing reference to food: "'Do not work for the food that perishes, but for the food that endures for eternal life, which the Son of Man will give you. For it is on him that God the Father has set his seal'" (John 6:27). Those who hear Jesus ask him for a sign similar to what took place when Israel left Egypt:

> So they said to him, "What sign are you going to give us then, so that we may see it and believe you? What work are you performing? Our ancestors ate the manna in the wilderness; as it is written, 'He gave them bread from heaven to eat.'" Then Jesus said to them, "Very truly, I tell you, it was not Moses who gave you the bread from heaven, but it is my Father who gives you the true bread from heaven. For the

bread of God is that which comes down from heaven and gives life to the world." They said to him, "Sir, give us this bread always."

Jesus said to them, "I am the bread of life. Whoever comes to me will never be hungry, and whoever believes in me will never be thirsty. But I said to you that you have seen me and yet do not believe. Everything that the Father gives me will come to me, and anyone who comes to me I will never drive away; for I have come down from heaven, not to do my own will, but the will of him who sent me. And this is the will of him who sent me, that I should lose nothing of all that he has given me, but raise it up on the last day. This is indeed the will of my Father, that all who see the Son and believe in him may have eternal life; and I will raise them up on the last day."

Then the Jews began to complain about him because he said, "I am the bread that came down from heaven." They were saying, "Is not this Jesus, the son of Joseph, whose father and mother we know? How can he now say, 'I have come down from heaven'?"

Jesus answered them . . . , "I am the living bread that came down from heaven. Whoever eats of this bread will live forever; and the bread that I will give for the life of the world is my flesh."

The Jews then disputed among themselves, saying, "How can this man give us his flesh to eat?" So Jesus said to them, "Very truly, I tell you, unless you eat the flesh of the Son of Man and drink his blood, you have no life in you. Those who eat my flesh and drink my blood have eternal life, and I will raise them up on the last day; for my flesh is true food and my blood is true drink. Those who eat my flesh and drink my blood abide in me, and I in them. Just as the living Father sent me, and I live because of the Father, so whoever eats me will live because of me. This is the bread that came down from heaven, not like that which your ancestors ate, and they died. But the one who eats this bread will live forever." (John 6:30–43, 51–58)

These words would be scandalous for the Jews who heard them. One of the dietetic prohibitions of the Law of Israel was eating an animal with its blood. Now Jesus tells them not only of drinking blood, but apparently of drinking human blood! His statement about eating his body is nothing less than savage cannibalism! The scandal is such that his own disciples say, "'This teaching is difficult; who can accept it?'" (John 6:60). As a result, "Many of his disciples turned back and no longer went about with him" (John 6:66).

In the ongoing discussion and sometimes bitter debate among Christians throughout the centuries regarding Jesus' presence in Communion, this passage in John 6 has played an important role. On the one hand, an absolutely literal interpretation would lead to the same objection of those first disciples who heard the words of Jesus: is it not forbidden to drink blood and eat human flesh? At the other extreme, a purely "spiritual" interpretation, as if Jesus were speaking only of having faith in him, leaves aside much of what the text says. In order to do justice to it, we have to go back to what Passover celebrated—back to what the people of Israel joined in once again every year in their paschal supper.

Regarding that meal, several elements should be taken into account. One is that the lamb and its blood were an essential element in the celebration itself. Just as in that first Passover, when the blood of the lamb was used to mark the doors of the houses of the children of Israel, thus now at each Passover celebration the blood of the lambs was poured on the altar at the Temple. After they left Egypt, God nourished the people in the desert through bread and flesh from heaven: manna in the mornings and quail in the evenings. For those who year after year celebrated the Passover meal, to say that they were the people of Israel was to affirm that they survived thanks to the blood of that first paschal lamb and to the manna that God gave them in the desert. This did not refer only to the past but also to the future, when God would once again feed the people with bread from heaven. The unleavened bread that was eaten in the days of Passover was a reminder that when the people of Israel left Egypt, they could no longer make bread as they had before, and that when bread was needed God sent them manna—bread from heaven. In some ancient texts manna is seen as the food of angels. This may be seen, for instance, in the Wisdom of Solomon, a text the Hebrew community in Egypt produced in the years preceding the birth of Jesus: "Instead of these things you gave your people food of angels, and without their toil you supplied them from heaven with bread ready to eat" (Wis. 16:20). Unfortunately, the extant Jewish writings explicitly connecting the Passover celebration with messianic expectation date from the time after Jesus. Such is the case of the Talmud, where Passover is not only a memory and an affirmation of the past, but also an announcement and a rehearsal of the future, when God would once again feed the people with bread from heaven. Possibly the most ancient Jewish writing where one finds this eschatological connection between the Messiah and the bread from heaven is the *Second Book of Baruch*, a document apparently written in Hebrew shortly after the fall of Jerusalem in the year 70, but existing only in a Syriac translation and in some Greek fragments. It is dated after 70 CE because it refers to the fall of Jerusalem—and no later than the middle of the second century, because at that time the Christian author of the so-called *Epistle of Barnabas* quoted it. Supposing then that this is a book written around the year 100, 2 Baruch is the most ancient witness we have to a connection between the promise of the Messiah and the bread that would once again come from heaven. There we read,

> And it will happen that when all that which should come to pass in these parts has been accomplished, the Anointed One will begin to be revealed. . . . And those who are hungry will enjoy themselves and they will, moreover, see marvels every day. For winds will go out in

front of me every morning to bring the fragrance of aromatic fruits and clouds at the end of the day to distill the dew of health. And it will happen at that time that the treasury of manna will come down again from on high, and they will eat of it in those years because these are they who will have arrived at the consummation of time. (2 Baruch 29:3, 6–8; J. H. Charlesworth, ed., *The Old Testament Pseudepigrapha* [Garden City, NY: Doubleday & Co., 1983], 630–31)

A NEW PASSOVER

Much of the foregoing is the background of what the Synoptic Gospels tell us about Jesus' institution of the Lord's Supper, as well as what the New Testament says about Communion itself. Later, when dealing with how ancient Christians celebrated the Supper, we shall see some elements of Hebrew tradition that continue into the Christian celebration to this day. However, while not forgetting the Jewish background of the institution of the Lord's Supper, we should also note that the Passover that Jesus celebrates with his disciples is quite different from any other Passover. Two main differences must be stressed to understand how what was originally an annual celebration of the Hebrew people became a frequent—usually, at least weekly—celebration among Christians.

The first of these differences has to do with who joined Jesus in this meal. Traditionally, the Passover meal was a family celebration, for it included a structure in which the younger ones present knew what they were to ask, others knew how they should answer them regarding their liberation from Egypt, the Psalms to be sung were known, and so on. The celebration often included some people who were not part of the family, because no Jew should be left alone to celebrate the Passover, and the lamb had to be entirely consumed. However, Jesus does not celebrate this Passover with his physical kindred, but rather with a group of disciples who scarcely understand his mission or his message, and who will abandon, deny, and even betray him. While the traditional paschal supper celebrated the bond of a common ancestry among the descendants of Israel, this new paschal meal that Jesus established celebrated the bond joining those who benefited from the blood of this new Lamb of God—a bond more permanent than any blood relationship. One might say, referring to the new birth of which Jesus speaks in John 3, that Communion signals not just the birth of a new person but also and above all the birth of a new family. Ever since that Last Supper, the followers of Jesus would gather to celebrate the bond of a new family joining those who, even though perhaps not all descendants of Abraham, are nevertheless heirs to the promises made to him.

All this fits into the manner in which the authors of the New Testament saw both the history of Israel and its dietetic and ritual laws. According to the New Testament, these were true acts of God on behalf of Israel, but they were also a shadow or a sign of this greatest act of God in Jesus. There, at that meal, Jesus offered himself as the sacrificial lamb that takes away the sins of the world and thus began a new exodus, offering himself as food and drink that nourish the faith and life of his people.

THE PRACTICE OF COMMUNION

When discussing baptism, we saw that the New Testament says very little about how it was administered, but we also followed a number of leads in various passages referring to baptism. The same is true of Communion. The institution of the Lord's Supper is told in all three Synoptic Gospels, as well as in 1 Corinthians. The repetition of that story in these diverse sources indicates that it was retold every time Christians gathered to break bread—much as in a traditional Passover meal the story of the liberation of Israel is retold. But, particularly in 1 Corinthians—whose date is earlier than any of the Gospels—other hints appear as to how Communion was celebrated. In that letter, Paul's concern is not what the believers may be thinking during Communion, but rather the way that Communion may affirm or distort the new reality it is supposed to commemorate and demonstrate.

The letter shows clearly that the divisions in Corinth were in part theological (1 Cor. 3:4–23), in part due to the almost incredible sins of some (1 Cor. 5:1–13), and in part a result of the enmities that festered among them (1 Cor. 6:1–8). But apparently the point at which all these various problems came to the surface was Communion:

> Now in the following instructions I do not commend you, because when you come together it is not for the better but for the worse. For, to begin with, when you come together as a church, I hear that there are divisions among you; and to some extent I believe it. Indeed, there have to be factions among you, for only so will it become clear who among you are genuine. When you come together, it is not really to eat the Lord's supper. For when the time comes to eat, each of you goes ahead with your own supper, and one goes hungry and another becomes drunk. What! Do you not have homes to eat and drink in? Or do you show contempt for the church of God and humiliate those who have nothing? What should I say to you? Should I commend you? In this matter I do not commend you!
> (1 Cor. 11:17–22)

This shows that, at least on some occasions, when those early Christians gathered to celebrate the Supper it was not a matter of taking a bit of bread and some wine. The Supper was what the name literally means: an entire meal. For the meal, each brought what they could, and it was expected that they would share. What bothers Paul is that the Corinthians are gathering, but are not sharing, so that while some eat in excess, others go hungry. Later we will come across common meals usually called *agapes*, "[meals of] love." Although Paul does not use that name to refer to the meal itself, the entire thirteenth chapter of 1 Corinthians, shortly after the above quoted passage, is the well-known praise of love (*agape*), which is his response to the evil that is destroying the church in Corinth. After declaring the nature of that evil in chapter 11, Paul explains in chapter 12 that the diversity of gifts makes it possible for all members to be part of the same body, each with its own function. Then, in chapter 13, he offers what he calls "a still more excellent way."

We know of agapes from other sources. Jude 12 refers to people who are "blemishes on your love-feasts." The same name is given to such suppers in 1 Peter—although only in the *Codex Vaticanus*. When speaking of Communion, the *Didache* uses language that implies that this was still a full meal: "After you are filled, thus give thanks" (*Didache* 10.1; ANF 7:380).

What is not clear is the exact relationship between Communion and an agape. While the meal that Paul is discussing in 1 Corinthians is obviously a full meal, he also suggests that any who are hungry should eat at home (1 Cor. 11:22).

The main conclusion to be drawn from these data is that determining the relationship between the Lord's Supper and the agapes is impossible. On this point, there is no scholarly consensus. Some hold that originally the Lord's Supper took place within the context of a banquet or agape. Others insist they were two different celebrations. All that can be said is that no one answer is completely convincing. Furthermore, if we remember that most often liturgical development did not move from an original unity to a greater diversity, but the opposite, it is quite possible that the apparently contradictory witnesses reflect different practices in various churches or areas. Quite possibly also, as churches grew in numbers, it became more difficult to celebrate an entire meal together. In that case, the church would gather to celebrate Communion only with bread and wine, and smaller groups of believers might then gather in various places to eat a full meal together. What comes across clearly is that eating together was of great importance for that church, even when they could not share an entire meal. These two different necessities—eating a full meal in the company of other believers and somehow sharing Communion with all believers—could be met by separating the Lord's Supper from the fuller meal of an agape.

In the next part of this book, when discussing the second century, we shall see that the agapes continued for quite some time, at least in certain areas. In any case it is important to stress that throughout the New Testament, even when speaking of a full meal, the bread and the wine have particular significance. This may be seen in the instructions of the *Didache* regarding the common meal:

> Now concerning the Eucharist, give thanks in this way. First, over the cup: We give thanks to you, our Father, for the holy vine of your servant David, which you made known to us through your Servant Jesus. To you be glory forever. Over the bread: We thank you, our Father, for the life and knowledge which you made known to us through your Servant Jesus. To you be glory forever. Even as this broken bread was scattered over the hills, and gathered together has become one, so let your church be gathered together from the ends of the earth into your kingdom, for yours is the glory and the power through Jesus Christ forever. (*Didache* 9.1–4; ANF 7:379–80)

Note that in this prayer over the bread the emphasis is not on the bread as the physical body of Jesus, but rather on the unity of the church as the body of Christ, which will come to fruition at the end, when this church is "gathered together from the ends of the earth into your kingdom." Note here also the wine precedes the bread, which is not the most common practice today, and differs from what Paul and the Synoptic Gospels say about the institution of the Lord's Supper. Once again, this points to the variety of practices in ancient Christian worship.

In the *Didache*, the above-quoted passage continues with a prayer of thanksgiving:

> But after you are filled, give thanks in this fashion: We thank you, holy Father, for your holy name which you caused to dwell in our hearts, and for the knowledge and faith and immortality which you made known to us through Jesus your Servant. To you be glory forever. You, almighty Master, did create all things for your name's sake. You gave food and drink to humanity for enjoyment, that they might give thanks to you. But to us you freely gave spiritual food and drink and life eternal through your Servant. Before all else we thank you that you are mighty. To you be glory forever. Remember, Lord, your church, to deliver it from all evil and to make it perfect in your love. Gather it from the four winds, sanctified for your kingdom which you have prepared for it. For yours is the power and the glory forever. Let grace come. Let this world pass away. Hosanna to the God of David. If any are holy, let them come; if any are not, let them repent. *Maranatha*. Amen. (*Didache* 10.1–6; ANF 7:380)

Notably absent in all of this is any reference to the death and resurrection of Jesus, to the cross, or to the empty tomb. This may be explained in two ways, and determining which of the two is correct is impossible. On the one hand, the cross may not be mentioned here because it is taken for granted that the narrative of the institution of the Supper will have been read before these various prayers—in other words, that the author is giving instructions only regarding those things that are not widely known already. On the other hand, it is also possible that what we have here is a practice different from what we see in other documents of the time. In such case, this would be an adaptation of the Hebrew Seder, now with repeated references to Jesus. In other words, the *Didache* may be understood as an addition or direction regarding what is to be said after telling the story of the institution of Communion, or it may simply reflect a practice that diverged from the rest of the church. Once again, the historical data are not enough to decide for one of these two alternatives. Clearly, though, the *Didache* believes in the importance of fasting on the sixth day of the week. This was a day to remember and reflect on Jesus' crucifixion, which did not have to be stressed again on the celebration of resurrection that took place every first day of the week.

Again, the section on Communion is preceded by what seems to be a manual of instructions for the preparation for baptism. The *Didache* makes it very clear that baptism is necessary before partaking of Communion: "But do not let anyone eat or drink of your Eucharist except those who have been baptized into the name of the Lord. About this also the Lord has said, 'Do not give what is holy to the dogs'" (*Didache* 9.5; ANF 7:380).

Even while acknowledging a vast variety of opinions and practices, stressing the corporate dimension of the early church's understanding of Communion is important. Just as baptism is not a private matter, but an incorporation into the body of Christ through the action of the Holy Spirit, so also Communion nourishes and unifies the body, again by virtue of the same Spirit. The center of this event is not that the individual is fed, but rather that the community as a whole is nourished. Once again, if baptism is a grafting of this individual into the body of Christ, Communion may then be understood as a process whereby the branches that are grafted onto the True Vine are nourished by the sap of that Vine.

The Judeo-Christian church lived by its memory of the cross—of the sacrifice of the Lamb of God that was at the very center of its faith. However, in Communion it was a matter of remembering not only the past but also the future. That promised future was the growing unity among Christians themselves that the sacrament entails, all leading to the great feast of the marriage of the Lamb—the Risen Christ—of which Communion was a foretaste.

In Revelation (22:20) and 1 Corinthians (16:22) we come across the Aramaic expression *maranatha*. This can be variously translated as "come, Lord" or as "the Lord comes." The same formula appears also in the *Didache* (10.6). Since all of these books were originally written in Greek, finding Aramaic in them is surprising. This is one of the few words that Christians who spoke Greek, rather than translating them into that language, kept in their original Hebrew or Aramaic—among them, "amen" and "alleluia." There is every indication that *maranatha* was used particularly in connection with Communion. Both 1 Corinthians and Revelation were written to be read out loud to the congregation before celebrating Communion. Both in 1 Corinthians and in Revelation, this formula appears at the end, and seems to be opening the way for Communion itself. The *Didache* offers a slightly different situation, for *maranatha* appears after the instructions regarding Communion. But even there it is used in connection with an invitation to the table: "If any are holy, let them come; if any are not, let them repent. *Maranatha*. Amen" (*Didache* 10.6; ANF 7:380). As the expectation of the immediate return of Jesus receded, this word progressively disappeared from Christian vocabulary, only to be rediscovered more recently precisely as a way to emphasize the eschatological expectation of the return of the Savior.

The theme of Communion as a foretaste of the wedding feast of the Lamb leads us to a fairly common element in ancient Christian worship that today is mostly forgotten: the certainty that, as the church presently praises God on earth, there is also in heaven a great and eternal praise. This point is clear in the book of Revelation where, after addressing the seven churches in Asia in the first three chapters, in the fourth John turns his sight heavenward and describes the worship that takes place there. There we find the sublime vision of the One seated on the throne from which come "flashes of lightning, and rumblings and peals of thunder," surrounded by "twenty-four thrones, and seated on the thrones are twenty-four elders, dressed in white robes, with golden crowns on their heads" (Rev. 4:4–5). There are also "four living creatures," reminiscent of the Seraphim in Isaiah 6, who constantly and endlessly sing, "Holy, holy, holy, / the Lord God the Almighty, / who was and is and is to come" (Rev. 4:8). The elders cast their crowns before the throne, and they too lift a song of praise. Anyone today who is aware of traditional hymnody will recognize in this scene the inspiration for the hymn "Holy, Holy, Holy."

John's vision is a reflection of the early church's understanding of the relationship between its own worship and what takes place in heaven. The eschatological dimension of worship as a foretaste of the wedding feast of the Lamb is also a participation and preparation for the great act of worship of which all will partake on the final day.

This connection between earthly and heavenly worship may be seen throughout the history of ancient Christian worship. At approximately the same time that John was writing Revelation, the church in Rome and its bishop Clement were writing a letter to the Corinthians that includes these words: "Let us consider the whole multitude of his angels, how they stand always ready to do his will. . . . And let us therefore, conscientiously gathering together in harmony, cry to him earnestly as with one mouth, that we may be partakers of his great and glorious promises" (*Ep. to the Corinthians* 34; ANF 1:14). Quite probably, this was a continuation and adaptation of some practices of Jewish worship—practices of which we still hear echoes in the *Kedusha* of Hebrew morning prayers.

This vision of earthly worship as an extension and foretaste of heavenly worship remains valid today, as is seen whenever, before Communion, many believers say or sing words such as, "Therefore, with angels and archangels, and with all the company of heaven, we magnify and glorify thy holy name, saying: Holy, holy, holy, Lord God Almighty, heaven and earth are full of thy glory. Glory be to thee, O Lord most high! Amen."

PART II

From 100 to 313 CE

7

New Circumstances

AN INCREASINGLY GENTILE CHRISTIANITY

The first part of this book, dealing with what we have called the Judeo-Christian period—a time when practically all Christian believers were either Jews or "God-fearers"—ended approximately in the year 100. By that time, Christians had been officially expelled from the synagogues by action of the Sanhedrin in Jamnia, under the leadership of Gamaliel II. In most cases, long before being expelled, Christians had left the synagogues, where they would find a biblical interpretation that differed significantly from theirs. Therefore, an important characteristic of the period that began with the second century would be the continuation of the process of differentiation between Christianity and Judaism. This process would include extreme and bitter polemics and recrimination, and part of the debate would be on Christianity's claim that it was an heir to the faith of Israel. The debate would continue through the centuries, leaving a profound and frequently tragic imprint both on the church and on the Jewish people. For these reasons, Christian documents from that period display a constant anti-Jewish polemic whose attacks would become increasingly harsh and prejudiced. When reading these documents, it is important to remember that they are generally not attacks against Jews as a people or a race, but are rather attempts—often misguided—to make a clear distinction between Judaism and Christianity.

In order to understand the context of that polemic, one must also remember that Judaism and Christianity at the time were both proselytizing religions. The ancient pagan gods were in clear decline. It was not just Jews and Christians who criticized them, but also many of the most distinguished thinkers among the pagan population itself. Ancient polytheism simply no longer met the deepest needs of much of the population. In such circumstances, Christianity and Judaism—radically monotheistic religions, each proposing a style of life different from the generally accepted mores—found themselves in competition. Thus, when today we read what a Christian wrote at that time regarding Judaism, this is part of a constant polemic between two religious options vying for the respect and perhaps even adherence of the rest of the population.

The dominant theme in Christian theology during the first century had been the relationship between Israel's faith and that of the church. Practically all those very early Christians were either Jews or Gentiles who had been God-fearers, and therefore participants in much of the life of the synagogue. What they saw in Jesus Christ and they now announced was not the birth of a new religion but rather the culmination of the ancient faith of Israel and the fulfillment of the promises made to Abraham and his descendants. The tensions and adjustments that this implied are clearly seen in the New Testament. In the Gospels we frequently find Jesus in conflict with Jewish authorities. This does not mean that he rejected Judaism but rather that he claimed to understand it better than those authorities—which is the reason his criticism of their attitudes and actions was generally based on the Law of Israel. The New Testament presents a constant discussion of how Gentiles who accepted Jesus as the Christ should relate to Jews and to Judaism itself. Did they have to keep the dietary laws? Must males be circumcised? Such questions seemed to be answered repeatedly, only to emerge once again: Philip baptizes the Ethiopian, which does not seem to produce any great controversy. But Peter baptizes Cornelius and his household, which leads to a controversy in Jerusalem that seems to have led a final decision. Even so, the leaders of the church in Jerusalem have to gather once again in order to decide what they are to do about the Gentiles who have been converted thanks to the ministry of Paul and his companions. Even later, as Paul tells the Galatians, Peter himself wavered regarding the possibility of eating with Gentile believers.

As we come to the second century, things are different. Quite possibly still most Christian believers are either Jews or former God-fearers. But now a breach has occurred between Judaism and Christianity. The Sanhedrin has declared that Christians are heretics and has expelled them from the synagogues. Christians insist that Jews are the ones who misinterpret Scripture. The debate and the dialogue would continue and become ever more bitter and virulent. The conflict was not only a theological matter, for there was also a proselytizing competition between Judaism and Christianity, each seeking to fill the vacuum left by the failure of ancient religions. Therefore, much of the Christian polemic against Judaism is not really addressed at Jewish readers, but rather seeking to persuade the population at large that their religious quest is best met by Christianity rather than by Judaism. This argument would eventually develop into an attack against the Jews as a people or a race, and thus into true anti-Semitism. Two particular circumstances led to the tragedy of Christians becoming anti-Semitic. The first was that Judaism lost its proselytizing impulse and became practically a hereditary religion. In consequence, attacks against Judaism were no longer attacks on that religion, but rather on the race that followed it. The second tragic circumstance was that, beginning early in the fourth century and after that for more than a millennium and a half, Christianity had the support of European society and governments, with the result that anti-Semitism led to the persecution and the wholesale massacre of Jews.

Christians also debated among themselves what should be done regarding the ancient religion of Israel, particularly its Scriptures. One of the marks of the general religious disquiet of the time was the search for spiritual realities that could somehow overcome the difficulties and anxieties of material life. Within the field of philosophy, Platonism, with its proposal of a higher world of pure ideas of which the present world is only an imperfect copy, was very attractive. Among the masses, religious alternatives that proposed a life beyond death—a life that would leave behind the pain and misery of the present life—were particularly attractive. One such example among many was the religion of Isis and Osiris that had spread out from Egypt. Originally, in the land of the Nile, the myth of Isis and Osiris had been one way to explain the periodic fertility of the Nile, and also a religion promising immortality to the pharaoh and the aristocracy—who were supposedly descendants of the gods. But now in its more popular form, that tradition became a way by which—through a rite of initiation and a particular lifestyle—believers were promised eternal life after death. Other religions and gods similarly promised liberation from the limitations of matter and entry into eternity: Mithras, Attis and Cybele, the Great Mother, and many others.

In contrast with those various religions, Judaism and Christianity both had Scriptures that spoke of physical creation as the work of a good God, and of human history as the scene of God's action. However, Christianity itself took various forms, including some that, joining the quest of the times for "spiritual" reality and its negative view of all that was material, abandoned the very notion of the material creation as the work of God. Such attitudes prevailed among Christian Gnostics, but their main exponent—and the one posing the greatest challenge to the church—was Marcion. This man, the son of a bishop in what is now the northern coast of Turkey, gained many followers, particularly in the western areas of the empire.

Apparently Marcion sought to propose a more "spiritual" version of Christianity and to leave aside the "materialism" of Judaism. This led him to reject the Scriptures of the god of Israel. He did not deny the existence of such a god, or that he had been revealed in the Scriptures of Israel. What he held was that the god of Israel is a lesser being, and not the supreme God and Father of Jesus Christ. That Jewish god is not only inferior, but also ignorant and vengeful, so that this material world, his creation, is imperfect. Upon it he has imposed the laws that appear in the sacred books of Israel. In contrast, the true and supreme God, whom Jesus Christ reveals, is only interested in spiritual reality, and is forgiving rather than rewarding and punishing.

Clearly, this found little support in the Scriptures of Israel—which Marcion therefore rejected. There, God not only proclaims laws and promises rewards and punishment, but is also a God whose mercy is everlasting. In the Gospels, Jesus speaks not only of grace and forgiveness, but also of the gnashing of teeth and of an eternal fire prepared for the devil and his angels. This leads Marcion to declare that among the early disciples and the writers who are now included in the New Testament the only ones who truly understood the message of Jesus were Paul and his companion Luke. Thus, while rejecting the entire Old Testament, Marcion proposed a canon that was limited to the Gospel of Luke and Paul's Epistles—although purging from these writings any reference to the ancient religion of Israel or its Scripture, for Marcion claimed that such references were mere interpolations that someone had introduced in the texts to distort and falsify their teachings. Obviously, the church at large rejected Marcion's theories and doctrines.

Apparently, similar ideas circulated before Marcion's time, for they seem to be behind what we read both in 2 Timothy and in 2 Peter: "All scripture is inspired by God and is useful for teaching, for reproof, for correction, and for training in righteousness" (2 Tim. 3:16). And "So also our beloved brother Paul wrote to you according to the wisdom given him, speaking of this as he does in all his letters. There are some things in them hard to understand, which the ignorant and unstable twist to their own destruction, as they do the other scriptures" (2 Pet. 3:15–16).

If we take into account the circumstances of the time, it is not surprising that Marcion and others left aside the Hebrew Bible and attempted to create a new one. In the synagogues the Scriptures of Israel were read and interpreted in such a way as to reject the notion that Jesus fulfilled the promises of God. Ever more distant from the synagogues, churches included in their worship a similar time, usually before Communion, in which they read and applied Scripture, but now as pointing to Jesus. While most Christians and churches continued reading the Hebrew Bible—usually in the Greek translation known as the Septuagint—and added to it letters and other writings that could be attributed to the apostles and other early Christian leaders, other Christians and churches were more inclined to replace the Hebrew Scriptures by the newer Christian writings. This is what Marcion did, and apparently others before him.

This accelerated a process that was already underway: the development of structures and principles of authority that would help decide between truth and error. In this, Judaism had moved ahead of Christianity, for already by the end of the first century, with the leadership of the new Sanhedrin in Jamnia, Judaism advanced toward uniformity. An important step in this evolution was the determination of the Hebrew canon, also by the leadership in Jamnia. In the case of Christianity, we have already seen in the *Didache* the concern over discerning between true and false apostles and prophets. In Clement's *Epistle to the Corinthians*, late in the first century, we see the beginning of the development of hierarchical authorities that would eventually provide Christianity with a measure of unity similar to what Judaism found through the Sanhedrin in Jamnia.

Part of the same quest for uniformity was the formation of the canon of the New Testament, while at the same time affirming and stressing the authority of Hebrew Scripture. As we saw when discussing Judeo-Christianity, from an early date it became customary to read in worship the messages of an apostle or some other distinguished leader. This was done out loud so that the entire congregation could receive the message. The extant documents do not say exactly which materials were read in worship. But during the course of the second century, and even later, there was a vast conversation and interchange among the churches in various areas leading to the determination of which Christian books should be considered Scripture. This is not the place to follow the process of the formation of the canon of the New Testament. It should suffice to say that, although in earlier times some churches knew a particular gospel better than the others, and gave it priority, already by the end of the second century the present list of four Gospels was generally accepted, and to it were added Acts and the main apostolic Epistles. However, some lists still included books that would not be part of the final canon, or did not include some of the "universal" Epistles. Thus, even though this may surprise us, the first extant list of books of the New Testament that exactly coincides with what today practically all churches accept is no earlier than the year 367 CE. There was a general consensus much earlier, but this is the earliest document where we find exactly the same list as is used today.

Most important—and frequently forgotten—is that, in the process of discussing the authority of these books, the question was not primarily which books could be used to prove doctrine or defend theological positions, but rather which books should be read and explained in worship. In other words, the matter of the canon was posed basically within the context of worship. In this the early church showed it understood what we often forget: that one of the main functions and results of worship is the formulation of faith—along with the formation of character and the development of the identity of the people of God.

THE CHURCH BEFORE STATE, SOCIETY, AND CULTURE

Roman authorities seem to have become cognizant of the rise of Christianity from an early date—certainly by the time of Nero, and possibly earlier, when Claudius had the Jews expelled from Rome because of the disturbances because by a certain "Chrestus" (which seems to refer to the debates among Jews regarding Christ). But Nero and Claudius both apparently thought that Christianity was simply one more sect within Judaism. In the second century the authorities began feeling the need to develop policies regarding this new and expanding religion. Since it was no longer seen as a form of Judaism but as a different religion, the existent laws and policies regarding Judaism could not serve as a guideline for policies regarding Christianity. We know of that need thanks to a letter that Pliny the Younger, governor of Bithynia in what is today Turkey, wrote to Emperor Trajan approximately in the year 112, and to the instructions that he received. We return to this correspondence later. What is important at this point is that Pliny was concerned because "this contagious superstition is now reaching no longer only the cities, but also the villages and countryside" and because the pagan temples are "practically abandoned" (*Epistle* 20). In his letter Pliny reports on what he has learned about Christians and their worship. This makes it the most ancient pagan document that we have regarding Christian worship.

The significance of that letter is not only in the information it provides about Christian worship and practices, but also in that it received from Trajan an answer that established the policy of the empire on Christianity for quite some time. It was customary, when an emperor wrote a letter to a provincial governor giving instructions that could be used for other governors, to have the imperial instructions circulated throughout the empire. Therefore, the instructions that Trajan gave Pliny in response to his questions became the common practice in various areas of the empire. In a few words, the main point of Trajan's instructions was that the state's resources should not be wasted in seeking out Christians, but that if some were accused of being Christians and refused to abandon their faith, they were to be executed. This policy continued over most of the second century. It led some Christians to write "apologies" or defenses of the faith, for the imperial policy meant that the fate of Christians depended to a large extent on the opinion that people had of them. People who believed the evil rumors about Christian beliefs and practices would be more inclined to accuse Christians before the authorities. When this happened, a believer had to choose between apostasy and martyrdom.

Since our interest here is not the persecutions but rather the worship of the church, it is unnecessary to review the development of persecution through the centuries. Suffice it to say that persecutions in general were neither constant nor universal, breaking out in one place or another simply because somebody accused a neighbor or another person of being Christian, or because Christians were blamed for a particular calamity. For instance, in the mid-second century, Marcus Aurelius, famous for his wisdom and admiration for Stoic philosophy, unleashed the persecution of Christians because he considered them stubborn and because they were blamed for a series of invasions, epidemics, and floods. Later, when Septimus Severus was emperor, Christians were once again persecuted because they were considered stubborn in rejecting the worship of the Unconquered Sun above all other gods. In the mid-third century, when Decius occupied the imperial throne, general persecution once again broke out, now in a more systematic fashion, because the emperor was convinced that the economic and moral decline of the empire was due to the abandonment of the old gods, and therefore decreed that everyone must have a certificate proving that they had sacrificed before the altars of the gods. This was actually the first general and systematic persecution of Christianity within the Roman Empire. Although that persecution ceased after the death of Decius, and the church once again enjoyed periods of relative peace, attempts by Roman authorities to stop the growth of Christianity became ever more frequent and sophisticated. Knowing the importance Christians gave to the sacred books, the authorities ordered that all such books be confiscated and destroyed. Knowing also the significance of the church's leadership, persecution now focused on pastors and other leaders, rather than believers in general. Since the witness of martyrs seemed to strengthen the church, by the early fourth century what authorities sought was to force Christians to reject their faith, and therefore Christians were tortured in a vast variety of ways. Seeking to stop the expansion of Christianity, conversion was forbidden. All of this led to the "Great Persecution" early in the fourth century, when all the resources of the government were employed to stop the growth of Christianity.

Such was the situation until the year 313, when in the so-called Edict of Milan emperors Constantine and Licinius put an end to persecution, thus opening a new chapter in the history of Christianity.

The period we are now entering is framed between the year 100—when it became clear that Christianity was rapidly moving beyond the bounds of Judaism and devout God-fearers, when persecution became the stated imperial policy—and the year 313, when persecutions generally ceased. Between those two dates, we have a persecuted yet growing church; an increasingly hostile state; and rather extensive and significant literature defending Christianity or attacking paganism, Judaism, and a number of eventually rejected views within Christianity itself. These various writings are our main source for the study of Christian worship during this period.

THE SOURCES

The growing interest in Christianity, and opposition to it, among imperial authorities and by society in general resulted in our having the earliest pagan documents referring to Christians and their faith. There certainly was concern over Christianity among Roman authorities during the previous period. This was probably the reason for the expulsion of Jews from Rome by Emperor Claudius. Slightly later, Nero and society at large were sufficiently aware of the existence of Christianity that Christians could be blamed for the fire that ravaged Rome. But now, early in the second century, the number of pagan documents that show an interest in Christianity increases. One of the most remarkable is the already mentioned epistle from Pliny to Trajan, and the emperor's response. We discuss it more fully later. Other pagan documents would soon appear that help us understand how culture and society in general looked upon Christianity. One of them is the writing of an unknown philosopher by the name of Celsus, who wrote a scathing attack on Christianity, *The True Logos*—which could also be translated as "true word," "true treatise," or "true reason." This work is known only because Christian theologian Origen refuted it, and in so doing quoted it extensively. There are also important attacks on Christianity in the writings of the famous physician Galen and the Neoplatonic philosopher Porphyry—of whose work *Against Christians* only fragments remain. To these may be added a number of brief mentions of Christians and their beliefs in other documents.

Besides those pagan documents, when we come to the second century, Christian sources become more abundant and extensive. During the first half of the century, the most significant are the group of writings commonly known as the "Apostolic Fathers," and another group usually discussed under the heading of "Greek Apologists of the Second Century." Among the former, we have already referred to the *Didache* and to Clement's *Epistle to the Corinthians*. As we now enter the second century, we find important resources in the other Apostolic Fathers: Ignatius of Antioch, Polycarp of Smyrna (and the acts of his martyrdom), the so-called *Epistle of Barnabas*, the anonymous *To Diognetus*, the *Shepherd* of Hermas, and the fragments of Papias of Hierapolis. Among them is also often included the *Second Epistle of Clement to the Corinthians*, improperly named, for it is neither Clement's nor an epistle, but rather a sermon of an unknown author—and therefore perhaps the most ancient extant Christian sermon. Among the apologists, the outstanding figure, and the one who tells us most about worship and about Christian polemics against Judaism, is Justin Martyr—so named due to the manner of his death. But there are also important data in the writings of Aristides, Tatian, Athenagoras, and Theophilus of Antioch. The writings of the apologists are particularly valuable because—in contrast to the New Testament and other early Christian documents—they do not take for granted that their readers know much about Christianity, and therefore tell us much about its worship and other practices. For instance, when we read about Communion in Paul's Epistles, what we are reading was addressed to people who regularly participated in Communion, and therefore they did not need to be told what was done during it. This makes it difficult for us today to understand exactly what Paul is saying. But when an apologist such as Justin wrote about Communion addressing pagan readers, he had to say more about it—and therefore he offers information that we would not otherwise have.

In addition to these sources, we also have a series of documents that are usually classified as apocryphal gospels, acts, and apocalypses. These are generally expressions of popular religiosity, and often depart from what would soon become Christian orthodoxy. (For instance, most of the so-called *Acts* of various apostles show a strong opposition to marriage and insist on total sexual abstinence—what came to be known as "Encratism.") Some of these documents seem to have been written in the second century, while most are much later.

Also in the late second century we shall come across the writings of Irenaeus of Lyon, Clement of Alexandria, and the pioneer of Latin Christian theological vocabulary, Tertullian of Carthage. Each of these represents a different theological current, but all of them left a profound imprint on the church and its worship. Among their writings are treatises on baptism, repentance, and the Lord's Prayer, as well as others that help us understand the process of preparation for baptism, the place of the agapes or love feasts in the life of the church, and other similar matters.

Slightly later, in the third century, an explosion takes place in the number of Christian documents that have made it into our time. Just to mention one particular case, in the famed *Greek Patrology* edited by J. P. Migne, there are nine volumes of the works of Origen, while all that remains from an earlier time occupies seven volumes. And in the parallel Latin Patrology there are, after two volumes on Tertullian—whose life overlapped the end of the second century and the beginning of the third—two of Cyprian, one of Arnobius, and two of Lactantius. Most of these writers continued the apologetic tradition of the second century, but also wrote on other matters. Cyprian's vast epistolary, besides some sixty letters of his, includes also synodical letters that he probably also wrote, as well as letters he received. This large body of literature includes a number of treatises devoted specifically to various aspects of worship, and also a wealth of other references to worship and to devotion.

The early third century has also bequeathed to us what may well be the most important document for the study of Christian worship at the time, the *Apostolic Tradition* of Hippolytus. Hippolytus, who clashed with several successive bishops in Rome, and who claimed to be the legitimate bishop of that city, is now considered a saint by the Roman Catholic Church, as well as an antipope! Although it was always known that he was a prolific author, until a relatively recent time his only important surviving work was his *Refutation of All Heresies*. But scholars have now come to a consensus that an ancient book that was initially known as the *Egyptian Ecclesiastical Order* is actually a work of Hippolytus that was thought to be lost, the *Apostolic Tradition*. Later, other translations of the same work into various languages have made it possible to reconstruct the original Greek text, of which much is still lost. This thus becomes the most ancient surviving document discussing liturgical matters in some detail. Since Hippolytus himself was a staunch conservative, whose conflict with the bishops of Rome had to do with his conviction that they were introducing undue innovations, one may well suppose that what Hippolytus wrote early in the third century reflected what had been done for some time earlier, and therefore late in the second century. Also, as we shall see later, while this writing proves the antiquity of many liturgical practices, it also corroborates the diversity and complexity of practices both in public worship and in private devotion.

From this wealth of resources that we will be able to use in the following chapters, one may safely conclude that the period to which we now turn is characterized by a process leading to a measure of uniformity. Part of that process is the establishment and development of an ecclesiastical hierarchy, so that now some believers—holding titles such as those of bishop, presbyter or elder, and deacon—will be in charge of not only the administration of the church but also its teachings and its worship. Bishops will also have the important function of serving as the bond of unity among churches—which is also the reason why, particularly beginning in the third century, we still have fairly extensive epistolaries containing the correspondence of the outstanding leaders of the church. Part of this process of moving toward uniformity is also the formation of the canon of the New Testament. And as we shall see in the chapter on baptism, creedal formulae appeared that would serve as a means to test the orthodoxy of anyone claiming to be a Christian. The same process led to the quest after a measure of uniformity in worship. That striving for unity is more difficult to see and to study when it comes to the matter of methods and styles of preaching and biblical interpretation (chapter 8), but it will be clear in what we now know about baptism (chapter 9) and Communion (chapter 10). In chapter 11, closing this second part of our study, we deal with the development of the Christian calendar, the places and spaces devoted to worship, and several other subjects—including music, on which unfortunately little is known.

8

Preaching

In the mid-second century, in an apology or defense of the faith addressed to Emperor Titus and to other important figures—in fact, to the entire Roman people—Justin Martyr describes Christian worship to show that nothing in it may be considered illegal or immoral, despite rumors to the contrary:

> On the day called Sunday all who live in cities or in the country gather together in one place. The memoirs of the apostles or the writings of the prophets are read, for as long as time permits. Then, when the reader has finished, the president verbally instructs and urges the imitation of these good things. (*1 Apol.* 67; ANF 1:186)

A generation later, Tertullian would declare that "preaching is the first thing, baptizing comes later" (*On Baptism* 14; ANF 3:676). Elsewhere, he writes that "wherever . . . the true Christian rule and faith are, *there* will also be the true Scriptures and their exposition" (*Presc. ag. Heretics* 19; ANF 3:251–52). His basis for this claim is that the church "unites the law and the prophets in one volume along with the writings of the evangelists and apostles. From this she drinks in her faith" (*Presc. ag. Heretics* 36; ANF 3:260).

Thus, during the period we are now studying, preaching was an essential part of worship. When we study various elements of worship in the early church, we see differences from place to place and from church to church, but such differences are much more remarkable when it comes to preaching. As we saw in the previous chapter and as reappears throughout part 2 of our study, the church was seeking greater uniformity in its teachings, its rites, and its organization. However, such uniformity is much more difficult to attain in preaching, since preachers have their own styles and even different views as to the nature of good preaching. Therefore, in this chapter, rather than

111

attempting a general description of Christian preaching from the second century and up to the early years of the fourth, we shall try to show the diversity of preaching through a series of concrete examples—all of them preaching the same gospel of Jesus Christ, but each with its own style, concerns, and perspective.

As to the sources available for the study of preaching during that time, one must begin by acknowledging that the sources that we have, particularly during the second century, are very similar to those from the earlier period. Just as much of what was said regarding preaching during the Judeo-Christian period is based on the letters of Paul and others written to be read in churches, so in this later period—particularly during the second century—letters often served as sermons. Since preaching is by its very nature oral and circumstantial—having to do with the challenges before the church at a particular time and place—very few sermons from the earlier part of this period have come to us. Also, partly due to the nature of a sermon, often dealing with passing circumstances, very few were written. If they were written, this was probably done on perishable material, and there was little interest in circulating or copying such sermons for posterity.

Despite all this, we do have a few sermons or homilies from the second century that are useful, if not for describing all preaching at that time, at least to show its diversity. Furthermore, as we enter the third century we have the immense literary production of one of the greatest Christian scholars of all time, Origen. On the basis of what other authors quote or mention, almost six hundred of Origen's homilies were estimated to be in circulation in ancient times. Of these, fewer than two hundred have survived. At any rate, when studying preaching in the third century, Origen deserves particular attention.

LETTERS AND SERMONS

In part 1, when dealing with Judeo-Christianity, we saw that the Epistles in the New Testament may well be considered sermons, for they were intended to be read out loud before the congregation. When Paul wrote to the Corinthians, he was not addressing a few among them but the entire church in that city, and he expected that his letter would be read before the church. In the Epistles to the Colossians and to Philemon, who was a member of the church in Colossae, it was clearly expected that both letters would be read out loud to the church. In other words, what Paul says to Philemon regarding how to deal with Onesimus was not simply a private message to Philemon but would also be known by the entire church in Colossae, which on hearing that letter would also learn something about what it means to be sisters and brothers in Christ.

The same is true in the second century. Early in that time frame, on his way to martyrdom in Rome, Ignatius, bishop of Antioch, wrote seven letters—six of them to churches and one to Polycarp, the young bishop of Smyrna. Just as Paul's letter to Philemon was addressed to the whole church, the letter that Ignatius sends to Polycarp is addressed not only to him but to the entire church, as may be seen in the salutations at the end. We know that these letters of Ignatius were read not only in the churches to which he originally sent them but also in other nearby churches. Soon someone collected them, and they began to circulate jointly as a corpus. Somewhat later, at the end of the period we are now studying, Eusebius of Caesarea, in an extensive chapter regarding Ignatius and his works, declared that whenever the bishop of Antioch reached a new place on his way to Rome, he would exhort the churches there, encouraging them to avoid error and to keep the apostolic tradition. According to Eusebius, it was in order to make sure that they followed his instructions that Ignatius wrote his letters:

> As he traveled through Asia under the strictest military surveillance, he strengthened the parishes in the various cities where he stopped by preaching and exhortation. He warned them above all to be on their guard against the heresies that were then beginning to prevail. He urged them to hold fast to the tradition of the apostles. Moreover, he thought it necessary to attest to that tradition by writing, to give it a fixed form for greater security. So when he came to Smyrna, where Polycarp was, he wrote an epistle to the church of Ephesus, in which he mentions Onesimus, its pastor. He wrote another to the church of Magnesia, situated on the Maeander, in which he mentions again a bishop Damas. Finally, he wrote one to the church of Tralles, whose bishop, he states, was at that time Polybius. (*Church History* 3:36.4.5; NPNF2 1:167–68)

Eusebius notably refers to Ignatius as preaching and teaching both orally and through his letters. That Ignatian preaching, echoes of which resound today through his letters, shows both his firm faith and his interest in relating that faith to the circumstances of each place. This may be seen in his famous letter to the Romans, where he faced his impending martyrdom and asked the Romans not to intervene on his behalf: "Allow me to become food for the wild beasts, through whom it will be granted me to attain to God. I am the wheat of God. Let me be ground by the teeth of the wild beasts, so that I may be found the pure bread of Christ" (*Ep. to the Romans* 4; ANF 1:75). But it may also be seen in less dramatic fashion in his other letters, where he shows a constant concern over the unity of the church and the authority of the bishop.

Some letters dealing with momentous events, such as a martyrdom, soon circulated and were used as exhortations read in church, much as a sermon.

Long years after Ignatius died as a martyr, Polycarp, who was the young bishop of Smyrna when Ignatius wrote to him, had become an old man when the time came for his martyrdom. We know the details of that event because the church in Smyrna, where Polycarp had spent most of his life, wrote to the church in Philomelium sending an account of Polycarp's martyrdom. At the very beginning of that letter, one notes that it is intended to be circulated widely and read throughout the churches: "The Church of God that sojourns at Smyrna, to the Church of God sojourning in Philomelium, and to all the congregations of the Holy and Catholic Church in every place: Mercy, peace, and love from God the Father, and our Lord Jesus Christ, be multiplied" (*Martyrdom of Polycarp* Salutation; ANF 1:39).

As a sign of the importance given to such documents and to their integrity as they were copied and circulated, the last lines of the oldest remaining manuscripts of this document are worth quoting:

> These things Caius transcribed from the copy of Irenaeus (who was a disciple of Polycarp). He himself had been an intimate of Irenaeus. And I Socrates transcribed them at Corinth from the copy of Caius. Grace be with you all.
> And I again, Pionius, wrote them from the previously written copy, having carefully searched into them. (*Martyrdom of Polycarp* 22; ANF 1:43)

The second-century church continued the custom, which it had received from apostolic times, and ultimately from the synagogues, of devoting time during worship to the reading, interpretation, and application of Scripture. Likewise, when there were distinguished visitors they were invited to speak about Scripture and the meaning of faith. We have seen this during Paul's early ministry, in Antioch of Pisidia. This was what Paul continued doing through his letters—addressed to those in a particular city who had accepted his message regarding Jesus. And now leaders such as Ignatius continued the same practice.

Near the end of that century, Tertullian would do likewise, when—possibly around 197 CE—he addressed a group of prisoners who were being readied for martyrdom. Tertullian's message to them has clear homiletical traits. He opens his exhortation as follows:

> To the blessed ones who are about to be martyrs: Our Mother the Church has supplied some of your physical needs from her bountiful breasts, and the brothers and sisters are giving you assistance out of their own private means. Accept also from me some nourishment for your spiritual needs, for it is not good for the flesh to feast while the spirit starves. It is right that the flesh which is weak should be

supplied, but that does not mean that that which is weaker still should be neglected. I have no right to exhort you, but even gladiators are encouraged not only by their coaches but also by those unskilled in the audience who cheer them on. Yes, anyone among the onlookers can yell out suggestions that may prove useful. My first such word to you, blessed ones, is that you do not grieve the Holy Spirit, who has entered this prison with you. If the Spirit had not gone with you, you would not be there now. Try your utmost, therefore, to keep the Spirit there. Let the Spirit lead you to your Lord. The prison, indeed, is the devil's house as well. The devil's family lives there. You have come within these walls for the very purpose of trampling the wicked one underfoot in his own house. You had already completely overcome him outside in a pitched battle. Do not now let him have any reason to say to himself: "Now they are in my domain. I shall tempt them to have defections or dissensions among them." Let the devil fly from your presence and skulk away to his own abysses, shrunken and weak, like a snake that has been outcharmed or smoked out. Do not give him any success in his own kingdom in creating dissension among you. Let him find you armed and fortified with peace, for peace among you is battle with him. (*To the Martyrs* 1; ANF 3:393)

Note that what is stressed here is the importance of peace and love among those who are about to witness to Christ through their death. The call is not so much to remain firm in their faith as it is to remain firm in peace and concord. Were a brave witness of individual strength to be moved by pride or the quest for notoriety, this would be a victory for evil. Here is one more example of what we have seen repeatedly of the collective and corporate nature of Christian life and worship.

THE PREACHING OF HERMAS

One of the documents included among the Apostolic Fathers is the *Shepherd* of Hermas. This book had such authority that some considered it Scripture, and *Codex Sinaiticus*—one of the most ancient manuscripts that we have of the New Testament—includes part of it. Hermas does not seem to have held any position within the hierarchical structure, but his brother Pius was bishop of Rome from 141 to 155. His book, the longest among the Apostolic Fathers, is not really a book in the sense of following an argument or expounding a particular position, but is rather a collection of "visions," "commandments," and "similitudes" that do not seem to follow a logical order, and sometimes become rather repetitive. There is every indication that these are a compilation of what were originally separate prophecies or sermons of Hermas in the church in Rome. We need not discuss its contents here. Suffice it to say that the main concern of this preacher is the problem of sins committed after baptism. What is important is to note that the style of preaching that we find here is different from the letters of Paul or of Ignatius. What Hermas presents is a series of visionary experiences through which he conveys a message to the church—a message that, consisting so much in visions and revelations, may well not have been entirely pleasing to the hierarchy, including his own brother.

Practically any passage of this book would serve to show Hermas's understanding of his task. A good example is near the end of the series of "visions," where the "Shepherd" first appears who has given his name to the entire book. Hermas recounts his experience:

> After I had been praying at home I sat down on my couch, and a man entered. He was glorious in appearance, dressed like a shepherd in a white goatskin. He had a pouch on his shoulders and a rod in his hand. He greeted me and I returned his salutation.
>
> He sat down beside me and said: "I have been sent by a most venerable angel to dwell with you all the rest of your days."
>
> I thought that he had come to tempt me, and I said to him: "Who are you? For I know the one to whom I have been entrusted."
>
> He said to me: "Do you not know me?"
>
> I answered: "No."
>
> He responded: "I am that shepherd to whom you have been entrusted."
>
> And while he was speaking his figure was changed and then I knew that it was he to whom I had been entrusted. Immediately I became confused, and fear took hold of me. I was overpowered with deep sorrow that I had spoken to him so wickedly and foolishly.
>
> But he answered and said to me: "Do not be confused, but receive strength from the commandments I am going to give you. For I was sent to show you again all the things you saw before, especially those useful to you. First, write down my commandments and similitudes, and other things that I will show you. For this purpose I command you to write down the commandments and similitudes: first, that you may read them easily, and be able to keep them."
>
> So I wrote down the commandments and similitudes, exactly as he had ordered me. If then, when you have heard these, you keep them and walk in them, and practice them with pure minds, you will receive from the Lord all that he has promised you. But if, after you have heard them, you do not repent but continue to add to your sins, then you shall receive from the Lord the opposite things. All these words the shepherd, even the angel of repentance, commanded me to write. (*Shepherd* Vision 5; ANF 2:18–19)

In brief, what we have in the *Shepherd* of Hermas is a collection of what seem to have been originally a series of sermons or prophetic utterances—"prophetic" not in the sense of predicting the future, but rather in the sense of conveying a message from God. Most of these are fairly short, and seem to be a summary of longer sermons or homilies. In general, they are much more symbolic than either Paul or Ignatius, and in this sense they are closer to the Revelation of John.

THE *SECOND EPISTLE OF CLEMENT*

Among the Apostolic Fathers there is, besides the already discussed letter of Clement to the Corinthians, another document claiming to be a second letter by the same author to the same audience. Scholars agree that this document is not the work of Clement, and that is not really a letter addressed to the Corinthians. It is rather a homily—perhaps even the earliest sermon in the strict sense that we have, for it may well date from 140 CE. It is clear that here we are leaving the Judeo-Christian world, for its author makes it clear that both he and his hearers are former pagans:

> We were deficient in understanding, worshiping stones and wood, gold, silver, and brass—the work of human hands. Our whole life was nothing else than death. We were blind, and though there was such darkness before our eyes, we have received sight. Through His will we have laid aside the cloud that enveloped us. For He had compassion on us, and mercifully saved us. He saw the many errors in which we were entangled, as well as the destruction to which we were exposed. We had no hope of salvation except it came to us from Him. For He called us when we were not, and willed that out of nothing we should attain a real existence. (*Second Epistle of Clement* 1; ANF 10:251)

Beginning with Isaiah 54:1, this preacher rejoices in the growth of Christianity among this people who did not know God: "our people seemed to be cast out from God, but now, through believing, we have become more numerous than those who are reckoned to possess God" (*Second Epistle of Clement* 2.3; ANF 10:251)—that is, Gentiles who know Christ are now more numerous than the children of Israel. This provides us with a sample of what must have been the main theme of early Christian preaching, claiming that the promises of the prophets have been fulfilled in Jesus—although sometimes arguing that Jews err in not accepting Jesus as the Messiah, and sometimes arguing that, even though Jesus has come into the world only recently, Christianity has deep roots that go far beyond the most ancient roots of pagan beliefs.

The rest of the sermon includes the arguments that eternal life is much more important than the passing life of this world, and that whatever we do with our body in this life is of eternal significance. Regarding the first, this unnamed preacher declares that "the sojourning in the flesh of this world is but brief and transient, but the promise of Christ is great and wonderful: the rest of the kingdom to come, and life everlasting" (*Second Epistle of Clement* 5.5; ANF 10:252). As to the second point, the importance of the body, he writes,

> And let no one of you say that this very flesh shall not be judged or rise again. Consider in what state you were saved, in which you received sight, if not while you were in the flesh. We must therefore preserve the flesh as the temple of God. As you were called in the flesh, so you shall also come to be judged in the flesh. As Christ the Lord who saved us, though he was first a spirit and became flesh, and thus called us, so shall we receive the reward in this flesh. (*Second Epistle of Clement* 9; ANF 10:253)

After a series of similar expectations, the document ends with words that show that it is indeed a sermon:

> Therefore, brothers and sisters, let us believe. In a trial of the living God we strive and we exercise in the present life, so that we may obtain the crown in the life that is to come. No one of the righteous received fruit quickly, but waited for it. For if God gave the reward of the righteous in an instant then it would be commerce we practiced and not godliness. It would be as though we were considered righteous because we followed after gain rather than following after godliness. For this reason the divine judgment baffled the spirit of the unrighteous and made the bonds strong.
>
> To the only God, invisible, Father of truth, who sent forth to us the Savior and Author of immortality, through whom He also manifested to us the truth of the heavenly light, to Him be glory forever and ever. Amen. (*Second Epistle of Clement* 20; ANF 10:256)

THE *EPISTLE OF BARNABAS*
AND ALEXANDRINE ALLEGORY

Another document among the Apostolic Fathers bears the title of *Epistle of Barnabas*, but it is neither an epistle nor the work of Paul's companion Barnabas. It seems to be a sermon. In that case, it could vie with *Second Clement* for the honor of being the oldest existing Christian homily. However, even if it were older, it could not compete with *Second Clement* in theological depth, elegance, logical order, or rhetorical value. Just as the two epistles bearing the name of Clement were given such authority that they appear in the *Codex Alexandrinus* of the New Testament, so is the *Epistle of Barnabas* included in the *Codex Sinaiticus*. The "document of the two ways" that appears in the *Didache* is also part of the *Epistle of Barnabas*—with the difference that in the first of these the two paths are of life and of death, in the latter they are the paths of light and of darkness. Also, while in the *Didache* the "document of the two ways" appears at the beginning, thus indicating that it had a catechetical function before baptism, in the *Epistle of Barnabas* it appears at the end, thus leading some to conclude that it is a later addendum to the original document.

The style of this *Epistle of Barnabas* is dense and confused. The author seems to know something about the rules of ancient rhetoric and applies them with such repetition and rigidity that it has provoked one of its translators into Spanish (Daniel Ruiz Bueno) to declare that the book is tedious and that translating it represents a true work of literary abnegation.

Scholars tend to attribute it to an anonymous believer, probably in Alexandria or nearby. Their main reason is its exaggerated use of allegory, for which Alexandria would soon be known. This is of one piece with the document's repeated attack on Judaism and its laws, for by means of allegory it becomes easy not only to leave aside, but even to condemn and ridicule any literal interpretation of the Scriptures of Israel as well as Judaism itself. What this false Barnabas says regarding circumcision shows what he thinks about the rest of the Law of Israel: "God declared that circumcision was not of the flesh, but they sinned because an evil angel deluded them" (*Ep. of Barnabas* 9.4; ANF 1:142).

The anti-Jewish tone of this letter, supported by an allegorical interpretation of the Scriptures of Israel, is one of the worst examples of what Christians wrote against Judaism in those early centuries of the history of the church. The author is convinced that God has cast Israel aside because of its sins. He even goes as far as to declare that "the Son of God therefore came in the flesh for this purpose: that He might bring to a head the sum of the sins of those who had persecuted His prophets to the point of death" (*Ep. of Barnabas* 5.1; ANF 1:140).

The result of all this is an allegorical interpretation that borders on the ridiculous and is clearly ill-informed of matters that could very easily be disproven. In order to show this, it suffices to quote what this author says about the dietary laws of Israel, often grounding it on gross zoological errors:

> Is there not a command of God that they should not eat these things? There is, but Moses spoke with a spiritual reference. For this reason he named the swine, as though he were saying: "Do not join with people who are like swine." For when they live in pleasure they forget their Lord; but when they are in need, they acknowledge the Lord. And in the same way, the swine, when it has eaten, forgets its master; but when hungry it cries out. On receiving food it is quiet again. . . .

Also, "You shall not eat the hyena." He means, "You shall not be an adulterer, or a corrupter, or be like them." Why? Because that animal annually changes its sex, and is at one time male, and at another female. . . .

Behold how well Moses legislated. But how was it possible for them to understand or comprehend these things? We then, rightly understanding his commandments, explain them as the Lord intended. For this purpose he circumcised our ears and our hearts, so that we might understand these things. (*Ep. of Barnabas* 10; ANF 1:143–44)

Such an allegorical interpretation was not an original invention of the anonymous author of this homily, for it actually had its forerunners in some of the best Jewish intellectuals in Alexandria, who used allegory in order to show that the Scriptures of Israel were full of wisdom similar to that of the great Greek philosophers. In a way, what the *Epistle of Barnabas* does is simply to take some of the ancient arguments of Alexandrine Jewish intellectuals against the pagans and turn them into an attack on Judaism itself. By the end of the second century, Christians in Alexandria were convinced that the best biblical interpretation had to follow along similar lines.

These tendencies were encouraged and strengthened by the most important Alexandrine theologian of all times, Origen, who was a master of allegorical interpretation, and whose writings echo much of the *Epistle of Barnabas*. In a passage that is parallel to the earlier quote from Barnabas, Origen explains Israel's dietary laws in similar fashion, although without Barnabas's crass factual errors:

If, according to this understanding, we say that the supreme God has proclaimed the laws to human beings, I think that the legislation will seem worthy of the divine majesty. But if we stand by the letter and according to that we accept what is seen by the Jews or the multitude as the written law, I would be ashamed to say and to confess that God gave such laws. For human laws, for instance, either of the Romans, or the Athenians, or the Lacedemonians, seem more elegant and reasonable. But if the Law of God is received according to this understanding that the Church teaches, then clearly it surpasses all human laws and is believed to be truly the Law of God. And so, with these firstfruits for the spiritual understanding, as we reminded you, let us speak briefly about the clean and unclean animals.

It says, "All cattle that parts the hoof and has hoofs and chews its cud among the cattle, these you will eat. Moreover, you will not eat from those which chew the cud and do not part the hoofs and have hoofs. The camel, because it indeed chews the cud but does not part the hoof, is unclean for you. The hare because it chews the cud but does not part the hoof is unclean for you; and the hedgehog because it chews the cud and does not part the hoof is unclean for you; and the swine," etc. Therefore, it determines that these kinds of animals, which seem to be partly clean and partly unclean, not be eaten. For example, "the camel" seems to be clean "because it chews the cud," but it is called "unclean" from the fact "that it does not have a parted hoof." After these it names now both "the hare" and "the hedgehog" and also it indeed says those "chew the cud" but do "not part the hoof." But it makes another list of these which, on the other hand, certainly "part the hoof" but "do not chew the cud."

Therefore, let us first see who these are that "chew the cud and part the hoof" which it calls clean. I think that one is said to chew the cud who pays heed to knowledge and "meditates day and night on the Law of the Lord." But hear how it was stated in the text: "Whatever parts the hoof and chews of the cud." Therefore, "he chews the cud" who applies those things which he reads according to the letter to the spiritual sense and he ascends from the lowest and visible to the invisible and higher things. But if you meditate on the divine law and you apply what you read to a precise and spiritual understanding, but your life and your deeds are not such that they have the capacity for distinguishing between the present life and the future, between this age and "the age to come," unless you discern and separate these things with the proper reason, you are a confused camel, who, when you receive understanding from meditation of the divine law, you do not divide nor separate the present and the future and do not discern "the narrow path" from "the wide path."

But let us explain still more clearly what is said. There are those who with their mouth take the testament of God and, although they have the Law of God in their mouth, their life and deeds are greatly different from their words and their sermons. "For they speak and do not do." About these the prophet says, "But God said to the sinner, 'Why do you interpret my righteousness and take my testament in your mouth?'" Therefore, you see how this one who has the testament of God in his mouth chews the cud. But what is said to him in the following? "But you hated discipline and you cast my words behind you." In this it clearly shows this one indeed "chews the cud" but "does not part the hoof," and for this reason whoever is such as this is unclean.

And again, there is another one, either of those who are outside our religion or of those who are with us, who indeed "part the hoof" and so advance in their lives that they prepare their deeds for the coming age. For many both learn thus from the philosophers and believe there is a future judgment. For they are aware of the immortal soul and they confess a reward is reserved for all good people. Some of the heretics do this, and inasmuch as they expect it, they have a fear of the future judgment and they temper their deed more cautiously as being liable to be examined in the divine judgment. But neither of these "chews the cud" nor "applies the cud."

For hearing what was written in the Law of God, he does not meditate on it and apply it with a keen and spiritual understanding. But when he hears something, he immediately either disdains or despises it and does not look for what valuable understanding is concealed in the more common words. And indeed those die "who part the hoof" but "do not apply the cud." But you who want to be pure, hold your life in conformity and harmony with knowledge, and your deeds with understanding, that you may be pure in each, that "you apply the cud" and "divide the hoof" but also that "you may produce" or "you may cast away" the hoofs. (*Homilies* 7.5.7–6.5; FoC 83:147–49)

The passage continues with a long list of similar details regarding various dietary laws. However, what is quoted suffices to see how Origen—as well as the long tradition of allegorical interpretation inspired by him—deals with various difficulties that the text may present by reading what would otherwise be difficult—or, as he would say, "shameful"—in what he calls a "spiritual" manner.

This sort of interpretation that we find in both the *Epistle of Barnabas* and Origen eventually became part of Christian traditional hermeneutics in general, but was a particular characteristic of theology produced in Alexandria and other regions where Platonism was dominant. In these areas, part of the interest of Christian interpreters would be to show that the Scriptures of Israel, whose laws many declared senseless, actually offer wise principles that any rational person should follow. There is no doubt that such interpretations did bring more than one Gentile to faith, for much anti-Christian propaganda was precisely that their books were senseless and even ridiculous. Such was the case of Clement of Alexandria, a teacher and forerunner of Origen who declared that, following a long quest for "the true philosophy," he met a Christian who could offer that philosophy by means of a spiritual interpretation of Scripture. Later this would also be the case of Augustine, for whom the allegorical interpretations of Ambrose had the same effect.

This points to one marked difference between the use of allegory in the *Epistle of Barnabas* and in Origen: The former uses allegory as an escape from profound thought—to the point that he does not even seem to have taken the time to check on popular rumors regarding various animals. Origen, on the other hand, makes use of the best knowledge of his time to be able to dialogue and, if necessary, debate with the foremost among his contemporary intellectuals. It is impossible to know Barnabas's intended audience; but it is difficult to think that they would be highly educated and informed people. Origen was addressing the intellectual elite, and therefore his fame spread to such an extent that people came from distant lands to hear his lectures—among them, the emperor's mother. Furthermore, Origen's "spiritual" interpretation did not lead him to set aside the text of Scripture, but exactly the opposite. If words have hidden meetings, it becomes necessary to pay careful attention to each of them and to make certain that one uses the best possible biblical text. This is why Origen, while making headway as a philosopher and defender of the faith among the intellectual elite, also spent long hours in careful study of the Bible, to the point that one could well say that he was the first biblical scholar whom the church produced. According to some of his contemporaries, he knew the Bible by heart since he was a child. His *Hexapla*, a Bible that placed the text and several translations in six parallel columns, also included a series of diacritical marks that served to show variants in the texts. As a result of this careful study of Scripture, Origen's allegorical interpretation, although often departing from the literal meaning of a text, generally results in conclusions that are faithful to the general message of Scripture. This may be seen in the following homily on Luke 4:14–20, well worth quoting is its entirety:

> First of all, "Jesus, full of the Holy Spirit, returned from the Jordan and was led by the Spirit into the desert for forty days." When he was being tempted by the devil, since he was still to struggle against him, the word "spirit" is put down twice without any qualification. But, when he has fought and overcome the three temptations that Scripture mentions, then see what is written of the Spirit, emphatically and carefully. The passage says, "Jesus returned in the power of the Spirit." "Power" has been added, because he had trodden down the dragon and conquered the tempter in hand-to-hand combat. So "Jesus returned in the power of the Spirit to the land of Galilee, and reports about him went out to the whole surrounding region. And he was teaching in their synagogues, and was glorified by all."
>
> When you read, "He was teaching in their synagogues and was glorified by all," beware of thinking that only they are blessed, and of believing that you have been deprived of his teaching. If the Scriptures are true, then the Lord speaks not only there, in the congregations of the Jews, but today too, in this congregation. And Jesus teaches not only in this congregation, but in other gatherings, and in the whole world. He seeks instruments through whom he can teach. Pray that he will find me, too, well tempered and fit for singing! At the time when mortal men need prophecy, Almighty God seeks prophets, and finds them—for example Isaiah, Jeremiah, Ezekiel, and Daniel. So Jesus seeks instruments through which he can teach his word or instruct the people in the synagogues and be glorified by all. Jesus is "glorified by all" more now than at that time when he was known in only one province.
>
> Thereupon, "he came to Nazareth, where he had been reared, and, according to custom, he entered the synagogue on the Sabbath day, and stood up to read. And the book of the prophet Isaiah was given to him. And he opened the scroll and found the place where it is written, 'The Spirit of the Lord is upon me. For this reason he anointed

me.'" It was no accident that he opens the scroll and finds the chapter of the reading that prophesies about him. This too was an act of God's providence. For Scripture says, "A sparrow does not fall into a net without the Father's willing it," and, "The hairs of the head" of the apostles "have all been counted." So perhaps this too should be thought to have happened not by accident or by chance, but by the providence and disposition of God. Precisely the book of Isaiah was found, and the reading was no other but this one, which spoke about the mystery of Christ: "The Spirit of the Lord is upon me; for this reason he anointed me." For it is Christ who says these words.

So we should consider what those things are that he spoke through the prophet and later proclaims about himself in a synagogue. He says, "He sent me to preach the Gospel to the poor." The "poor" stand for the Gentiles, for they are indeed poor. They possess nothing at all: neither God, nor the law, nor the prophets, nor justice and the rest of the virtues. For what reason did God send him to preach to the poor? "To preach release to captives." We were the captives. For many years Satan had bound us and held us captive, and subject to himself. Jesus has come "to proclaim release to captives, and sight to the blind." By his word and the proclamation of his teaching the blind see. Therefore, his "proclamation" should be understood ἀπὸ κοινο (apo koino) not only of the "captives" but also of the "blind."

"To send broken men forth into freedom . . ." What being was so broken and crushed as man, whom Jesus healed and sent away? "To preach an acceptable year of the Lord . . ." Following the simple sense of the text, some say that the Savior preached the Gospel in Judea for only one year, and that this is what the passage "to preach an acceptable year of the Lord and a day of retribution" means. But perhaps the divine word has concealed some mystery in the preaching of a year of the Lord. For, other days are to come, not days like those we now see in the world; there will be other months, and a different order of Kalends. Just as those will be different, so too will there be a year pleasing to the Lord. But all of this has been proclaimed so that we may come to "the acceptable year of the Lord," when we see after blindness, when we are free from our chains, and when we have been healed of our wounds.

But, when Jesus had read this passage, he rolled up "the scroll, gave it to the servant, and sat down. And the eyes of all in the synagogue were fixed on him." Now too, if you want it, your eyes can be fixed on the Savior in this synagogue, here in this assembly. For, when you direct the principal power of seeing in your heart to wisdom and truth, and to contemplating God's Only-Begotten, your eyes gaze on Jesus. Blessed is that congregation of which Scripture testifies that "the eyes of all were fixed on him"! How much would I wish that this assembly gave such testimony. I wish that the eyes of all (of catechumens and faithful, of women, men, and children)—not the eyes of the body, but the eyes of the soul—would gaze upon Jesus. For, when you look to him, your faces will be shining from the light of his gaze. You will be able to say, "The light of your face, O Lord, has made its mark upon us." To him is glory and power for ages of ages. Amen. (*Homilies on Luke* 32; FoC 94:130–33)

In this brief homily, Origen clearly analyzes the passage and its meaning masterfully. While making use of allegorical interpretation, he dives into the biblical passage and leads his audience to participate in the experience that the text narrates. He does not address his audience as individual believers but rather as a corporate congregation, and in so doing he takes them to the experience in that synagogue, relating it to what the congregation is experiencing at that point. Thus, this is not an allegorical interpretation that ignores the text; on the contrary, it relates the text with the present life, and the experience of those who were in the synagogue with the experience of the congregation that now hears the message.

MELITO OF SARDIS

Melito, bishop of Sardis late in the second century, must have been a renowned apologist. Near the year 170, he wrote an apology addressed to Emperor Marcus Aurelius that, on the basis of the few existing fragments, seems to have been a literary jewel. Unfortunately, that apology and practically all else he wrote has disappeared. Thanks to a fortunate discovery several decades ago, a homily of his was found whose existence was known through various citations, but that had been lost.

This homily, commonly known as *On Passover* or *Paschal Homily*, is a semi-poetic interpretation of much of the history of Israel, all seen as a sign pointing to Christ. It is important to realize that this is not an allegorical interpretation. What we have here is the already described typological interpretation—that is, one that accepts the events narrated and the laws prescribed in the Scriptures of Israel as historical realities, but at the same time sees in them types, signs, shadows, or announcements of what was to come.

The emphasis on the cross and the victory of Jesus in this homily, as well as the name that it has traditionally been given, may lead to the conclusion that the homily was preached at the annual paschal celebration. This is a reasonable conjecture—but still only a conjecture, for the homily could have been preached any other Sunday between the reading of Scripture and the celebration of Communion.

Given the nature of this homily, the best way to understand it is to quote some extensive portions of it. After a brief introduction that lets us know that the story of the first Passover has been read, Melito says,

Know therefore, beloved,
how this mystery
is both new and old,
everlasting and temporary,
perishable and imperishable,
mortal and immortal.
Such is the mystery of the Passover:
it is old in the law,
but it is new in the Word;
passing as a figure,
eternal thanks to grace;
perishable because the lamb was slaughtered,
and imperishable because of the life of the Lord;
perishable because of the tomb,
immortal because of the resurrection of the dead.
The law is old,
but the Word is new;
the figure, passing,
but the grace, eternal.
The lamb can perish,
but the Lord is imperishable.

. . . .

And the law was made Word.
And the old was made new.

. . . .

This is the mystery of the Lord,
from ancient times shown as a type
and suffering as a figure;
but now believed because it has been fulfilled,
even though some believe it to be new.
Because the mystery of the Lord is new and is also old:
old because of the law,
yet new because of the grace.
Study the type,
and in it you will see him, its fulfillment.
To see the mystery of the Lord,
look at Abel, like him killed;
at Isaac, like him bound;
at Joseph, like him sold;
at Moses, like him exposed;
at David, like him persecuted;
at the prophets, like him suffering for Christ.
And look at the lamb slain in Egypt,
by whose blood Egypt was struck down,
and Israel was saved.

Melito, *On Pascha* 2–4, 7, 58–60

What we see in this sermon is an eloquent example of typological interpretation. Melito's interpretation illustrates what Justin had earlier declared in his debate with Trypho: "the Holy Spirit sometimes brought about that something should be done as a type of the future" (*Dial. with Trypho* 114.1; ANF 1:256). Justin's view—that the Holy Spirit speaks not only by means of words but by actions—clearly differs from the allegorical interpretation of the *Epistle of Barnabas*, for it affirms that the laws and ceremonies of ancient Israel were certainly given by God, and not, as Barnabas would say, by an evil angel; at the same time those laws and ceremonies announced a new exodus and a people that would now include the Gentiles.

As we come to the end of this chapter we can see that preaching took a variety of forms during the second and third centuries: Some spoke in visions and parables whose meaning had to be explained—as did Hermas. Some—such as the unknown author of the *Epistle of Barnabas*—took the Scriptures of Israel as a starting point for allegorical interpretations whose wild flights often had little to do with reality. Others focused their attention on the events and laws of the Hebrew Scripture as signs pointing to Christ and to the church—as we have seen in the case of Melito. Still others sought to prove that Christianity agreed with the best philosophy of their time by means of an erudite allegorical interpretation of Scripture—a task in which Origen excelled.

Thus, while the church as a whole was seeking greater uniformity by developing a canon of the New Testament, increasing the authority of the hierarchy, formulating baptismal creeds to affirm a common faith over against views considered heretical, and in many other ways, preaching itself was far from such uniformity, often reflecting different purposes, audiences, and contexts. There is, however, one point that appears repeatedly in the few sermons and other documents that we have from that time: their purpose is to interpret Scripture so as to help the congregation see itself as part of a vast people of God that, like ancient Israel, marches as a single body toward the future that God has promised.

9

Baptism

NEW CONDITIONS: THE CATECHUMENATE

The transition from Judeo-Christianity to a church composed mostly of Gentile converts had important consequences for the practice of baptism. When we read in Acts that immediately after the outpouring of the Holy Spirit on Pentecost thousands were baptized, we often forget that throughout that first century those who joined the church through baptism were mostly Jews. Those who were Gentiles by blood, such as the Ethiopian and the centurion whom Philip and Peter baptized, respectively, were at least God-fearers—they were people who for some time had known and followed the Scriptures and the faith of Israel, although they had not become Jewish proselytes. For both Jews and God-fearers, what was required for Christian baptism would be the conviction that, as the apostles announced, in Jesus the promises made to Israel regarding the Messiah had been fulfilled. Such people did not need any instruction regarding monotheism, a world created by God, or other similar doctrines. They did not need to be taught that this God requires righteousness, justice, and love. Nor did they need to be taught about the history of Israel, which for God-fearers could now become their legacy through baptism.

All of this would change rapidly as Christianity began making inroads into the pagan Gentile population. When people who had been formed in the polytheism of the dominant culture and understood only the morality of that culture decided to join the church, they could not simply be received without further ado. It was necessary for such people to have at least a basic knowledge of Christian doctrine and life—and even such knowledge would not be enough, for they would also have to make a number of adjustments in both their private and their public lives. They also had to learn the history of

Israel, and how God's acts in that history could serve as the basis for a present recognition of God's presence and action both in church and in society. In the mid-third century, Cyprian—originally a Gentile—declared that "we already begin to consider the patriarchs as our parents" (*On Mortality* 26; ANF 5:475). A believer was now an heir and part of a particular history—the history of the people of God. Learning that history and tradition, and understanding the relationship between those events and their own experience, required from Gentile converts dedication and study.

This radical change in circumstances led to a growing emphasis on teaching or catechesis. Teaching was doubtlessly always important for Christianity, as seen in Paul's words to the Galatians: "Those who are taught the word must share in all good things with their teacher" (Gal. 6:6). Likewise Luke tells Theophilus that he is writing "so that you may know the truth concerning the things about which you have been instructed" (Luke 1:4). As already stated, the earlier part of the *Didache*—the "document of the two ways"—seems to have been conceived as a manual of instruction for the faithful. But now in the second century, the required instruction went far beyond a few moral teachings such as that document proposed. What was now needed was an entire process of instruction and preparation for baptism. Two additional factors made this necessary. First, some people at the time collected religious experiences and initiations in various cults. This is clear in the novel *Metamorphoses* or *The Golden Ass*, by Lucius Apuleius, which is partly a satiric mockery of such practices. Over against such attitudes, the church had to make certain that people would not join them out of mere curiosity, or simply seeking a new religious experience. A second important reason for developing a system for preparation for baptism was that, at a time when persecution was always a possibility—and often a reality—people receiving baptism should be sufficiently firm in their faith so as not to abandon it under either social pressure or perhaps even threat of death. The very fact that between periods of persecution there were also times of relative peace for the church could easily lead some to request baptism in times of peace and then abandon the church and its faith in times of persecution.

The result of these conditions was a process for preparing people for baptism that continued evolving throughout the entire period we are studying. Since the word "catechesis" means "teaching," those who were undergoing such instruction were called "catechumens," and the process itself was the "catechumenate."

As is also the case with many of the subjects that we study here, the development of the catechumenate was a process that moved slowly from an original diversity in the direction of greater uniformity. In general, during the time we are now studying, the catechumenate varied from place to place and time to time. Only in the next period, after the year 313, did a relatively uniform catechetical process emerge. This is particularly true of the various stages in the catechumenate, or the classification of catechumens according to their advancement. What is clear is that during the second century it became common to call people preparing for baptism "catechumens," be it in Rome, Carthage, Alexandria, or Antioch—the four great cities of the empire where the church was particularly strong—and that set an example that other churches followed.

The task of following the developing catechumenate from the second century until the beginning of the fourth is made difficult by that diversity, but also by the scarcity of written sources. Documents dealing with the manner in which church life is to be organized, and therefore also with the catechumenate, are commonly known as "church orders." Of all such documents that we have, leaving aside the already mentioned *Didache*, the only one that precedes Constantine and therefore falls into this particular period is the *Apostolic Tradition* of Hippolytus. This document dates from the early third century and deals with preparation for baptism, but also with baptism itself as well as with Communion. Therefore it is a fundamental source for our study of baptism and Communion in part 2 of our study. Since Hippolytus was a conservative who wrote trying to keep or restore what he thought had always been done, the common opinion is that, although his writing dates from the early 200s, it actually describes what was already done in Rome late in the second century. But this does not necessarily mean that what Hippolytus describes was also the practice in other places. As to other church orders, several of them, even though written in the fourth century, quite possibly are referring to what was already being done in the third—but this is not easy to determine, and therefore such documents must be used carefully.

After such caveats, one can still affirm that the catechumenate began developing fairly early in the period we are now studying. Already, as early as the second century, Justin Martyr wrote,

> All those who are persuaded and believe that what we teach and say is true, and who wish to be able to live accordingly, are told to pray and implore God with fasting for the remission of their past sins. And we are praying and fasting with them. Then they are brought to a place where there is water, and they are reborn in the same way in which we ourselves were reborn. (*1 Apol.* 61; ANF 1:183)

These few words show that there was a period of preparation for baptism, requiring not only repentance and fasting but also instruction and accompaniment ("we are praying and fasting with them"). During that time a catechumen was to learn Christian teachings in matters not only of doctrine but of actual life, so as to be able to "live accordingly." From the rest of Justin's writings we see that he considered it very important that Christians know the history of Israel, which was a type or figure that was now being fulfilled in the church. But Justin does not tell us how long the period of instruction, repentance, and fasting lasted.

Some fifty years after Justin wrote his *Apology* in Rome, a scholar by the name of Pantenus settled in Alexandria. According to Eusebius of Caesarea, there Pantenus led the "school for the faithful." Whether this was a cat-echetical school preparing people for baptism, or rather a center of study and discussion for those who were already members of the church, is not clear. Somewhat later Clement arrived there. He was originally from Athens, but since he spent most of his life in Alexandria, he is usually known as "Clem-ent of Alexandria." Before reaching this latter city, Clement had followed a long intellectual pilgrimage seeking "the true philosophy." Clement first, and then Origen, led the school in Alexandria—although there is some debate as to whether there was a single school formally established, or rather a succes-sion of distinguished teachers whose schools have later been conflated into the "catechetical school of Alexandria." Apparently, when the persecution of Septimus Severus forced Clement to leave the city the school was closed. But there is no doubt that catechesis was of great importance for Clement, because commenting on the passage where Paul tells the Corinthians that he gave them milk to drink rather than meat to eat, Clement says,

> We may regard the proclamation of the Gospel, which is widely dis-persed, as milk. Faith becomes a solid foundation through teaching. Teaching is more substantial than hearing, and it gives to the soul itself nourishment that is solid like meat. (*The Instructor* 1.6; ANF 2:219)

Somewhat later, Origen, who was then eighteen years old, was put in charge of the training of catechumens. As his fame grew, Origen founded a school similar to those of the classical philosophers, while the training of catechumens was left to Heraclas, his former disciple and later bishop of Alex-andria. By the end of the second century there was clearly in Alexandria a fairly well-developed educational program that included the preparation of catechumens for baptism. Origen refers to this program when he compares what is required to enter a philosophical school with what is required to enter into the church:

> Let us see if Christians are not better than the philosophers in urging multitudes to practice virtue. The philosophers teach in public and have no choice as to their listeners. Anyone who chooses to can stand and listen. Christians, however, as far as possible, test the souls of

those who wish to become their hearers. After instructing them in private, before they enter the community, they make sure they have given sufficient evidence that they desire to lead a virtuous life. Then they are introduced, and now there are two classes: one of those who are beginners needing further purification, who have not yet received the sign of complete purification; and the second, those who have shown to the best of their ability that they desire only those things approved of by the Christians. Among these people some are appointed to check on the lives and behaviors of the ones who wish to join. This prevents scandals from entering the public assembly; but it allows those who truly wish to be virtuous to be welcomed whole-heartedly, so that they can become even better. (*Ag. Celsus* 3.51; ANF 4:484–85)

The entire passage and its context lead to the conclusion that the second group to which Origen refers are the baptized, among whom some are given the task of overseeing and teaching others—the catechumens.

In Carthage, which was the center of imperial power in North Africa, there was a clear distinction between the catechumens and the baptized, as may be seen in Tertullian's criticism of heretics and others who have left the church. According to Tertullian, among such people, "it is doubtful who is a catechumen, and who a believer; they have all access alike, they hear alike, they pray alike—even heathens, if any such happen to come among them" (*Presc. ag. Heretics* 31; ANF 3:263).

Tertullian's words lead us to consider, first, who the catechumens were; second, how their entrance into the catechumenate was signaled; and, finally, their participation in the worship of the church. On the first matter, the initial requirement was that the person seeking admission into the catechumenate be apt for it. This would exclude anyone who was not ready to lead the life that was expected of believers in Christ. In this context, the words of Hippolytus are clear:

New converts to the faith, who are to be admitted as hearers of the word, shall first be brought to the teachers before the people assemble. And they shall be examined as to their reason for embracing the faith, and they who bring them shall testify that they are competent to hear the word. Inquiry shall be made as to the nature of their life; whether a man has a wife or is a slave. If he is the slave of a believer and he has his master's permission, then let him be received; but if his master does not give him a good character, let him be rejected. If his master is a heathen, let the slave be taught to please his master, that the word be not blasphemed. If a man has a wife or a woman a husband, let the man be instructed to content himself with his wife and the woman to content herself with her husband. But if a man is unmarried, let him be instructed to abstain from impurity, either by lawfully marrying a wife or else by remaining as he is. But if any man is possessed with demons, he shall not be admitted as a hearer until he is cleansed.

Inquiry shall also be made about the professions and trades of those who are brought to be admitted to the faith. If a man is a panderer, he must desist or be rejected. If a man is a sculptor or painter, he must be charged not to make idols; if he does not desist he must be rejected. If a man is an actor or pantomimist, he must desist or be rejected. A teacher of young children had best desist, but if he has no other occupation, he may be permitted to continue. A charioteer, likewise, who races or frequents races, must desist or be rejected. A gladiator or a trainer of gladiators, or a huntsman [in the wild-beast shows], or anyone connected with these shows, or a public official in charge of gladiatorial exhibitions must desist or be rejected. (*The Apostolic Tradition of Hippolytus* 16; trans. B. S. Easton [Cambridge: Archon Books, 1962], hereafter *Ap. Trad.*)

This text continues along the same lines, excluding those who are pagan priests, soldiers, magistrates, magicians, astrologers, diviners, and sorcerers. Finally, it adds that this list is not complete, and that those making decisions as to who will be admitted to the catechumenate will have to do so under the guidance of the Holy Spirit.

While the *Apostolic Tradition* says that candidates are to present themselves before the teachers, according to the *Clementine Recognitions*, a document that may well date from the third century—but more probably from the fourth— and seems to reflect what was being done in Syria, the candidate is to appear only before the bishop.

As to how a person's admission to the catechumenate was signaled, the texts of the time say little. However, church orders from the fourth century may well reflect what was being done earlier. Apparently, in Rome it was customary to pronounce an exorcism over the candidates while blowing on their face. They were then anointed with the sign of the cross on the forehead, and a bit of salt that had been blessed was placed in their mouths. Possibly in other parts of Italy hands were placed on the ears of the candidates, and a prayer made asking that they be able to hear and properly live what they were to be taught. In North Africa, where there were close connections with Italy, the new catechumen was marked with the sign of the cross and the imposition of hands. In the Greek East, neither salt nor oil were used, but hands were imposed on the new catechumens while prayers were made for them. No matter where, this was normally done in the presence of the gathered congregation. As time went by, particularly in the fourth century, such practices would become more uniform.

On the participation of catechumens in worship, all extant texts lead to the conclusion that they were allowed to be present during the first part of worship, when Scripture was read and explained—what eventually was called the "service of the Word." But they were excluded from the second part of worship, where Communion was celebrated—the "service of the Table." This seems to be an ancient custom, for already in the *Didache* there is a clear instruction: "Let no one eat or drink at your Eucharist who is not baptized into the name of the Lord" (*Didache* 9.5; ANF 7:380). At least in some areas, space was set aside for the catechumens, who were allowed to remain in the service after those who were only "hearers" or interested people were dismissed, which took place after the reading and explanation of Scripture. In Hippolytus's *Apostolic Tradition*, at the time of the kiss of peace, which was a sign of peace and reconciliation among believers, catechumens were not allowed to participate, for it was considered that their kiss was not pure. In some areas—at least in Syria—apparently the catechumens did share a kiss among themselves, but this was not yet considered equal to the holy kiss of peace that believers shared. (In all cases, the kiss was only among people of the same gender.) Then, after a special prayer for them and the imposition of hands—normally by the teacher who led their instruction—the catechumens were dismissed, and only the baptized remained. Also, some ancient documents suggest that catechumens are to listen carefully to the reading of Scripture and its explanation, and to remember the questions that they have in order to pose them later to their teachers or catechists.

As to the duration of the catechumenate, there were also variations. The passage from Justin quoted above only speaks of the order of events to be followed to be baptized, but not of the time this would take. The *Apostolic Tradition* says that this should be at least three years, although it also allows for exceptions: "Let catechumens spend three years as hearers of the word. But if a man is zealous and perseveres well in the work, it is not the time but his character that is decisive" (*Ap. Trad.* 17). Many texts mention various reasons for shortening the catechumenate. Even after the fourth century, when greater uniformity was sought, such practices differed among various areas.

In the middle of the third century—apparently first in Rome and in the West, then in the rest of the church—the custom arose of setting aside a few weeks at the end of the catechumenate during which instruction would come directly from the bishop. This period of instruction ended with what was called "the giving and returning of the creed" (*traditio et redditio symboli*). In this process the catechumens were taught the creed, and they would then "return" it to the teacher, showing that they understood and accepted the essentials of Christian faith. This was an important part of the preparation for baptism, for in the act itself of being baptized a catechumen had to affirm that creed. (The creed used in Rome was what historians now call the "Old Roman Symbol," to which other phrases were later added to become the present "Apostles' Creed.")

It is impossible to know the details of the process whereby the giving and returning of the creed became a common practice. Certainly by the fourth century almost all churches brought the catechumenate to a close with that giving and returning.

Once this process of instruction was complete, the candidate was ready to receive baptism.

THE ADMINISTRATION OF BAPTISM: PLACE AND TIME

The New Testament says nothing about where or when people are to be baptized. We are not told where those who accepted Peter's preaching on the day of Pentecost were baptized. In the story of Philip and the Ethiopian, the latter is baptized at a place on the roadside where there is water. As to Cornelius and his household, once again we are not told where the baptism took place. The *Didache* prefers running water, although it allows for the use of still water and even—if water is scarce—for the pouring of water over the neophyte's head. One may well suppose that in the earliest times people were baptized in any river or other water that was available. It is impossible to tell when the custom began of baptizing people naked, but quite probably this custom led to the desire to have more private places where baptism would be conferred. We have already referred to pools that were available for similar uses in Jerusalem and throughout the Holy Land, and the early Christians quite likely used those pools as baptisteries.

Archaeological excavations have uncovered numerous pools or other basins that could have been used for baptism. However, the earliest baptistery that has been discovered and whose date can be determined with some certitude is among the ruins of the city of Dura, on the banks of the Euphrates—also known as Dura-Europos—in a house built early in the third century. Around the year 240 the house became a meeting place for Christians. The architecture of the house itself is that of a typical Roman residence. One of its rooms has a baptistery that is slightly over a meter and a half long, nearly a meter wide and not as deep. On the basis of these dimensions, one may well suppose that the neophyte would enter the water, but the person baptizing remained outside—although some also suggest that probably the person to be baptized would only kneel in the water and then have water poured over the head.

The entire room was covered with fresco paintings that have been partly restored. On the wall behind the baptistery itself is an image of the Good Shepherd surrounded by his flock. There are also representations of the temptation in the garden of Eden and of the resurrection, as well as of some miracles of Jesus and of the victory of David over Goliath, and others having to do with water and therefore more directly related to baptism—Jesus and Peter walking over the water, and the Samaritan woman by the well.

Although this is the oldest baptistery that can be clearly dated, other pools in similar places may well have been baptisteries. Later, particularly as the fourth century advanced, baptisteries would begin taking shapes allusive to various meanings of baptism—some in the shape of the cross; others in the shape of a coffin, signifying death and resurrection with Christ; others in the shape of a womb, allusive to the new birth, and so forth.

As to the time when people were baptized, the book of Acts provides several examples of people who were baptized whenever they asked for it. As the catechumenate developed, baptism was usually done on Easter Sunday, although other dates were added later—particularly Pentecost. Some suggested that baptisms should be offered more frequently. Hesitation regarding these matters may be seen in the following words from Tertullian:

> The Passover is a more than usually solemn day for baptism because that is when the Lord's passion, into which we are baptized, was completed. It would be appropriate to interpret figuratively the fact that when the Lord was about to celebrate the last Passover, he said to the disciples who were sent to make preparation, "You will meet a man carrying water." He points out the place for celebrating the Passover by the sign of water. After Passover, Pentecost is a joyous time for baptizing, because within this season the Risen Lord repeatedly proved to his disciples that he had risen, and the hope of the coming of the Lord was pointed to indirectly. . . . However, every day is the Lord's; every hour, every time, is appropriate for baptism. There may be a difference in the solemnity but there is no distinction in the grace. (*On Baptism* 19; ANF 3:678)

THE ADMINISTRATION OF BAPTISM: THE RITE ITSELF

After considering how people were prepared for baptism, we must now deal with the ceremony itself insofar as it is possible to reconstruct it. This is particularly difficult because among believers themselves there was a certain resistance to divulge the secrets of baptism and Communion—what some historians have called "the arcane of the sacraments." Unfortunately, the only contemporary document we have indicating what was done during baptism, and in what order it was done, is Hippolytus's *Apostolic Tradition*. Once again, this document was written early in the third century, although it possibly reflected what was being done late in the second. The warning must be repeated here that what Hippolytus says is what was done in Rome—and not necessarily elsewhere. On the other hand, the early translations of the work of Hippolytus into other languages, some of them made as far away as Egypt, would seem to show that what Hippolytus describes here was well received and probably followed in other lands.

Besides the work of Hippolytus, another important document discussing baptism is a very brief treatise of Tertullian titled *On Baptism*. This work, written before the one by Hippolytus, is the only document from before the time of Constantine that focuses on a particular sacrament. Tertullian wrote it in order to refute the objections of a certain Quintilla, who rejected baptism, claiming there could be no relationship between washing the body with water and washing the soul for salvation. Unfortunately, given the polemical nature of this writing, Tertullian takes for granted that his readers know what baptism is, how it is administered, and the rites that accompany it, and therefore whatever he says on these matters is only in passing. In any case, one of the most interesting points of data that Tertullian provides is the simplicity of baptismal rites:

> There is absolutely nothing which makes the human mind more stubborn than the simplicity of the divine works. These works seem so simple in the act as compared to the greatness of what is promised through the act. Such simplicity: without pomp, without any great novelty in preparation, and finally, without expense, a person is dipped in water. A few words are uttered, the person is sprinkled with the water, and then they rise again. They are not much (or not at all) cleaner, so the attainment of eternity because of this act is all the more incredible. I would be a deceiver if I did not say that the idols gain credit and authority precisely because of the circumstance and preparation and expense of their ceremonies. O miserable incredulity that denies to God God's own properties of simplicity and power! (*On Baptism* 2; ANF 3:669)

This might lead us to think that baptism as Tertullian knew it would be a rather simple rite, consisting only of dipping a person and pronouncing a formula. But as we read the entire treatise we find mentions in passing of several other ritual actions—for instance, anointing the neophyte. Thus, in using Tertullian's treatise as a source to understand the administration of baptism as he knew it, one must read between the lines, noting his agreements and differences with what Hippolytus says. Due to its polemical character, this treatise is more useful to understand Tertullian's theology of baptism than to learn how baptism itself was practiced. For this reason, even risking a measure of anachronism, here we discuss the administration of baptism as Hippolytus presents it, comparing it with Tertullian's work in order to note the agreements and differences between the two. Beside these two main sources, we shall also refer to brief notices in the literature of that time when possible.

Those preparing for baptism are now coming to the end of a long period of instruction—according to Hippolytus, three years. Before being baptized, there would be an examination or scrutiny to make certain that they "have lived soberly, whether they have honoured the widows, whether they have visited the sick, whether they have been active in well-doing" (*Ap. Trad.* 20). Then, having passed that scrutiny, they would be ordered to bathe on the fifth day of the week (Thursday), to fast on the sixth (Friday), and to gather with the bishop on the seventh (Saturday). When they were kneeling before the bishop, he would impose hands on them and pronounce an exorcism ordering the evil spirits to abandon the person and never come back. Then the bishop, after blowing on the faces of those to be baptized, would anoint their forehead, ears, and nose. They would then spend the entire night in vigil, listening to readings and receiving further instruction. At dawn there would be a prayer blessing the water, which if possible should be running water.

Then Hippolytus describes baptism itself:

> They shall remove their clothing. And first baptize the little ones; if they can speak for themselves, they shall do so; if not, their parents or other relatives shall speak for them. Then baptize the men, and last of all the women; they must first loosen their hair and put aside any gold or silver ornaments that they were wearing; let no one take any alien thing down to the water with them. (*Ap. Trad.* 21)

(Regarding being naked for baptism, the church in Dura-Europos had a separate room where people could undress as they awaited their turn—men apart from women. One may suppose that other churches had similar arrangements.)

This text is the most ancient to include instructions regarding the baptism of children who are as yet incapable of speaking for themselves. During the first two centuries, the silence in the existing texts is almost absolute. It certainly is not mentioned in the New Testament or in the Apostolic Fathers or the Apologists of the second century. In the account by Hippolytus, he seems to take for granted that such baptisms were a generally accepted custom that needed no defense. Surprisingly, at about the same date, practically at the other end of the empire, Origen also seems to take this practice for granted, for he uses it as a way to prove universal sinfulness:

> Little children are baptized "for the remission of sins." Whose sins are they? When did they sin? Or how can this explanation of the baptismal washing be maintained in the case of small children, except according to the interpretation we spoke of earlier? "No man is clean

of stain, not even if his life upon the earth had lasted but a single day."
Through the mystery of baptism, the stains of birth are put aside.
For this reason, even small children are baptized. "For unless born
of water and the Spirit one cannot enter the kingdom of heaven."
(*Homilies on Luke* 14.5; FoC 94:58–59)

Later in that century, now on the north coast of Africa, a certain bishop
Fidus suggested that newly born children should not be baptized, for it was
best to wait until the eighth day after their birth, following the example of the
circumcision of the children of Israel. The matter was discussed in a synod
gathered in Carthage, apparently in 251. Their response may be found in a
letter to Fidus from Cyprian, bishop of Carthage:

> But as to the case of infants, whom you say ought not to be baptized
> on the second or third day after their birth: you say we should follow
> the ancient law of circumcision and not baptize a newly born child
> until the eighth day. In our council we all felt very differently. We
> did not agree with your way of thinking but rather we judged that the
> mercy and grace of God should not be refused to any human child. . . .
> Therefore, dearest brother, this was the opinion of our council: that
> no one should be hindered from baptism and the grace of God by us,
> for God is merciful and kind and loving to all. This should be true
> particularly in the case of infants and the newly born; they deserve
> more from our help and from the divine mercy, since from their very
> birth they weep and lament and do nothing but entreat. (*Epistle* 64, *To
> Fidus*, 2, 6; ANF 5:353–54)

Remarkably there seems to have been no movement of protest against
infant baptism. The first objection to such a practice appears in Tertullian's
On Baptism, written several decades before the texts of Hippolytus and Origen quoted above. Tertullian always had a legalistic and moralizing inclination that eventually led him to Montanism. His work *On Baptism* seems to
have been written before that final step, when he broke away from the rest
of the church. But such legalistic tendencies may already be seen in what he
says about the age at which people should be baptized. After complaining
that some are ready to administer and to receive baptism without sufficient
thought, he says,

> And so, taking into account the circumstances, the disposition, and
> even the age of each individual, the delay of baptism is to be pre-
> ferred. This is especially true in the case of little children. Why is
> it necessary—if baptism itself is not so necessary—that the sponsors
> are also put in a dangerous position? They might not be able to carry
> out their promises because of their own mortality. The child might
> develop an evil disposition and yet they were the sponsors. The Lord

does indeed say, "Let the children come to me." Let them come, then, while they are growing up. Let them come while they are learning where to come. Let them become Christians when they are able to know Christ. Why does the innocent period of life hurry to the remission of sins? More caution is exercised in worldly matters; so now one who is not to be trusted in earthly things is trusted with what is divine! Let them know how to ask! At least then you would seem to have given "to him that asks." (*On Baptism* 18; ANF 3:678)

Up to this point, Tertullian says simply seems to be arguing against infant baptism. But then he continues,

This is an equally strong reason for postponing the baptism of the unmarried—in whom there is the ground of temptation. This is equally true of those who have never married because of their age as of the widowed because of their freedom. Baptism should be deferred until they marry or are more fully strengthened in continence. (*On Baptism* 18; ANF 3:678)

Thus, while Tertullian objects to the baptism of infants, his reason is not that he believes such baptism to be invalid, but rather that he understands baptism as a washing of all sin committed before it, but not after. On that basis, he believes that baptism should be postponed until a time when all the sins of youth have been left behind. In a word, his objection is not that children cannot have faith, but rather that they have not yet reached the age of major sins, and therefore their baptism should be postponed until they have passed that age. By so doing, the baptismal washing will be valid for all those other sins. The purpose of baptism is not to prevent sin. As he says elsewhere, "We are not washed in order to stop sinning, but because we have stopped, since in our heart we have already been washed" (*On Repentance* 6; ANF 3:662).

Returning then to the narrative of the events and rites connected with baptism, Hippolytus has said that baptism is to be administered in a certain order: first children, then men, and finally women. But in saying this, Hippolytus himself is moving ahead of his narrative, for he then tells us what happens before baptism. According to Hippolytus, at the beginning of the rite the bishop is to pray over two vessels of oil, which Hippolytus calls "the oil of thanksgiving" and "the oil of exorcism." The candidate is then brought before the one who is to perform the baptism, who orders him or her to say, "I renounce thee, Satan, and all thy servants and all thy works." Immediately he is anointed with the oil of exorcism and with the words "Let all spirits depart far from thee" (*Ap. Trad.* 21). Tertullian also mentions this ceremony, usually called the "renunciation," although according to him this takes place in the presence of all the congregation: "When we are going to enter the water, but a little before, in the presence of the congregation and under the hand of the president, we solemnly profess that we disown the devil, and his pomp, and his angels" (*On the Crown* 3; ANF 3:94). Beginning in the fourth century, documents attesting to such renunciations are common.

After the renunciations, and declaring allegiance to Christ, the candidate enters the water and is asked, "Dost thou believe in God, the Father Almighty?" After the response, "I believe," the candidate is submerged—or perhaps has water poured over the head, for the text does not say, although total immersion is most probable. Then follows the next question:

> Dost thou believe in Christ Jesus, the Son of God, who was born of the Holy Ghost of the Virgin Mary, and was crucified under Pontius Pilate, and was dead and buried, and rose again the third day, alive from the dead, and ascended into heaven, and sat at the right hand of the Father, and will come to judge the quick and the dead?

After answering, "I believe," the candidate is submerged again. Then follows a third and final question: "Dost thou believe in the Holy Spirit, the holy church, and the resurrection of the flesh?" After a third answer, "I believe," there is a final submersion (*Ap. Trad.* 21).

Obviously, what is being asked is very similar to what today we call the Apostles' Creed. Other clauses would later be added to that earlier formula (the Old Roman Symbol), thus developing into the creed we know today. Also note that in the second century—particularly in the writings of Tertullian and Irenaeus—similar formulae appear that are often called "the rule of faith." In any case, it seems clear that the creed was originally presented in an interrogative form, and was used as a way to test the faith of the neophyte at the very moment of baptism. Also, once again remember that what Hippolytus says refers particularly to Rome, and other places would use different formulae, although all the ones that have survived have a Trinitarian structure based on baptism in the name of the Father, the Son, and the Holy Spirit.

According to Hippolytus, when the neophyte leaves the water and is dressed, there is a further anointing, this time with the oil of thanksgiving and in the name of Jesus Christ. In order to understand the significance of this, it is necessary to remember that the title of "Christ" means "Anointed"— which is why sometimes confirmation, which involves anointment, is called "chrismation." Thus, by anointing the neophyte, the church proclaims that this person now has been anointed in the name of the Anointed. Tertullian also mentions this anointing, relating it to the ancient practice of anointing priests with oil.

Tertullian says that this anointing is followed by the imposition of hands and a prayer asking for the blessing of the Holy Spirit (*On Baptism* 7–8; ANF

3:672–73). Hippolytus says something similar, that the neophyte is to be anointed on the forehead and the following words pronounced: "I anoint thee with holy oil in the name of the Lord, the Father Almighty, and Christ Jesus and the Holy Ghost." Each person being anointed is saluted with the words "The Lord be with thee," to which the neophyte responds, "And with thy spirit" (*Ap. Trad.* 22).

Finally, the neophytes are taken to join the congregation, which has been gathered at a different place. Now for the first time they are allowed to participate in the "prayer of the faithful" and in Communion, from which they had been excluded until then. We return to what happens then in our next chapter.

SOME THEOLOGICAL ISSUES

Although it is not possible here to examine the entire course of theology regarding baptism, certain matters must be discussed—some because of their own intrinsic interest, and some because they show the theological reasons for various rites connected with the administration of baptism. We have not discussed five basic issues that often emerge in discussions of baptism and need to be clarified before moving on to its meaning. Given the nature of these questions, in some we have found it necessary to go beyond the chronological limits of this part 2, and to say something of later discussions.

Why Was Jesus Baptized?

The first of these questions is why Jesus went to be baptized by John, for John's baptism was for repentance, and Jesus had no reason to repent. Reading the remaining fragments of some of the apocryphal gospels, we see that this question was posed as early as the second century. One example may be found in the so-called *Gospel of the Hebrews*, which Jerome quotes—as does also a document falsely ascribed to Cyprian. There Jesus is seen "confessing his own sin . . . and forced by his mother Mary, practically against his will, to receive the baptism of John."

Other similar passages could be quoted. Probably the most interesting among them—and the one that later had constant echoes in early Christian theology—is a comment by Ignatius of Antioch, at the very beginning of the period we are studying. According to Ignatius, Jesus was "baptized, that by His passion He might purify the water" (*Ep. to the Ephesians* 18; ANF 1:57). When referring to the "passion" of Jesus, Ignatius means not only the sufferings of the cross but also the incarnation itself. The passion of Jesus began with the incarnation. Therefore, what Ignatius is saying is that the Word of God made flesh, by the very act of entering the baptismal waters, empowered those waters.

What Ignatius said early in the second century reappears in the fourth century in other authors, particularly in Asia Minor, Syria, and Egypt. In Egypt, Cyril of Alexandria would write that "by being baptized Jesus blessed the waters and purified them in our favor. He did not need holy baptism for the remission of sins, but now we receive that remission from him" (*On Luke* 3.21). In Asia Minor, Gregory of Nyssa affirmed that thanks to Jesus' baptism in the Jordan the waters of the river have become the source from which the grace of baptism flows throughout the world (*On the Baptism of Christ* 7). And in Syria Ephrem Syrus explained that, since the Holy Spirit was in Jesus, by receiving baptism Jesus mixed the waters with the Spirit, so that now when a body enters the baptismal waters the soul also receives the gift of the Spirit (*Sermon on the Lord* 55). This is part of a long theological tradition, particularly in the Greek-speaking church, according to which by his very presence in the world the Word of God incarnate has imparted holiness to the world itself. At any rate, significantly, according to Ignatius, John's baptism of Jesus gives power to every baptism in water and in his name.

At least by the early second century, Ignatius and others were convinced that baptism was much more than a symbolic action or a witness the person being baptized gave before those present. In some way that the authors do not claim to explain or determine, the waters of baptism are joined with the new birth. Something similar appears in the continuation of the passage of Justin where he speaks of believers preparing for baptism. Referring to baptism itself, Justin writes,

> Then we bring them to a place where there is water, and they are born again in the same way that we ourselves were reborn. For in the name of God, the Father and Lord of the universe, and of our Savior Jesus Christ, and of the Holy Spirit, they then receive the washing with water. (*1 Apol.* 61; ANF 1:183)

The passages affirming the relationship between baptism and the new birth or regeneration are too numerous to quote. Most of them are based on Jesus' words that "no one can enter the kingdom of God without being born of water and Spirit" (John 3:5). Others refer to baptism as a "seal"—sometimes in contexts that relate such a seal with the master's brand that was burned on a slave's flesh. Some slightly later texts relate baptism with the circumcision of the children of Israel—to which we shall return, and have already seen in the case of Cyprian's response to Fidus.

Baptism for the Dead

A second question is the matter of baptism for the dead. In his first Epistle to the Corinthians, trying to convince doubters that there is a resurrection, Paul asks them, "If the dead are not raised at all, why are people baptized on their behalf?" (1 Cor. 15:29). This is the only biblical reference to such a practice, and apparently Paul not only accepted but even used it to strengthen his argument. We find some discussions on the subject during the period we are now studying. Late in the second century, Tertullian accused the followers of Marcion and Cerinthus of practicing baptism for the dead. Tertullian himself, through a hermeneutical sleight-of-hand, claims that Paul is speaking of the expectation that the present body will die, and that therefore when people are baptized in their body they are also baptizing that which will die: "To be 'baptized for the dead' therefore means to be baptized for the body. As we have shown, it is the body that dies. What, then, shall those who are baptized for the body do, if the body does not rise again?" (*Ag. Marcion* 5.10; ANF 3:449).

It is impossible to solve the matter of baptism for the dead in Corinth with the data that are available today. Most probably what they did was, not just to be baptized for anybody who had died even though they never knew faith, but rather to be baptized in the place of people who were ready for baptism, but died before receiving it. Even this is mere conjecture. Certainly, these few words in 1 Corinthians are the only ancient text indicating this practice. Quite possibly these words of Paul reflect what he knew was being done in Corinth, and to which he did not object. It certainly was not the general practice of the church.

Requirements for the Validity of Baptism

Once again, much of the development of worship in the first few centuries is a quest for a measure of uniformity. In part 1, when discussing the *Didache*, we saw concern over people who called themselves apostles or prophets and used such titles for their own gain. As we come to the second century, that concern continues and becomes even stronger. It is reflected in the letters of Ignatius regarding subjects such as marriage, Communion, the care of widows, and—of interest for us here—baptism. Regarding this subject, Ignatius says, "Without the bishop it is not lawful either to baptize or to celebrate a love-feast" (*Ep. to the Smyrneans* 8.2; ANF 1:90).

Later, near the end of the second century, Tertullian wrote regarding those authorized to administer baptism:

> To conclude this brief subject, let us remember to give proper obser-
> vance to the giving and receiving of baptism. The bishop, who is the
> chief priest, has the right to give baptism. Next, with the permission
> of the bishop, presbyters and deacons may baptize. In this way, the
> honor and the peace of the church is preserved. In addition, even lay-
> men have the right to baptize, for what has been equally received can
> be equally given. (*On Baptism* 17; ANF 3:677)

On this point, Tertullian seems to agree with Ignatius, for what is important
is not who administers baptism but that it be done orderly and with proper
authorization. (We must also note that, referring to the legends regarding
Paul and Thecla, Tertullian declared that, since women do not have the right
to speak, they do not have the right to baptize.)

Tertullian also poses a question that shortly thereafter would lead to a
harsh controversy between the church in Carthage and that in Rome. The
question is whether heretics and schismatics have the right to baptize—that
is, whether their baptism is valid. Tertullian does not think so, for their God
is not the same, and "therefore their baptism is not one with ours either,
because it is not the same" (*On Baptism* 17; ANF 3:676). Apparently, this was
the traditional position on this matter in the church of North Africa, where
it was customary to baptize again anyone who had received baptism from any
community that was not part of the church that other bishops acknowledged
and authorized. In Rome the custom was the opposite; the baptism administered by groups considered heretical or schismatic was deemed valid as long
as it was done in the name of the Triune God and with water. What was then
necessary was simply to have the bishop anoint those baptized in such groups
so that they could receive the Holy Spirit. Without that anointing, their baptism was considered imperfect. A few decades later, in the mid-third century,
these contrasting practices led to a controversy between Cyprian, bishop of
Carthage, and his colleague in Rome, Stephen. Although tension had long
been present between them, the controversy came to the surface when, after
a synod of the bishops of the province of Africa, Cyprian wrote to Stephen
letting him know what had been decided:

> That those who were dipped elsewhere outside of the Church, and
> have been stained with the taint of profane water among heretics and
> schismatics, ought to be baptized when they come to us and to the
> Church. It is a small matter to "lay hands on them that they may
> receive the Holy Spirit," unless they receive also the baptism of the
> Church. (*Ep.* 71.1, *To Stephen*; ANF 5:378)

While Cyprian was communicating to Stephen the decision of the African
bishops, Cyprian also let Stephen know that he did not expect Stephen to

agree, "since each bishop in the administration of the Church has his free will. He shall give an account of his conduct to the Lord" (*Ep.* 71.3; ANF 5:379). Stephen insisted that all must follow the same policies as Rome, to which Cyprian responded harshly. Stephen's death, and soon thereafter also Cyprian's, lessened the tension, although the differences between Rome and North Africa regarding the baptism of heretics continued. It is not possible to determine the exact time when the African church changed its practice, but by the fourth century all had clearly reached the conclusion that any baptism done in water and in the name of the Trinity was valid, no matter who administered it. All that should be required in the case of people baptized by schismatics or heretics was for the bishop to receive them formally into the church by anointing them.

There were also disagreements regarding what was called "clinical" baptism—a name derived from the Greek word *klínē*, meaning "bed" or "couch"—sometimes administered to people on their deathbeds. In such cases, baptism was not by immersion but rather by placing water on the head. Ancient texts indicate that, while the church accepted this practice in exceptional cases, some considered it unsatisfactory. In at least one case, some insisted that one who had been baptized on what was expected to be his deathbed and then survived could not be a bishop. In one of his letters, Cyprian tells a certain Magnus,

> You have asked, dearest son, what I thought of those who obtain God's grace in sickness and weakness. That is, are they to be considered legitimate Christians, since they were sprinkled and not washed with the saving water? On this point, I don't want to let anyone think that I am judging those who think or act differently. As far as my poor understanding goes, I do not think that the divine benefits can be mutilated or weakened [because of less water]. If the giver and receiver of baptism act in full faith, then what is drawn from the divine gifts is not less in that case. For the sacrament of salvation is a washing away of sins, not in the way that filth is washed away from the skin or in the ordinary washing of the body. . . . In a very different manner is the heart of the believer washed. The human mind is purified by the merit of faith not by ordinary washing. (*Ep.* 75.12; ANF 5:400–401)

Cornelius, the bishop of Rome, had similar concerns regarding the baptism of schismatic leader Novatius, although his doubts did not have to do directly with baptism itself, but rather with his not having been anointed after baptism as a sign of the presence of the Holy Spirit:

> Having been freed by the exorcists, he fell into a severe sickness. Since he seemed about to die, he was baptized by sprinkling while he was on his sickbed. That is, if we can say that such a person did receive

it. And when his sickness was over he did not receive the other things which the laws of the Church require. He was not even anointed by the bishop. Since he did not receive this sealing, how could he receive the Holy Spirit? (Eusebius, *Ch. Hist.* 6.43.14–15; NPNF2 1:288–289)

On this particular issue, it was eventually decided that baptism was valid even if a neophyte had not been anointed.

Baptism and Martyrdom

In ancient Christian literature one repeatedly finds the notion that martyrdom is like a second baptism. Tertullian declares it clearly:

> We have indeed a second font, though it is one with the first. This is a font of blood, just as the Lord said: "I have a baptism to be baptized with," although he had already been baptized. He had come "by means of water and blood," just as John had written, that is, that he might be baptized with water and glorified by blood. Therefore we also are called by water and chosen by blood. These two baptisms he sent out by the wound in his pierced side, so that those who believed in blood might be bathed with the water, and that those who had been bathed in the water might also drink the blood. This is the baptism which both stands in the place of washing of the font when that has not been received, and restores the fontal washing when it has been lost. (*On Baptism* 16; ANF 3:677)

This understanding of martyrdom as another form of baptism served two functions: first, it made it possible to tell believers who were preparing for baptism and found themselves about to suffer martyrdom that they would be counted among the baptized. Second, particularly in the Western church, where there was much concern regarding sins committed after baptism, martyrdom came to be a second chance for those who had fallen after their baptism. What was absolutely necessary was that martyrdom should not be sought; it was to be left in the hands of God. Those who offered themselves for martyrdom—called the "spontaneous"—were not considered true martyrs.

Baptism and Circumcision

Finally, a theme that appears in the third century but need not be discussed here is the relationship between circumcision and baptism. The main biblical text quoted in relation to this point is Colossians 2:11–12: "In him also you were circumcised with a spiritual circumcision, by putting off the body of the flesh in the circumcision of Christ; when you were buried with him in baptism, you were also raised with him through faith in the power of God." The difficulty was that, while this passage refers to both circumcision and baptism, their relationship is not made clear. The same is true of some passages in ancient Christian literature where reference is made to circumcision and to baptism. However, most of these passages, like the one in Colossians, do not categorically say that baptism has taken the place of circumcision, a concept that became common in the fourth century. The importance of this question lies in the matter of infant baptism, for if baptism is tantamount to a new circumcision, and in the Law infants are to be circumcised on their eighth day, the same would seem to apply to baptism.

The earliest clear case where the connection between circumcision and baptism is applied to the age at which infants are to be baptized is in the already discussed correspondence between Cyprian and Fidus. Although they agreed on the baptism of infants, the point of the discussion was whether such baptism should wait until the eighth day after birth, following the model of circumcision, as Fidus suggested. A possible reason for the decision that Cyprian reported to Fidus may have been a concern that baptism should take place when the church was gathered for worship, so that the neophytes—infants or adults—could immediately partake of Communion. This desire would then lead to the insistence that baptism should normally take place on a Sunday.

A VARIETY OF PERSPECTIVES

A careful reading of the existing ancient texts shows that the manner in which baptism was understood largely depended on the understanding of sin and the human condition. In the western areas of the Roman Empire, the tendency soon developed to view sin as a debt that had to be paid, or a stain that had to be washed. Within that context, baptism came to be the manner in which that stain is removed, or the means by which the merits of Jesus are applied in payment for the debt of sin. This is the reason Tertullian suggests that baptism should be postponed until after the sins of youth are past. As he sees matters, since the stain can only be washed once, it is best to delay the washing until it is truly necessary; or, since there is only one baptism to pay for the debt of sins, it should be applied after the debt has become considerable. Since this view of sin became characteristic of the Western church, that section of the church was soon involved in a series of debates as to how to address sins committed after baptism. Eventually, this would lead to the evolution of the entire penitential system, which chronologically falls far beyond the limits of this study.

Another view, particularly prevalent in Alexandria, saw sin as an obfuscation, ignorance, or forgetfulness. We forget or do not know that we are children of God, and because of that forgetfulness we disobey. If this is the nature of sin, what takes place in the new birth is actually an illumination, an awakening to a new vision. Along these lines, at a later time baptism would often be viewed simply as a symbol of our true being, or as a reminder of it.

Finally, particularly in Syria and Asia Minor, sin was seen as a sort of oppression, a slavery to the powers of evil. Being human means being part of a humankind whose head is Adam, and therefore being forced to follow him along the path of evil. Being a sinner means being a slave of Satan. Within this perspective, the work of Jesus Christ is to defeat the powers of evil—Satan, death, and sin—and to create a new humanity whose head is Christ himself. He is the New Adam, and those who follow him are the new humankind. From this perspective, baptism and the new birth are the means by which one becomes part of the body of Christ, of this new humanity that thanks to him will overcome the powers of evil. Baptism then is best understood as a grafting whereby the branch is joined to the vine and is nourished by it. When baptism is seen as a grafting, sin committed after baptism certainly damages the grafted branch, but does not destroy it, nor does it require a new grafting.

While the first of these three main perspectives was deeply influenced by Roman emphasis on law and order, the second reflects the impact of Platonic philosophy on the thought of the church, and the third is rather a continuation of what we have already seen in part 1 of this study. For this reason, while the first perspective is particularly interested in the law of God and obeying it, and the second focuses attention on the immutable truths of God, the third stresses God's action in human history as seen in Israel's history and in the fulfillment of God's promises in the church. Although soon the first of these types of theology prevailed in matters having to do with morality and ethics, the second prevailed in discussions having to do with doctrines, while the third was mostly noticeable in worship—particularly in baptism and Communion.

This may be seen in Tertullian's treatise *On Baptism*. While Tertullian himself clearly reflects the first of these three types of theology, his understanding of baptism involves a typological interpretation characteristic of the third type. Not only Tertullian but most ancient writings on baptism interpret it by referring to points in the biblical narrative in which water plays an important role. The first is creation itself. Within that context, Tertullian affirms that the presence of the Spirit moving over the waters of creation was a type or announcement of the presence of the Spirit in the waters of baptism:

> Thus the nature of water, sanctified by the Holy One, thereby received the power of sanctifying. Let no one say: "Are we then baptized with

the very water which existed in the first beginning?" Not with that water, of course, except as the *genus* is the same, but the *species* are varied. But what is an attribute of the *genus* appears also in the *species*. Accordingly, there is no difference between those whom John baptized in the Jordan and those whom Peter baptized in the Tiber. . . . All water, therefore, by virtue of its pure origin, has the sacramental power of sanctification after the invocation of God. The Spirit immediately comes from the heavens and hovers over the water, sanctifying it and giving it the power to sanctify. (*On Baptism* 4; ANF 3:670–71)

Tertullian sees in the flood and in the dove that signals the end of punishment a shadow or announcement both of the death of the old humanity in baptismal waters and of the gift of the Holy Spirit with the anointing of the neophyte. Like other ancient writers, Tertullian stresses the biblical narrative of the exodus as a type or figure of baptism. The result of divine intervention at that time was freeing Israel from the Egyptian yoke—and this too is a type or figure of what would happen through the redeeming work of Christ and Christian baptism:

What figure more [than water] is completely fulfilled in the sacrament of baptism? The nations are set free from this world by means of water, that is, they are freed from the devil, their old tyrant. They leave him quite behind, overwhelmed in water. (*On Baptism* 9; ANF 3:673)

The passage continues with other passages having to do with water, such as the episode of the bitter waters of Mara that turned sweet by the presence of the tree—just as the bitterness of sin is destroyed by the tree of the cross—and the water from the rock in the desert.

COMMON POINTS

Having distinguished between three basic approaches to the question of the meaning of baptism, it is important to stress at least three common points in baptismal theory and practice during the period we are now studying. The first of these has to do with the relationship between baptism and the new birth, a matter on which the extant texts show unusual unanimity. All the ancient Christian writers on this matter see an unequivocal connection between baptism and the new birth. They do not go to the extreme of claiming that baptism causes such new birth—which is usually attributed to the Holy Spirit. But neither do they say that baptism is only an affirmation of faith by the person receiving it, symbolizing a new birth that has already taken place. On this intermediary position there seems to have been a certain consensus.

The second point to note is that the vast majority of ancient texts stress the corporate nature of baptism. Baptism does not have to do only with a person's conversion, but also and most of all with how that person becomes part of a single body and a single people. Both in the Gospel of John and in Romans this is expressed through the image of grafting. In John 15 it is the grafting of a branch on a vine. In Romans 11 it is the grafting of a wild olive branch on a good root. In the first case, the branches are grafted onto the True Vine, Christ. In the second, the branch is grafted onto the root of the people of God. In both cases, life depends on the connection with the root. The same imagery lies behind the frequent use of the word "member" in the New Testament and in ancient Christianity. Today that word has lost much of its meaning, for being a "member" of something simply means being part of a membership list. But in its original sense a "member" was precisely that: part of a body. Within that context, baptism does not simply connect the member with Christ, but also with that vast number of other members who jointly form the body of Christ and live thanks to their joint relationship with him. Quite likely, when a connection was made between baptism and circumcision this had to do precisely with this communal dimension of baptism. Circumcision was a sign of being part of the people of Israel. Likewise, baptism is a sign of being a part of this people of God that is the church.

Third, as Tertullian points out, the anointing that took place at the time of baptism was connected to Israel's ancient practice of anointing priests. Jesus is the Anointed and the High Priest, and those who are baptized in him are now anointed to be part of his priesthood. This is the fulfillment of the promise in Exodus 19:6: "'You shall be for me a priestly kingdom and a holy nation.'" There are abundant references to this in the New Testament, but probably the best known is 1 Peter 2:9: "You are a chosen race, a royal priesthood, a holy nation, God's own people." Note that this passage has abundant references to corporate realities: race, priesthood, nation, people. Likewise, in ancient Christian writings during the time of our study, we frequently hear that baptism is a becoming part of this people, race, or nation—and this people has a priestly function, as we shall see.

As we come to the end of this chapter, it may be helpful to think about baptism now not from the point of view of the pastors and theologians who have been quoted, but from the point of view of the person receiving it. From a very early date, those who had not been baptized were not allowed to partake in Communion, or even to be present at it. The ones now receiving baptism had been attending the service of the Word and preparing for baptism for a long time—according to Hippolytus, three years—in order eventually to be admitted into the rest of the service. Through baptism, they were now becoming members of the body of Christ and therefore able to participate with him in a holy meal. They had been told very little about the Supper, for baptism and Communion were both considered so sacred that they should not be discussed with the uninitiated. The ceremony itself of baptism had not been described or explained to them beforehand, and they knew little about the significance of each of the actions or rites that they would undergo. What was clear to them was that from this point on they would be members of the body of Christ and would share in his death and resurrection.

Now, after long years of waiting, after rigorous discipline, after the renunciations, after their baptism and their anointing, they would finally be allowed to join the rest of the congregation in parts of the worship service that until then had been forbidden to them.

Let us then close this chapter accompanying the neophytes who are processing to join the rest of the church, and see in our next chapter what would take place there.

10

Communion

At the end of chapter 9, we left the neophytes at the moment when they were being led from the place of their baptism to where the congregation was gathered. One must remember that for those neophytes this would be the first time that they would be present for Communion. Until then, following ancient instructions that appear already in the *Didache*, after the reading and the explanation of the Word all the catechumens were dismissed, as well as any other person who was not baptized.

THE PRAYER OF THE FAITHFUL

While describing what happens after baptism, Hippolytus adds a few words that would be of great significance for the neophytes: "Immediately they will join in prayer with all the people, since this had not been allowed earlier" (*Ap. Trad.* 22). This might surprise us, for these neophytes had been attending church and participating in much of its worship for quite some time, and had been preparing for baptism for years. It seems inconceivable that in all that time they would not have prayed with the rest of the church. Furthermore, Hippolytus himself has earlier instructed that before being dismissed from the service of the Word, the catechumens are to pray, separately from the rest of the congregation. They are also to be dismissed by their teachers, who bless each one by placing a hand on their head and praying over them (*Ap. Trad.* 18–19). What Justin had said more than half a century earlier is more explicit, and helps us understand what is happening:

> After we have thus washed the one who has been convinced of our teachings and agreed to them, we bring him or her to the assembly of those we call brothers and sisters. There we all offer prayers for ourselves, for the newly baptized, and for everyone in every place. We do this so that, having learned the truth, we can be counted worthy by our works. Also, we want to be found good citizens and keepers of the commandments, so that we may be saved with an everlasting salvation. (*1 Apol.* 65.1; ANF 1:185)

The same emphasis on the prayer of the faithful as a culminating point after baptism is found in Tertullian's discussion of baptism:

> You come up from that most sacred font of your new birth, and for the first time you spread your hands in the house of your mother. Together with your brothers and sisters you ask from the Father, you ask from the Lord, that his own specialties of grace and the distribution of gifts may be given to you. (*On Baptism* 20; ANF 3:679)

On the basis of these data from Justin, Tertullian, and several others, it is clear that what Hippolytus forbids before baptism is not that the catechumens and others pray. What is prohibited is for them to participate in a special prayer in which only baptized believers join—a prayer commonly called "the prayer of the faithful" or "the prayer of the people." This was a far-reaching prayer, which usually began by praying for the believers themselves and for the neophytes, and then turned to prayers for all others throughout the world. It was, in a word, a priestly prayer or a prayer of intercession—for the task of a priest is precisely to lead the people before the heavenly throne. Tertullian shows the nature and scope of such prayers:

> We are a body knit together by a common religious profession, by the unity of discipline, and by the bond of a common hope. We meet as an assembly, a congregation that offers up prayer to God as a united force. We may wrestle with God in our supplications. This is a violence in which God delights. We also pray for the emperors, for their ministers, and for all in authority. We pray for the welfare of the world, that there will be peace, and for the delay of the final consummation. (*Apol.* 39; ANF 3:46)

(Today we may be surprised that those Christians prayed "for the delay of the final consummation." Their purpose was to have more time to reach more people with the gospel before the day of judgment.)

Elsewhere, Tertullian explains that part of the reason why Christians pray for the empire and its leaders is that these, even when they persecute Christians, have an important role: "When there is a disturbance in the Empire, we will also feel the commotion that affects others. Even though we are not disorderly, we will be in places affected by calamity" (*Apol.* 31; ANF 3:42).

In another passage (*To Scapula* 4), Tertullian witnesses to the power of these priestly prayers. According to him, when on an expedition into Germanic lands, Emperor Marcus Aurelius and his troops were sorely tried by extreme drought, Christians among the imperial troops prayed, and God sent rain.

We have no detailed descriptions of the form and content of these prayers during the time we are now studying. The *Apostolic Constitutions*, a document from the fourth century seemingly written in Syria, may well reflect what was already being done in the third century. There we read that after all who are not baptized, and others who are doing penance for their sins, are dismissed, the leader should say, "All we of the faithful, let us bend our knee; let us all entreat God through Jesus Christ; let us earnestly beseech God through His Christ." This is followed by a list of petitions, culminating with a long "prayer for the faithful" (*Apostolic Constitutions* 8.12; ANF 7:485–86). Somewhat earlier, Tertullian had spoken of the attitude that should prevail in such prayers:

> Our prayers are more commendable to God when we pray with modesty and humility. We do not raise our hands too loftily, but moderately and becomingly. Even our face is not lifted too boldly. For the publican who prayed with humility and dejection not only in his words but also in his countenance went his way more justified than the shameless Pharisee. Our voices also should be subdued. If we were to be heard because of the noise we created, then what large windpipes we would need! But God listens not to the voice but to the heart, just as God is its inspector. (*On Prayer* 17; ANF 3:686)

At this point, recall that the neophytes were anointed at the time of their baptism, and the reason was that the priests of Israel were anointed. As a result, from that point on, every baptized believer had a priestly function and authority. This is what we find repeatedly in the New Testament in phrases such "kings and priests" or "royal priesthood." However, this priesthood is not a private authority or the responsibility of individual neophytes. This person has been anointed in the name of the Anointed. The only true priest is Jesus Christ. Those now baptized are also anointed in his name; and just as they now partake of his anointing, they partake of his priesthood. In a word, this body of Christ that is the church fulfills the promise: "'You shall be for me a priestly kingdom and a holy nation'" (Exod. 19:6). It was thus that the ancient church understood the universal priesthood of believers—not simply or primarily that each person could approach God directly, but rather the common priesthood of all the people through which it is to take all creation before the throne of the Most High. The priesthood of believers is above all a common priesthood, and the petitions of individual believers, according to their particular needs and interests, are placed under that common priesthood.

It may be difficult for us today to understand the importance of the "prayer of the faithful" for the faithful themselves. For those believers, our ancestors in the faith, a central element of Christian life was the deep privilege and mission of being part of the priestly people of God, of the body of the High Priest, Jesus Christ. Early in the period we are studying, Ignatius of Antioch wrote to the church in Ephesus:

> Let no one be self-deceived. If they are not at the altar, they are deprived of the bread of God. If the prayer of one or two possesses such power, how much more does that of the bishop and the whole Church! Those, therefore, who do not assemble with the Church, show a pride by which they condemn themselves. (*Ep. to the Ephesians* 5.5; ANF 1:51)

As a sign indicating the importance of the prayer for the faithful and its connection with Communion, an action of Bishop Gregory of Neocaesarea—better known as Gregory the Wonderworker—is significant. A Germanic invasion had wrought destruction to the area. After the invaders had left, Gregory wrote a *Canonical Epistle* establishing the actions to be taken regarding people who had profited from the invasion. Some people had followed the invaders as they were leaving the land and taken possession of the booty they abandoned along the way. Among these people, those who had on their own declared what they had done and had made restoration to the proper owners would be restored to "the privilege of prayer"—that is, although they still would not be allowed to partake of Communion, their attitude of repentance would be acknowledged by allowing them to be part of the prayer of the faithful. Those who took advantage of the reigning chaos to steal from their neighbors are to be excluded not only from Communion but also from the prayer of the faithful—that is, they are suspended from their participation in the priesthood of the people of God—until such a time as they have showed that they truly repent and have restored what they stole (*Canonical Epistle*, 5).

THE KISS OF PEACE

It was common in antiquity to kiss one another as a sign of respect or love. Our very word "adoration" comes from the Latin *adoratio*, which originally meant showing respect to the gods by throwing them a kiss. The Gospels and other ancient documents include references to a kiss as a sign of friendship, welcome, reconciliation, and respect—as well as the traitorous kiss of Judas. Later in the New Testament we find references to a kiss as a sign of love, fellowship, and reconciliation among believers. In Romans 16:16, Paul says, "Greet one another with a holy kiss." The same phrase appears, almost exactly with the same words, in 1 Corinthians 16:20; 2 Corinthians 13:12; 1 Thessalonians 5:26; and 1 Peter 5:14. Such repetition, not only in the Pauline corpus, but also in 1 Peter, would seem to indicate that during the first century the kiss of peace was one of the usual rites in Christian gatherings. In the second century, Justin says, "Having ended the prayers, we salute one another with a kiss" (*1 Apol.* 65.2; ANF 1:185). In the same century, slightly later, Tertullian writes that some who are fasting and therefore do not plan to partake in Communion "withhold the kiss of peace, which is the seal of prayer, after prayer is made with the brothers and sisters." He does not approve of this practice, for, "What prayer is complete if divorced from the holy kiss?" (*On Prayer* 18; ANF 3:686). Like Justin before him and Hippolytus later, Tertullian expected the kiss of peace to be shared immediately after the prayer of the faithful—except on Good Friday, when all would be fasting and therefore not sharing the kiss of peace would not be a sign of division, but rather of solidarity. The situation to which Tertullian refers in the texts quoted is somewhat different, for these are people who out of their own individual volition have decided to fast and therefore leave the meeting before the kiss of peace, for the kiss leads to Communion, which normally is to be understood as a festive occasion ending all fasts.

Obviously, the practice of sharing the kiss of peace lent itself to abuse. Roughly about the same time when Tertullian was emphasizing the importance of the kiss of peace, Clement of Alexandria was writing,

> Love is not proved by a kiss, but by kindly feeling. There are those who do nothing but make the church resound with a kiss, and yet they do not have love itself in them. For this very reason—the shameless use of a kiss, which ought to be mystic—causes foul suspicions and evil reports. The apostle calls the kiss holy. . . .
>
> But there is another unholy kiss, full of poison, counterfeiting holiness. Do you not know that spiders, merely by touching with their mouths, afflict victims with pain? And often kisses inject the poison of licentiousness. It is then very clear to us that a kiss is not love. For the love meant is the love of God. "And this is the love of God," says John, "that we keep God's commandments." We are not commanded to stroke each other on the mouth. (*Instructor* 3.11; ANF 2:291)

For these reasons, the kiss of peace was subjected to increasingly restrictive rules. The *Apostolic Constitutions* determine exactly where each person is to be, and insist that people kissing one another should be of the same gender:

"Then let the men give the men, and the women give the women, the Lord's kiss. But let no one do it with deceit, as Judas betrayed the Lord with a kiss" (*Apostolic Constitutions* 2.57; ANF 7:476). Possibly for the same reasons, the kiss of peace began disappearing, so that eventually it was limited to the clergy and, in monastic houses, to the residents.

THE OFFERTORY AND COMMUNION ITSELF

Both Justin in the second century and Hippolytus in the third affirmed that after the kiss of peace, bread and wine were presented to the person presiding in Communion. (Although today some churches call the collection of offerings the "offertory," in ancient times what was offered in the offertory was primarily the bread and wine for Communion.) Justin states it thus:

> Then bread and a cup of wine mixed with water are brought to the president of the brothers and sisters. He takes them and gives praise and glory to the Father of the universe, through the name of the Son and of the Holy Spirit. He offers thanks at considerable length for our being counted worthy to receive these things from God's hands. (*1 Apol.* 65; ANF 1:185)

And Hippolytus says,

> And then the offering is immediately brought by the deacons to the bishop, and by thanksgiving he shall make the bread into an image of the body of Christ, and the cup of wine mixed with water according to the likeness of the blood, which is shed for all who believe in him. (*Ap. Trad.* 23)

In another passage, Hippolytus adds a discussion of what may be included in the offertory, besides bread and wine. There he is describing the ordination of a bishop, to whom bread and wine are brought for him to bless. But he may also be presented with other offerings that should also be blessed, although with different words than those said over the bread and wine, apparently in order to show the singular significance of bread and wine in Communion. Although Hippolytus does not say that these are the only offerings that may be presented, he includes specific prayers over oil, cheese, and olives, which were apparently the most frequent items. After blessing each offering, the bishop was to say, "Glory be to thee, with the Holy Spirit in the holy church, both now and always and world without end. Amen" (*Ap. Trad.* 6).

Hippolytus says more about possible offerings, distinguishing between some that are acceptable and some that are not. Fruits such as grapes, figs, pomegranates, olives, pears, apples, berries, and others are acceptable. But for some reason that Hippolytus does not explain, melons, cucumbers, and other similar vegetables and fruits are not acceptable; the same is true of onions, garlic, or anything else that may have a strong smell. As to flowers, only roses and lilies are accepted. In the same passage Hippolytus includes a prayer of thanksgiving for the first fruits of the harvest (*Ap. Trad.* 28).

Back to Communion itself and to what Hippolytus says about it immediately after baptism, here he describes a rite that would take place only when the person was taking Communion for the first time. This included two extra cups, one with milk mixed with honey, and the other with water. Hippolytus explains their use as follows:

> And milk and honey mixed together for the fulfillment of the promise to the fathers, which spoke of a land flowing with milk and honey; namely, Christ's flesh which he gave, by which they who believe are nourished like babes, he making sweet the bitter things of the heart by the gentleness of his word. And the water into an offering in a token of the laver, in order that the inner part of man, which is a living soul, may receive the same as the body. (*Ap. Trad.* 23)

Other ancient texts also refer to a chalice of milk and honey given to the neophytes on their first Communion. Tertullian says that "when we are taken up (as newborn children), we taste first of all a mixture of milk and honey" (*On the Crown* 3; ANF 3:94). Elsewhere, almost in passing, he mentions the mixture of milk and honey in a list of various physical means by which God blesses people. In an ironic passage, Tertullian declares that even the Marcionites who despise physical things as the work of a lesser god, have not disdained to use

> the water which the Creator made which they use to wash their people, or the oil with which they anoint them, or the mixture of milk and honey they give to nourish them as children, or the bread by which he represents his own proper body. (*Ag. Marcion* 1.14; ANF 3:281)

The mixture of milk mixed with honey has clear typological significance, for just as upon crossing the Jordan the children of Israel entered into a land that flowed with milk and honey, now the neophytes have entered the land of promise. For this reason, just as baptism could only be received once, the chalice of milk and honey was only taken once, on that first occasion when the neophyte partook of Communion.

Justin provides us with the most ancient witness we have to the manner in which Communion was celebrated after the kiss of peace. He continues the narrative quoted above:

Then bread and a cup of wine mixed with water are brought to the president of the brothers and sisters. He takes them and gives praise and glory to the Father of the universe, through the name of the Son and of the Holy Spirit. He offers thanks at considerable length for our being counted worthy to receive these things from God's hands, and all the people give their assent by saying "Amen." . . . When the president has given thanks, and all the people have shown their agreement, those whom we call deacons give to all of us who are present the opportunity to partake of the bread over which the thanksgiving was said, and the wine mixed with water. They take a portion to those who are absent. (*1 Apol.* 65; ANF 1:185)

On the basis of this text and many others, it is clear that what people drank in Communion was wine mixed with water. On or about the year 255, Cyprian wrote a letter to his colleague Caecilius arguing this point:

Christ bore us all in that he also carried our sins. The water we understand to be the people, but the wine shows us the blood of Christ. When the water is mingled with the wine in the cup the people are made one with Christ, and the assembly of believers is associated and joined to the One in whom they believe. This union of water and wine is so mingled in the Lord's cup that the mixture cannot be separated any more. Nothing can separate the Church—that is, the people established in the Church, remaining faithful and firm in what they have believed—from Christ. Their undivided love will therefore keep them abiding in Christ and clinging to him. (*Ep.*, 62.13; ANF 5:362)

Apparently some preferred to take Communion in the morning with water without any wine. Cyprian says that the reason was that that they feared that when nonbelievers smelled the wine on their breath early in the morning, they would know that they were Christians, and could accuse them as such. Against such objections, Cyprian insists that Communion must be celebrated with a chalice of wine mixed with water, for "how can we shed our blood for Christ if we are ashamed to drink the blood of Christ?" (*Ep.* 62.15; ANF 5:362–63).

What Justin calls the "long prayer" over the bread and the wine is more technically known as the "anaphora." The most ancient anaphora that we have is the text from the *Didache* quoted in chapter 6. Among later anaphoras, the most complete as well as the most ancient is the one found in the *Apostolic Tradition* of Hippolytus. Note that Hippolytus says clearly that this prayer is only a sample, and the words of the prayer itself depend on the circumstances and the ability of the one offering the prayer. The rite begins with a dialogue between the leader and the congregation, then leading to the anaphora:

The Lord be with you.
And with thy spirit.
Lift up your hearts.
We lift them up unto the Lord.
Let us give thanks to the Lord.
It is meet and right.

We give thee thanks, O God, through thy beloved Servant Jesus Christ, whom at the end of time thou didst send to us a Saviour and Redeemer and the Messenger of thy counsel. Who is thy Word, inseparable from thee; through whom thou didst make all things and in whom thou art well pleased. Whom thou didst send from heaven into the womb of the Virgin, and who, dwelling within her, was made flesh, and was manifested as thy Son, being born of the Holy Spirit and the Virgin. Who, fulfilling thy will, and winning for himself a holy people, spread out his hands when he came to suffer, that by his death he might set free them who believed on thee. Who, when he was betrayed to his willing death, that he might bring to nought death, and break the bonds of the devil, and tread hell under foot, and give light to the righteous, and set up a boundary post, and manifest his resurrection, taking bread and giving thanks to thee said: Take, eat: this is my body, which is broken for you. And likewise also the cup, saying: This is my blood, which is shed for you. As often as ye perform this, perform my memorial.

Having in memory, therefore, his death and resurrection, we offer to thee the bread and the cup, yielding thee thanks, because thou has counted us worthy to stand before thee and to minister to thee.

And we pray thee that thou wouldest send thy Holy Spirit upon the offerings of thy holy church; that thou, gathering them into one, wouldest grant to all thy saints who partake to be filled with the Holy Spirit, that their faith may be confirmed in truth, that we may praise and glorify thee. Through thy Servant Jesus Christ, though whom be to thee glory and honour, with the Holy Spirit in the holy church, both now and always and world without end. Amen. (*Ap. Trad.* 4)

As each participant takes the bread, they are to be told, "The heavenly bread in Christ Jesus." To this the person receiving the bread responds, "Amen." When the cup is offered, each person is to take three sips, in the name of the Father, the Son, and the Holy Spirit (*Ap. Trad.* 23).

Hippolytus says nothing about how the service is to end, but about a century earlier Tertullian did say, "As the feast commenced with prayer, so with prayer it closes" (*Apology* 39; ANF 3:47). He also adds that after Communion all are to go out to do good works, a point to which we return in chapter 11.

After taking Communion that first time, the neophytes would continue receiving instruction and following a number of observances for a week—although most of what we know about this comes from writings of the fourth century, and not from the period we are now studying. Tertullian adds that after baptism the neophyte is to abstain from the daily bath for a week. Several authors speak of neophytes as newly born children who still need special care. In one of the versions of the *Apostolic Tradition* of Hippolytus, mention is made also of secret knowledge that the neophytes are to receive after their baptism; but there is no indication as to what those secrets might have been nor for how long the newly born were expected to continue under special care. All that we are offered is a rather cryptic quotation from the book of Revelation: "I will give a white stone, and on the white stone is written a new name that no one knows except the one who receives it" (*Ap. Trad.* 23). Some interpreters suggest that this may be the Lord's Prayer, which Hippolytus does not quote or discuss. In the next chapter we return to these neophytes or "babes" in the faith who must still continue in a special week of instruction.

SOME THEOLOGICAL ISSUES

As we come to the manner in which Communion was understood, the first point to be made is that, since there was in the surrounding culture a common tendency to think that material reality was either evil or not important, Christians strongly emphasized the physicality of the elements in Communion as a sign of the importance of physical reality—particularly the body. Irenaeus says it as follows:

> Those who despise the entire plan of God and reject the salvation of the flesh are completely wrong. They treat with contempt the regeneration of the body, maintaining that it is not capable of incorruption. But if the body does not gain salvation, then neither did the Lord redeem us with his blood, nor is the cup of the Eucharist the Communion in his blood, nor the bread which we break the Communion in his body. For blood can only come from veins and flesh, and whatever else makes up the substance of a human being. It is of that substance that the Word of God was actually made. By his own blood he redeemed us, as also his apostle declares, "In whom we have redemption through his blood, even the remission of sins." And as we are his members, we are also nourished by means of the creation. He himself grants us the creation, for he causes his sun to rise, and sends rain when he wills. He has acknowledged the cup, which is a part of creation, as his own blood. From it he bedews our blood. The bread which is also a part of creation, he has established as his own body, from which he gives growth to our bodies. (*Against Heresies* 5.2; ANF 1:528)

As we come to the end of this chapter, it is clear that for those ancient Christians Communion was not a mere memorial of Jesus Christ, but was actually a meeting with the risen Lord, a celebration of resurrection, and clearly a joyful occasion that not only joined each believer to the Lord, but also joined all of them with bonds that were often stronger than those of physical kindred. Those believers who joined in this meal were now part of a new family and—even more surprisingly—of a family that involved vast numbers of people whom they had never met, but with whom they were joined by a single Lord through participating in a single meal, the Lord's Supper or Eucharist.

This leads to the question of "the body of Christ." Over the centuries there has been much discussion on and many divisions have occurred because of the relationship between the body of Christ and Communion. The phrase itself "the body of Christ" has three important but distinct meanings. In the first place, it is the physical body of Jesus of Nazareth, the body that lived, died, arose, and now, transformed as we also shall be transformed (1 Cor. 15), is in the presence of the Father. Second, in some cases the phrase "the body of Christ" refers to the bread over which thanks have been given in Communion. (As the Greek word *eucharistía* means giving thanks, Communion is often called "Eucharist." In some ancient Christian writers we find what would be the equivalent of "eucharistized" bread.) It is in the second sense that the phrase "body of Christ" has been a matter of disagreements and schisms among Christians over the centuries. However, it is interesting and significant to note that neither in the New Testament nor in the most ancient Christian writers do we find any attempts to define clearly in what sense the bread of Communion is "the body of Christ." When we read those ancient writings trying to discover what that phrase meant—specifically, asking whether the bread is the body of Christ, or rather represents it—we find frequent affirmations of the extreme importance of Communion; but as to how this was to be understood, early statements are either ambiguous or seem to contradict one another. The importance of Communion for the early church is clear even in the most cursory reading of the epistles of Ignatius, who declares that the bread of Communion "is the medicine of immortality, and the antidote to keep us from dying. It causes us to live forever in Jesus Christ" (*Ep. to the Ephesians* 20; ANF 1:58). He even declares that one must confess "the Eucharist to be the flesh of our Saviour Jesus Christ" (*Ep. to the Smyrneans* 7.1; ANF 1:89). On the other hand, Hippolytus says that what happens when the bread and the cup are blessed is that they become "an image of the body and blood of Christ" (*Ap. Trad.* 23). Clement of Alexandria goes further by declaring, "The flesh figuratively represents to us the Holy Spirit, for the flesh was created by him. The blood points us to the Word, for as rich blood the Word has been infused into life. The union of both is the Lord, the food of babes" (*The Instructor* 1.7; ANF 2:220). Numerous quotations could be gathered; the important point is that these various authors were not asking how Christ is present in Communion, or in bread and wine. Among their many expressions, they never claim that the bread ceases to be bread in order to become flesh, even though they actually speak of the bread as "the body of Christ."

Third, the phrase "the body of Christ" often refers to the church. There is no doubt that early Christians were convinced that they were part of the body of Christ in this third sense, and also that they could not be members of that body without having received also the body of Christ in the second sense—that is, without participating in Communion.

In brief, the three meanings of the phrase "the body of Christ" are inseparable, and their mutual relationship may be understood in various ways. Apparently those early Christians were not interested in defining the manner in which Christ was present in Communion, but were certainly convinced that he was there.

If baptism is seen as a grafting whereby the branches are joined to the True Vine, Communion becomes like the sap that nourishes the branch. The notion of being a Christian by oneself, with no commitment to a community of believers, early Christians would have considered absurd.

Finally are two other points that merit serious consideration. The first is the Trinitarian nature of Communion itself, and of the prayers raised in it. In general those prayers address the Father, thanking him for the gift of the Son, and end with a petition asking the Holy Spirit to make it possible for this bread and wine to be a bond joining all to Christ as well as to one another.

A second point that must not be forgotten as a constant characteristic of worship in the early church is the vision of the present earthly worship as an imitation or shadow of the heavenly worship in which believers will eventually participate. Thus, Tertullian declares that when we say, "Hallowed be thy name," we must remember that we are speaking of the One to whom the heavenly host sings, "Holy, holy, holy." And then he adds,

> We also are candidates for angelhood, if we succeed in deserving it. Therefore we begin even while we are still on earth to learn by heart that song that hereafter will be raised to God. We are learning the function of future glory. (*On Prayer* 3; ANF 3:682)

11

Times, Places, and Practices

Worship is not limited to what is said and done during the time when the church is gathered. It also has to do with the times and the places in which the church worships, and a necessary part of worship is also the manner in which it is reflected in the daily life of worshipers, both in its ethical dimensions and in its disciplines of devotion. Therefore we look first at the calendar that worship followed in the church, then move to the places where the church gathered to worship, and finally to some brief comments regarding women's participation in worship and music, and the manner in which all of this was also reflected in the daily life of believers.

THE TIMES: SUNDAY

In part 1, we saw that from its very beginning the church gathered to break bread on the first day of the week, because it was the day of the resurrection of its Lord. There were also two other reasons for gathering on that first day of the week—Sunday—that appear repeatedly in the period we are now studying, and therefore may well have existed during the first century, even though we have no explicit documents to prove it.

The first of these two other reasons for gathering on the first day of the week was that, in the story in Genesis, the first day of the week was the beginning of creation. This is parallel to what happened with the resurrection of Jesus, which began the new creation. Justin expresses it as follows:

> We all hold our common assembly on Sunday. It is on this first day that God made the world by changing darkness and matter. It was

> on this same day that Jesus Christ our Savior rose from the dead. He
> was crucified on the day before that of Saturn [Saturday], and on the
> day after that of Saturn, which is the day of the Sun, he appeared to
> his apostles and disciples. He taught them these things, which we also
> have submitted to you for your consideration. (*1 Apol.* 67; ANF 1:186)

(Since in these lines Justin is addressing pagan readers, he names the days of
the week as his audience would. This is why he refers to the first day of the
week as "Sunday," or literally, "the day of the sun." For most Romans, the
most important day of the week was the day of Saturn. Had Justin said that
Christians used to gather on the first day of the week, his readers would have
been confused. For the same reason, rather than referring to the last day of
the week as "the seventh day," he calls it "the day of Saturn." In his *Dialogue
with Trypho*, who was a Jew, Justin calls these days the "first" and the "seventh" days of the week.)

The other reason the first day of the week had particular significance was
that, just as this day marks the beginning of a new week, it also marks the
beginning of eternity. Christians sometimes referred to eternity as the "eighth
day," as seen in the following lines from the *Epistle of Barnabas*:

> The Lord speaks: Your present Sabbaths are not acceptable to me.
> But what I have made is this, giving rest to all things: I shall make an
> eighth day, a new beginning of another world. Therefore we keep the
> eighth day joyfully. It is also the day on which Jesus rose again from
> the dead. After he had shown himself, he ascended to the heavens.
> (*Ep. of Barnabas* 15; ANF 1:147)

These two reasons making the day of the resurrection more significant
added even greater joy and a cosmic dimension to the celebration of Jesus'
resurrection. This was the day when the church celebrated God's gift as creator, the victory of Jesus over death, and the beginning of the experience of
eternity.

THE TIMES: EASTER

As we saw in chapter 4, early Christians developed a weekly calendar that centered on the first day of the week, the day of the Lord's resurrection. During
the first decades, when most Christians were Jewish in origin, it would have
been common for them to keep the Sabbath on the seventh day and then,
as the day ended with sunset, to gather again in order to break bread and
celebrate the resurrection of Jesus, which took place on the first day of the
week—that is, after sunset of the seventh day. But now, as Judeo-Christianity

was being left behind and most believers were originally Gentiles, it would be more difficult to gather after the sunset of the Sabbath. Making adjustments over generations, the people of Israel had found occupations and conditions allowing them to keep the Sabbath. For them, as well as for some of the God-fearers who came to accept Christianity, it would not be difficult to gather immediately after the end of the day of rest with its sunset. But as that first period passed, such a time to gather would be much more difficult for Gentile Christians. For society at large the seventh day of the week was a day of work like any other. A slave could not very well tell his master that tonight he would not work, because he had to gather with the church. An employee whose work required his presence in the evening could not excuse himself for religious reasons. Therefore, for practical reasons, the church began gathering, no longer after the sunset of the seventh day, but rather very early before sunrise on the first day.

Another factor contributed to this change. While Jews counted the end of a day and the beginning of the next from sunset, for Romans and most others the day was counted from midnight to midnight, as we do today. Therefore, a meeting after sunset on the seventh day of the week, which a Jew would clearly understand to be the first day, from the point of view of a Gentile Christian would no longer seem to be a meeting on the first day, but rather in the evening of the seventh.

For these two reasons, during the first decades of the period we are now studying, the time of meeting was slowly transferred, so that more and more Christians, rather than gathering after the sunset of the seventh day, would gather before dawn on the first.

During that time the church continued keeping the weekly calendar that we saw in chapter 4. The pivotal point of that calendar was the first day of the week, the "Lord's Day." This was a day of joy that above all celebrated the resurrection of Jesus Christ, but also the beginning of the very first creation and its culmination in the "eighth day." The sixth day, which today we call "Friday," was a day of fasting and penance, commemorating the crucifixion. Also the fourth day, "Wednesday," was a day of fasting, apparently because it was the day in which Judas sold Jesus for thirty pieces of silver.

It is not surprising that, even though each Sunday was a day for celebrating Jesus' resurrection, there was a special Sunday every year in which they celebrated that resurrection in a particular way. There was a connection between that particular Sunday and the Jewish Passover for chronological and typological reasons. As to chronology, in the Gospels there is a connection between Passover and the passion and resurrection of Jesus—although as to their exact relationship, the Synoptic Gospels differ from the Gospel of John. As to typology, the liberation of Israel through the blood of the lamb and that first Passover when the Israelites left Egypt was seen as an announcement, figure, or type of the liberation of believers from sin and death through the blood of the Lamb of God.

Two other developments during that period are of interest to us here. The first of these is that, at least in some circles, the connection began to be forgotten between the Christian paschal celebration and its Jewish roots in the Passover. In his sermon *On Pascha*, Melito of Sardis asks himself the reason for the name of "Pascha" for this feast; then, rather than going to its etymological roots in Hebrew, offers a false etymology based on the Greek word for "passion." (This does not mean, however, that Melito left aside the Hebrew roots of the celebration itself, for his entire sermon is a typological interpretation of the history of Israel as a type or announcement of what happened in Jesus.)

Origen, in a homily on the same subject, says that, although the common opinion is that "Pascha" is so named because of the passion of Jesus, in fact it derives from its Hebrew name and means "to pass over," as the avenging angel passed over the children of Israel on that first Passover. Later Eusebius of Caesarea, who was a student and follower of Origen's views, joined that correct etymology with a typological understanding of the connection between the Hebrew Passover and Christian life:

> At this point it may be useful to return to the subject of Passover and explain that in the beginning this was given to the Hebrews as a figure. In the first Passover, they took a sheep or lamb from their flocks and sacrificed it. Then they anointed the doors of their homes with blood so that the avenging angel would not enter them. After eating the meat of the lamb and having girded their loins, they took unleavened bread and bitter herbs with them. They went from one place to another, from Egypt to the desert. . . . For this reason of the angel bypassing them and their leaving Egypt this feast receives the name of Pascha. (*On the Paschal Solemnity* 1; PG 24:693)

Now, beginning in the second century, a series of controversies began on the exact date on which Christians should celebrate the resurrection of Jesus. It is impossible to know the method—or methods—that the early church followed in its first years to establish the annual celebration of Easter, although there is every indication that in general the Hebrew calendar was followed. At the beginning of the period we are studying, there were already two main practices regarding the date for the celebration of Christian Pascha or Easter. In Asia Minor and the surrounding area—which today is mostly part of Turkey—it was customary to follow the Hebrew calendar so that the day of resurrection was celebrated on the fourteenth day of the Hebrew month of Nisan. In other areas it was customary to celebrate the resurrection of Jesus always on a Sunday—apparently normally the Sunday after the fourteenth of Nisan.

What Eusebius of Caesarea tells us about the origins of this controversy is somewhat confusing. On the one hand, he quotes a lost book by Melito, apparently written around the year 169, in which he affirms that the paschal feast is to be celebrated on the fourteenth of Nisan. There is also a fragment from a writing of Apollinaris, bishop of Hierapolis, and therefore a neighbor of Melito. In that fragment the notion is rejected that Jesus ate with his disciples on the fourteenth of Nisan and therefore died on the fifteenth, normally known as the "great day of the unleavened bread." According to Apollinaris, "The 14th [of Nisan] is a true Pascha of the Lord, the great sacrifice that put the Son of God in the place of the Paschal Lamb" (PG 92:80). Therefore, on the basis of what Eusebius says and of the fragment from Apollinaris, it would seem that by the year 160 the controversy was already brewing. Eusebius himself, referring to the time when Victor was bishop of Rome—and therefore around the year 190 or slightly later—says,

> An important question arose at that time. The parishes in all of Asia came from an older tradition. They held that the fourteenth day of the moon, the day on which Jews were commanded to sacrifice the lamb, should be observed as the feast of the Savior's Passover. They therefore needed to end their fast on that day, whatever day of the week it happened to be. But that was not the custom of the churches in the rest of the world. They held to an apostolic tradition that had been followed up to the present time, that the fast should end on no other day but that of the resurrection of our Savior. (*Church History* 5.23.1; NPNF1 1:241)

This passage from Eusebius shows why the controversy was important. It was not just a matter of when such a significant event should be celebrated, but also of difficulties and confusion regarding worship itself. The Quartodeciman ("fourteenth-ist") party insisted that the resurrection of the Lord should be celebrated on the fourteenth of Nisan, no matter what day of the week this was. Their opponents affirmed that the resurrection of the Lord should always be celebrated on the first day of the week. Since it was customary to fast on the day of crucifixion, and to continue fasting until the day of resurrection, and it was common for Christians to travel from one city to another, this meant that when some were fasting in penance others in the same church would be celebrating. Since Rome was the place where people most frequently gathered from different areas, it is not surprising that it was the bishop of Rome who was most concerned over Quartodeciman practices. When Polycarp of Smyrna visited Rome, Bishop Anicetus tried to convince him to follow the Roman custom. However, when Polycarp resisted, Anicetus did not insist. In brief, what the apparently contradictory statements of Eusebius and others tell us is that these different practices had very ancient roots, and that what brought the difference to the surface was the growing contact between Christians who were used to celebrating the resurrection of Jesus always on Sunday, and those others who had been taught that they should celebrate it on the fourteenth of Nisan.

According to Eusebius, a long series of regional synods in Palestine, Rome, Pontus, and Gaul confirmed the practice of always celebrating the resurrection on a Sunday, and not necessarily on the fourteenth of Nisan. However, when Victor, then bishop of Rome, let them know of these decisions, the bishops of Asia, under the leadership of Polycrates, gathered in a synod that insisted on their ancient tradition. Victor answered with a series of letters threatening breaking communion with all believers in Asia. Such extreme measures did not gain great support in either the East or the West. Among others resisting Victor's threats, one was Irenaeus, bishop of Lyons in Gaul, who however hailed from Smyrna and therefore was an heir of the tradition of Asia Minor. Apparently many of his flock also came from the same background. Therefore, he and his church, placed as they were in the middle of other churches that did not accept their Quartodeciman tradition, were very concerned with the situation.

For this reason Irenaeus wrote a letter to Victor that Eusebius quotes extensively. It was a conciliatory letter, whose *irenic* spirit led Eusebius to comment that in it *Irenaeus* showed that he was well named. In this letter Irenaeus insisted on the possibility of observing different traditions without breaking communion or disturbing harmony. He pleads,

> The controversy is not only about the day of the fast but also about how it should be practiced. Some think they should fast one day, others two, and others even more. Also, some believe the day should be forty hours, day and night.
>
> This variety of observances is not new. It began long ago with our ancestors. It is quite likely that they were not totally accurate in the way they carried out the fast and they therefore developed a custom for their posterity from their own simplicity and peculiarity. Yet all these variations lived in peace. We also live in peace with one another; and the disagreements about the fast confirms the agreement in faith.
> . . .
> No one was ever cast out of the church because of the way they carried out the fast. The presbyters before you who did not observe it sent the eucharist to those of other parishes that did. (*Church History* 5.24.12–13,15; NPNF1 1:243)

Although Eusebius does not tell us what happened next, it seems probable that Victor decided not to break communion with believers in Asia. In any case, most of the churches in Asia slowly adopted the custom of the rest of the church.

This still did not solve the issue of when the resurrection of Jesus was to be celebrated. Even though the Quartodecimans had insisted on celebrating it on the fourteenth day of Nisan, and others thought that it should always be celebrated on a Sunday, both parties took as a starting point the date of Passover in the Jewish calendar. However, the Jewish calendar, based on the lunar year, did not coincide with a solar calendar, and therefore Jewish authorities had to determine each year when the month of Nisan began. Now, as tensions between Christians and Jews increased, many Christians did not think it proper to leave to Jewish authorities the task of deciding the most important date in the Christian calendar. Since the lunar year is significantly shorter than the solar year, it was necessary to make adjustments frequently. Furthermore, it was highly desirable to have all Christians celebrate the day of resurrection on the same day, and to know the date with sufficient time to prepare for the celebration itself. The mathematical problem was not simple, and many attempts were made at solving it. The first such attempt that is known was made by Hippolytus—whom we have met before as the author of the *Apostolic Tradition*. The table that Hippolytus prepared was engraved on a statue in his honor that was discovered in Rome in the mid-sixteenth century. There the date of Easter is calculated for each year from 222 to 334. But an inexactitude in the calculation of the duration of a year resulted in the date proposed by Hippolytus moving forward three days every sixteen years. Although at the beginning this was not noticeable, eventually it became clear that Hippolytus's calculation was in error.

None of the many other computations of the date for Easter prevailed, partly because the astronomical observations on which they were based were inexact. The most glaring example of this inexactitude was that the East and the West did not agree on the date of the spring equinox. The resulting disagreement would therefore continue for a long time, but this would lead us far beyond the limits of our study.

THE TIMES: TIMES SURROUNDING EASTER

Much of the Christian calendar as we now know it developed around the celebration of the resurrection of Jesus. From the very beginning, the church also observed the feast of Pentecost, when, according to Acts 2, the Holy Spirit was poured on the disciples. This feast was part of the Jewish calendar, taking place fifty days after Passover—which is the etymological origin of the name "Pentecost." Christians followed the same pattern, although now determining the date for Pentecost no longer following the Hebrew calendar, but simply placing it fifty days after Easter. Next to Easter itself, for quite some time Pentecost was the most important date in the Christian calendar. We see this in that catechumens who were ready to be baptized on Easter, but for some reason had to postpone their baptism, were baptized on Pentecost. The fifty days between Easter and Pentecost were then a time of celebration of the victory of Christ and of the adoption of believers as children of God by virtue of Jesus' resurrection and the outpouring of the Spirit. One other sign of the importance of this time is that during those days Christians were not supposed to kneel for prayer, but rather to stand, for now they were not approaching God as petitioners before a king, but rather as the adopted children of the king. On this point, Tertullian says, "We believe it is unlawful to fast or kneel on the Lord's Day. We also claim the same privilege from Easter to Pentecost" (*On the Crown* 3; ANF 3:94). And, early in the period that we shall discuss in part 3, the Council of Nicaea, gathered in 325 CE, decided, "Because some kneel on the Lord's Day and the days of Pentecost, this holy synod, in order to make the practice uniform, has decided that it is good that all prayer be done standing" (*Canon 20*; Mansi 2:677).

As is well known, between the resurrection of Jesus and Pentecost there was the ascension of Jesus, to which Luke refers both in his Gospel and in Acts. Among the authors of the time we are now considering, although there are frequent references to the ascension of Jesus, nothing is said about a particular day to celebrate it—thus leading to the conclusion that there was still no fixed date for celebrating the ascension.

While the great feasts of Easter and Pentecost are directly derived from the biblical witness, such is not the case with the period preceding Easter, which we now call "Lent." The earliest reference we have to a period of fasting in preparation for Easter is found in the already quoted letter from Irenaeus to Victor, bishop of Rome, which has reached us thanks to the long quotations of it by Eusebius of Caesarea. Naturally, since Easter was celebrated on a Sunday, it was always preceded by the already mentioned fast that began on the Friday of each week. Apparently, what led to the expansion of that brief period to the forty days of Lent was, on the one hand, an extension of the Friday fast before Easter, and on the other, the catechetical system. As to the first, if it was appropriate to fast in preparation for every Sunday, when the resurrection of Jesus was celebrated, it would seem entirely appropriate to have an extended period of fasting before the Great Sunday of Easter. As to the second, remember that several days before their baptism on Easter Sunday, the catechumens had a period of special instruction both on Christian doctrine and on the practice of Christian life. This involved also a period of fasting and spiritual discipline. Although the duration of this period varied from place to place, it was slowly fixed at forty days on the basis of the many times that this number appears in Scripture—particularly in connection with the years of Israel in the desert and the days of Jesus in the desert to be tempted. What's more, since the members of the church were expected to provide guidance and support to those preparing for baptism, that period when the catechumens were preparing for their own baptism became a time in which the entire church fasted in preparation for Easter Sunday. Fasting, however, did not include Sundays, which by their very nature were days of celebration and not of fasting—the reason the season of Lent is in fact longer than forty days.

THE TIMES: HOURS OF THE DAY

As we saw in part 1, as long as Christianity was mostly Judeo-Christian its followers kept at least the same hours of prayer that Judaism observed. Without mentioning fixed hours, the *Didache* tells its readers that they are to repeat the Lord's Prayer three times a day. During the period that we are now studying, there are numerous signs that the number of the hours of prayer increased. In his treatise *On Prayer*, Tertullian mentions the three hours of prayers that already were followed in the first century, but then adds others in which one should also pray, as well as particular circumstances requiring prayer:

> About the time: it would seem profitable to observe certain hours. I mean the common hours that mark the intervals of the day: the third, sixth, and ninth hours that Scripture seems to count more solemn than others. The first coming of the power of the Spirit on the gathered disciples was at "the third hour." Peter experienced his vision of the inclusive community when he went to the upper part of the house for prayer "at the sixth hour." The same apostle was going into the Temple with John at "the ninth hour," when he restored the paralytic to health. Although these instances are stated without any rule given for their observance, it can be said that it is a good thing to assume that it is a law to pray at least three times a day. This tears us away from our business as a duty. We see that Daniel did this also, in accordance with Israel's discipline. The three times a day is in honor of the Three: Father, Son, and Holy Spirit. These times are in addition to our regular prayers which are due without any urging, on the entrance of light and the coming of night. It behooves believers not to take food, or go to the bath, without praying first, for the refreshment and nourishment of the spirit takes precedence over those of the flesh, and heavenly things are before earthly ones. (*On Prayer* 25; ANF 3:689–90)

A few decades later, Hippolytus reaffirmed what Tertullian says here regarding the main hours of prayer:

Let all the faithful, whether men or women, when early in the morning they rise from their sleep and before they undertake any tasks, wash their hands and pray to God; and so they may go to their duties. But if any instruction in God's word is held [that day], everyone ought to attend it willingly, recollecting that he will hear God speaking through the instructor and that prayer in the church enables him to avoid the day's evil; any godly man ought to count it a great loss if he does not attend the place of instruction, especially if he can read. . . .

If at the third hour thou art at home, pray then and give thanks to God; but if thou chance to be abroad at that hour, make thy prayer to God in thy heart. For at that hour Christ was nailed to the tree; . . .

At the sixth hour likewise pray also, for, after Christ was nailed to the wood of the cross, the day was divided and there was a great darkness; . . .

And at the ninth hour let a great prayer and a great thanksgiving be made, such as made the souls of the righteous ones, blessing the Lord, . . .

Pray again before thy body rests on thy bed.

At midnight arise, wash thy hands with water and pray. And if thy wife is with thee, pray ye both together; but if she is not yet a believer, go into another room and pray, and again return to thy bed; . . .

It is needful to pray at this hour; for those very elders who gave us the tradition taught us that at this hour all creation rests for a certain moment, that all creatures may praise the Lord: stars and trees and waters stand still with one accord, and all the angelic host does service to God by praising Him, together with the souls of the righteous. . . .

And at the cockcrow rise up and pray likewise, for at that hour of cockcrow the children of Israel denied Christ, whom we have known by faith. (*Ap. Trad.* 35–36)

As Hippolytus himself later says, the purpose of such hours of prayer is to have Christ always in mind and thus to avoid being tempted and lost. However, it is also important to remember that the significance of these set hours for prayer has to do not only with private devotion and one's relationship with God, but also with having all the church praying at the same time—even when its members are dispersed in their various occupations. Note also that, according to Hippolytus, at midnight the entire creation praises God. In other words, prayer at set hours is intended not only to edify the individual believer but also to join the praise of the rest of the church as well as all of creation, and thus to reinforce the nature of the church as a priestly people, and of its worship as joining heavenly worship and rehearsing for it. When all believers pray at the same time, no matter whether they are physically together or not, that very action makes them one and strengthens their identity as a priestly people of God.

THE PLACES: HOMES, CHURCHES, AND CATACOMBS

Having discussed the calendar and the scheduled prayers, we now turn to the places where Christians gathered in order to worship. In Judeo-Christian times, we find in the New Testament abundant examples of churches gathering in the homes of believers. Some of these homes would have been large enough to have more than one story (see Acts 20:8). But as the Christian community grew in a city, it became necessary to meet in more than one house. In the acts of the martyrdom of Justin, when the prefect asks him where Christians meet, Justin answers,

> Christians meet where each one chooses and can. Do you suppose that we all meet in one place? Not true. The God of the Christians is not limited by place. God is invisible and fills the heaven and earth. God is worshiped and glorified by the faithful everywhere. (*Martyrdom of Justin* 2; ANF 1:305)

When the prefect insists, Justin simply gives him his address, but does not reveal other places. The entire dialogue seems to indicate that Christians had several meeting places in Rome, and that the authorities had difficulties locating them. Some calculations suggest that there may have been some twenty meeting places in Rome by end of the first century.

As time went by, some of these homes that were being used for meetings were entirely dedicated to serve as churches, and remodeled and decorated as such. Although there is no doubt that this took place much earlier in the main cities of the Roman Empire, the most ancient such residence converted to a church that archaeologists have been able to reconstruct and date is the already mentioned one in Dura—or Dura-Europos—which dates approximately from the year 240. However, although many other ruins exist that are difficult to date, as time passed the number of buildings devoted to worship certainly grew. In a legal suit between Paul of Samosata and the church, Emperor Aurelian—who reigned from 200 to 275—was called to make a decision regarding a church building. Eusebius tells the story as follows: "Emperor Aurelian was petitioned. He resolved the matter very justly. He ordered the building to be given to those whom the bishops of Italy and of the city of Rome should decide" (*Church Hist.* 7.30.19; NPNF2 1:316). The edict of Galerius in 311 decreed "that they may again be Christians. They may rebuild the places where they were used to assemble" (*Church Hist.* 8.17.9; NPNF2 1:340). The joint Edict of Milan issued by Constantine and Licinius in 313 likewise declared,

In addition, as far as Christians are concerned: in the past we gave some order concerning places used for their religious assemblies. However, now we will that anyone who has purchased such places, either from our exchequer or from anyone else, shall restore them to the Christians, without demanding any money or claiming a price. This is to be done immediately and unambiguously. We also will that those who have obtained any right to such places as a gift should also immediately restore them to the Christians. If such persons, who have either purchased a property for a price, or acquired it gratuitously, should feel that they are entitled to be reimbursed by us, they should apply to the judge of the district. (*On the Death of Persecutors* 48; ANF 7:320)

During most of this period, such meeting places were not called "churches." A "church" was the body of believers, not the building. Near the end of this period, well into the third century, we begin to find uses of "church" as referring to buildings where Christians gathered for worship. There is a connection between the change in terminology and Christianity's growth. When Christians met in a home, they could simply refer to the place by the name of the owner—for instance, "Prisca's house." This could no longer be done when there was a building devoted entirely to worship—which then became "the church."

Finally, when speaking of meeting places, one must mention the catacombs. Although they had an important place in church life in the early centuries, much of what has been said or implied about the catacombs is not exactly true. First, Christians were not the first to dig catacombs. In ancient Rome—and therefore also in most of the cities ruled by it—it was customary to incinerate bodies and forbidden to bury people within the city limits. Therefore, when in any of those cities there were people representing other cultures or religions that preferred to bury their dead, they had to do this beyond the city limits. The case of Rome is typical. Long before the time of Christ a large number of Jews had settled in Rome, and in order to bury their dead they and others of similar customs created subterranean cemeteries outside the city. Some of these cemeteries, which are now under the modern city of Rome, were then several miles away from the city itself. There the Jews, and later also Christians, buried their dead. Indeed, the first legal status that churches were allowed was as funerary societies.

Although Christians occasionally may have used the catacombs to hide from the authorities in times of persecution, the importance of the catacombs for them was not as a hiding place but rather that they held their dead brothers and sisters. On the anniversary of some of these people's deaths—particularly of martyrs, who had witnessed to their faith with their own lives—it was customary to gather at their tombs in order to celebrate Communion. This was done because it was necessary to show and to experience that the church is not only a group of people gathering in a particular place at a particular time, but it is also that great cloud of witnesses surrounding us, and that this entire church in the end times will be gathered from the ends of earth to celebrate the wedding feast of the lamb—a celebration that Communion foreshadows and announces.

The catacombs are also important because they are the main source we have for the history of Christian art. Some of them—notably that of Domitilla—contain frescoes and inscriptions dating from the time we are now studying, although most belong to a later time, when after the persecution believers set out to decorate the places where their ancestors in the faith rested.

MUSIC

Since the church was born from the synagogue and with the Temple as background, and in both Temple and synagogue psalms and other hymns were sung, it was quite natural for the church to do likewise. But in fact we can say very little about ancient Christian music, for few extant Christian texts offer anything about it. During the time we are now studying we begin finding more frequent references both to instrumental music and to singing. Writing to the Ephesians, and urging them to unity, Ignatius of Antioch uses the image of a choir—which he probably would not have done had there been no choral music in the church:

> Your justly renowned presbytery is worthy of God. It is fitted as exactly to the bishop as the strings are to the harp. Therefore, in your peace and harmonious love, Jesus Christ is sung. You become a choir, one by one. With harmonious love you take up the song of God in unison, so that you may with one voice sing to the Father through Jesus Christ. Thus, God may both hear you and see by your works that you are indeed members of his Son. Therefore, it is profitable that you live blamelessly in unity so that you may always enjoy communion with God. (*Ep. to the Ephesians* 4; ANF 1:50–51)

In the letter that Pliny wrote to Trajan regarding Christians, he tells the emperor that they gather to sing hymns to Christ as to a god. In refuting Celsus, who claimed that Christians were uncouth barbarians, Origen claims that, while Greeks pray in Greek and Romans do so in Latin, "Christians in prayer do not even use the precise names which divine Scripture applies to

God; but the Greeks use Greek names, the Romans Latin names, and every one prays and sings praises to God as he best can, in his mother tongue" (*Ag. Celsus* 8.37; ANF 4:653).

Every indication is that singing in the ancient church followed a single melodic line, commonly sung in unison. Elaborate music, with many different instruments, was regarded askance not only in worship but even in Christian agapes or banquets. Thus, Clement of Alexandria, commenting on such meals, writes,

> If people occupy their time with pipes and psalteries, choirs, dances, and Egyptian hand-clapping, and other such disorderly frivolities, they become quite immodest and intractable. They beat on cymbals and drums, and make noise on instruments of delusion. Plainly, it seems to me, such a banquet is a theater of drunkenness. (*Instructor* 2.4; ANF 2:248)

And further on he adds,

> Temperate harmonies are to be admitted. However, we are to banish as far as possible from our strong minds those liquid harmonies. Through pernicious arts in the modulations of tones, they lead to effeminacy and vulgarity. Grave and modest strains, however, say farewell to the turbulence of drunkenness. Immodest banquets are the place for chromatic harmonies, along with flowery and popular music. (*Instructor* 2.4; ANF 2:249)

Similar opinions may be found among other early Christian writers, who often connect singing with the phrase "with a single voice." Apparently, the very idea of polyphonic singing seemed to them a sign of division or disagreement. However, this did not exclude the possibility of antiphonal singing in which the congregation—or a second cantor—would respond to a leading cantor. Tertullian seems to be referring to antiphonal singing as he praises as ideal a marriage in which "between the two echo psalms and hymns. They mutually challenge each other as to which one shall chant better to their Lord" (*To His Wife* 2.8; ANF 4:48).

Little more can be said about Christian music at that time. The only document including intelligible musical notation is a Gnostic fragment found in Egypt early in the twentieth century. Since the method used in it is the same as was generally used in Greek documents, it is possible to decipher the music, which is just a few lines. It is a simple melody that may well be an example of what was used among orthodox Christians, but it is too short to generalize about the nature of Christian music at the time.

PRACTICES IN DAILY LIFE

The purpose of worship is not only to praise God but also to enable believers to lead lives that reflect and continue what is done, taught, and practiced in worship. This results both in a series of devout practices and in attitudes and actions within society. As to devout practices, when discussing what Tertullian says about prayer, we have seen that several particular times and situations call for prayer, even beyond the three traditional hours. Tertullian invites his readers to add to those three hours other prayers at the beginning and the end of the day, when saying farewell to a brother or sister, and before each meal and each bath. Prayer is preferably done while kneeling, except on Sundays and during the days of Pentecost, when one should stand in order to rejoice in the victory of Christ. Half a century later, Cyprian also affirmed other times in which he suggested that prayer was appropriate, besides the traditional hours:

> But for us, beloved brothers and sisters, besides the hours of prayer observed traditionally, both the times and the sacraments have increased in number. We must pray in the morning so that the Lord's resurrection can be celebrated by morning prayer. . . . Also we must necessarily pray at the setting of the sun and the end of day, for since Christ is the true day, as the earthly sun and day depart, we pray and ask that light may return to us again. We pray for the advent of Christ, which shall give us the grace of everlasting light. . . . But if according to the Holy Scriptures Christ is the true sun and the true day, there is no hour in which Christians ought not to worship God, frequently and always. We who are in Christ—that is, in the true Sun and the true Day—should pray with petitions throughout the whole day. And when, according to the laws of nature, the revolving night returns, there can be no harm in the darkness of the night to those who pray, because the children of light have the day even in the night. (*On the Lord's Prayer* 35; ANF 5:457)

In another passage, Tertullian says that such prayers are usually accompanied by the sign of the cross over one's forehead. This is the same sign with which the neophytes were anointed upon emerging from the baptismal waters, and therefore repeating it was a reminder that, by virtue of baptism, the believer now belongs to Christ and bears on the forehead, even though unseen, the sign of the cross. Tertullian makes it clear that this includes practically every activity:

> At every forward step and movement, at every going in and out, when we put on our clothes and shoes, when we bathe, when we sit at table,

when we light the lamps, when we lie on the couch or sit down, in all
the ordinary actions of daily life, we trace the sign upon our forehead.
(*On the Crown* 3; ANF 3:94–95)

In the mid-third century, Cyprian interpreted the doors in Egypt marked
with the blood of a lamb as a foreshadowing of the sign of the cross Christians
now carry on the forehead, for just as the children of Israel were saved by the
sign on the doors, "so also, when the world shall begin to be desolated and
struck, only those who are found in the blood and sign of Christ shall escape"
(*To Demetrianus* 22; ANF 5:464).

Another gesture that appears repeatedly both in the biblical text and in
the ancient church, and that is often connected to baptism and ordination,
is the imposition or laying on of hands. In the Old Testament, hands are
imposed on certain sacrifices (Exod. 29:10; Lev. 3:2), as well as for passing authority from one person to another (Num. 27:18), to bless someone
(Gen. 48:14–15), and to authorize priests and Levites (Num. 8:10). In the
New Testament, Jesus heals and blesses by laying hands on the sick (Matt.
8:3; Mark 1:41; 10:13–16). Peter and John lay their hands on the disciples
in Samaria so that they may receive the Holy Spirit (Acts 8:17). Ananias
restores sight to Saul by the imposition of hands (Acts 9:17). Saul and Barnabas are commissioned in the same way (Acts 13:3). Later we are told that
Timothy has received his authority by the laying on of hands from the council of elders (1 Tim. 4:14).

During the period we are now studying, the practice of laying on of hands
in a number of rites and circumstances continues. As we saw when discussing
baptism, Tertullian says that, after the neophyte is anointed upon leaving the
waters, there is an imposition of hands that invokes the blessing of the Holy
Spirit. Elsewhere, referring to the same action, he says that "the flesh is shad-
owed with the laying on of hands, so that the soul also may be illuminated
by the Spirit" (*On the Resurrection of the Flesh* 8; ANF 3:551). After that come
numerous passages that could be quoted insisting on the importance of the
laying on of hands after baptism in invocation of the Spirit.

In the *Apostolic Tradition* of Hippolytus, the imposition of hands is a means
of granting authority to certain leaders in the church, and of establishing
a distinction between them and others. According to Hippolytus, after
the people elect a bishop, in his consecration, other bishops present are to
impose their hands on him, invoking the coming of the Spirit, while the
elders remain standing and silent. Immediately one of these bishops, laying a
hand on the one being ordained, prays over him. Then the first action of the
new bishop is to lay his own hands on what has been offered for Communion
and to preside over Communion itself. This seems to be a way of indicating

that the bishop does not consecrate Communion on his own authority, but rather on the authority that he has received from the rest of the church (*Ap. Trad.* 2–4).

The ordination of an elder or presbyter is different, for in that case a bishop places his hand on the head of the ordinand while the other elders also touch him; Hippolytus does not explain exactly how, but clearly not by laying hands on his head, as does the bishop. In a deacon's ordination, only the bishop performs the laying on of hands, and Hippolytus explains that "he is not ordained to the priesthood but to serve the bishop and to carry out his commands" (*Ap. Trad.* 9). When the time comes to acknowledge a confessor—this is, someone who suffered as a Christian but was not killed, and therefore is not a martyr—either the deacons or the elders perform the laying on of hands, since the act itself of confessing the faith has already conferred the honor of an elder. But if the confessor is then to be made a bishop, there is an imposition of hands on him (*Ap. Trad.* 10).

In clear contrast with those who are to be bishops, presbyters, or deacons, others performing various functions are not to receive the imposition of hands. This is the case of readers, who are simply commissioned by being given the book; subdeacons; as well as those who have the gift of healing, whose authority does not have to be signaled, but will be manifested by deeds of healing.

In this context, what Hippolytus says regarding women who are to join the official group of widows does not mean simply that their husbands are deceased, but rather that they are to devote themselves to a life of celibacy and service to the community. According to the instructions of Hippolytus, for a woman joining the rank of widows, "Hands shall not be laid upon her because she does not offer the oblation nor has she a sacred ministry" (*Ap. Trad.* 11). The same is true of the rank of virgins, who will not receive the imposition of hands, since for their ministry keeping their own vocation is sufficient. What we may see in all this is what the New Testament already foreshadowed regarding this group of women devoted to special tasks within the church, and which is now officially recognized. When, early in the second century, Ignatius is writing to Christians in Smyrna, he says in the final salutations of his letter, "Salute the families of my brethren, with their wives and children, and the virgins who are called widows" (*Ep. to the Smyrneans* 13; ANF 1:92). The phrase itself, referring to some "virgins" who were also called "widows," suggests that already by that time when one spoke of "widows," this referred not only to women who had lost a husband but actually to a special group of women whom the church supported and who worked for the church. Polycarp is probably referring to them when he writes to the Philippians,

Teach the widows they are to be discreet, which the faith of the Lord requires. They are to pray continually for all, avoid slandering, evil-speaking, false-witnessing, love of money, and every kind of evil. They must know that they are at the altar of God, and that God clearly sees all things. Nothing is hid from God, not reasonings, not reflections, not any of the secret things of the heart. (*Ep. to the Philippians* 4; ANF 1:34)

By immediately preceding other recommendations regarding deacons and presbyters or elders, this statement about widows would seem to indicate that these are not simply women who have lost their husbands and need the support of the church, but a particular group of women who have decided to remain unmarried and serve the church.

In the third century, we have Cyprian's treatise *On the Dress of Virgins*, where he affirms that by their celibate life these women would not only attain a place in heaven, but are already freed from the curses pronounced on women in the book of Genesis:

Hold fast, O virgins! Hold fast to what you have begun to be. Hold fast to what you shall be. A great reward awaits you, a great compensation for virtue, the immense advantage of chastity. Do you wish to know what ills the virtue of continence avoids, what good it possesses? "I will multiply your sorrows and groans; in sorrow you shall bring forth children. Your desire shall be for your husband, and he shall rule over you." You are free from this sentence. You do not fear the sorrows and groans of women. You have no fear of child-bearing; nor is your husband lord over you. Your Lord and Head is Christ, after the likeness and in the place of the man. Your lot and your condition are equal to that of men. . . . What we shall be you have already begun to be. (*On the Dress of Virgins* 22; ANF 5:436)

These women are the background of all Christian monasticism, which originally moved much more rapidly among women than among men. Significantly, these women had a role to play within the Christian community, as seen in the *Apostolic Constitutions*, a fourth-century document one of whose main sources comes from the previous century. There the bishops are instructed,

Ordain also a deaconess who is faithful and holy, for the ministries for women. Sometimes he [the bishop] cannot send a deacon, who is a man, to women, because of unbelievers. You shall therefore send a woman, a deaconess, so that there will be no evil imaginings [by outsiders]. We need to have a woman, a deaconess, for many necessary actions. First, in the baptism of women: the deacon shall anoint only their forehead with the holy oil. After that, the deaconess shall anoint them. There is no need that the women should be seen by the men. In the laying on of hands by the bishop, he shall anoint her head, as the priests and kings were formerly anointed. This is not because those who are now baptized are ordained as priests, but because they are Christians, or anointed ones, from Christ the Anointed, "a royal priesthood, and a holy nation, the Church of God, the pillar and ground of the marriage-chamber." (*Apostolic Constitutions* 3.2; ANF 7:431)

Returning to the laying on of hands, we must add that this rite, besides conferring authority to another, was also used for other purposes. In the *Testament of the Lord*—a document from the late fourth century that may well reflect practices in the third—we are told that on dismissing the catechumens before Communion, hands are to be imposed on them. In the *Apostolic Tradition* (19) the teacher is to pray and lay hands on the catechumens as they are dismissed from the service. Also during that period, hands were laid on believers as a sign of forgiveness and reconciliation with the church. In 250 CE, Cyprian chided some confessors for claiming that people who had fallen into apostasy could be restored to the Communion of the church "before hands were laid upon the penitent by the bishops and clergy" (*Ep.* 10.1; ANF 5:291). Likewise, in his clash with Stephen, bishop of Rome, Cyprian criticized him for having declared that if a heretic who has been baptized decides to join the church, all that should be required is his or her repentance and the imposition of hands. Cyprian does not object to the imposition of hands, which has also been practiced in Carthage. His objection regards whether a heretic should be baptized anew, as we have already seen. In brief, even though differing on the matter of the baptism by heretics, Rome and Carthage agreed that the imposition of hands should signal their restitution to the church. (The common practice today, of dismissing the congregation with a benediction while holding the arms extended with the palms down, is an extension of the old custom of imposing hands for blessing.)

The impact of worship on daily life was not limited to these actions of devotion—frequent prayer, remembering one's baptism, the sign of the cross, and others—but was intended to be manifest also in the relations among believers and with the rest of society. The claim in Acts—that the first believers had all things in common and no one claimed that something was his own, but all were ready to share with those in need—echoes throughout the period we are now considering. This point may be seen in the literature itself, where the words of the *Didache* late in the first century are repeated almost verbatim in the *Epistle of Barnabas* several decades later: "You shall share in all things with your neighbor. You shall not call anything your own. If you are joint partakers in things that are incorruptible, how much more should you be joint sharers in things that are corruptible!" (*Ep. of Barnabas* 19; ANF 1:148). Something similar is found later in a document of uncertain date—but probably from the second century—*To Diognetus*:

> How will you love him who has first loved you? If you love Him you will imitate his kindness. . . . The one who distributes to the needy whatever has been received from God becomes a god to those to whom these things have been given. This is the way we become imitators of God. (*To Diognetus* 15; ANF 1:29)

This text indicates that the result of the love to God that is expressed in worship is an imitation of God expressed in human relations. Similar ideas appear in numerous passages. Writing to believers in Smyrna, Ignatius made a connection between withdrawing from the Eucharist and withdrawing from charity, for those who reject the Eucharist "have no regard for love; no care for the widow, or the orphan, or the oppressed; of the bond, or of the free; of the hungry, or of the thirsty" (*Ep. to the Smyrneans* 6; ANF 1:89).

Similar attitudes prevailed during all this time before Constantine's reign. Some four decades after Ignatius, Justin wrote,

> We who valued gaining wealth and possessions above everything else, now bring what we have to a common stock, and give to everyone who is in need. We who hated and destroyed one another because of our different customs, who would not live with those of a different tribe, now, since Christ has come, live with them as family. We pray for our enemies. We try to persuade those who hate us unjustly to live according to the good teachings of Christ. We want them to become partakers with us of the same joyful hope of a reward from God, the ruler of all. (*1 Apol.* 14; ANF 1:167)

Later in the second century, in a passage already cited, Tertullian says that a voluntary collection is gathered in worship meetings in order to help the needy. And near the middle of the next century, the third, Cyprian wrote an extensive treatise, *On Works and Alms*, in which he establishes a connection between helping the needy and baptism:

> The Holy Spirit speaks in the sacred Scriptures and says, "By charity and faith sins are forgiven." Obviously not those earlier sins, for those are forgiven by the blood and sanctification of Christ. Moreover, the Spirit says again, "As water quenches fire, so charity quenches sin." Here it is shown that in the washing of saving water the fire of Gehenna is extinguished. So by charity and the works of righteousness the flame of sins is subdued. Because in baptism the remission of sins is granted once and for all, constant and ceaseless work, following the likeness of baptism, once again brings the mercy of God. (*On Works and Alms* 2; ANF 5:476)

Although many other texts could be quoted, these should suffice to show the indissoluble relationship between worship and support for the needy. Therefore, we may move to one of the most concrete manners in which the ancient church sought to help the needy, the agape or love feast. In part 1 (chapter 6), we dealt with the agape within Judeo-Christianity, having to conclude that it is impossible to determine the exact process or time by which the agape became quite distinct from Communion. Now in the second century it is possible to affirm that, although there is still a connection between Communion and the agape feasts, the difference between them is becoming clearer. An unexpected witness of that distinction is the letter of Governor Pliny to Emperor Trajan regarding Christian practices. According to Pliny, his inquiries had led him to conclude that Christians would meet before sunrise in order to sing hymns to Christ and to commit to doing good, and that later they gathered again to share in a meal—although according to Pliny this latter meeting had been suspended in view of the laws forbidding secret societies. The first important conclusion to be drawn from this report is that, by that time, early in the second century, Christians appear to have distinguished clearly between the worship service before dawn and another meal that took place later—what eventually came to be known as the agape. A second conclusion is that, at least in this particular case, meeting for a meal seemed to be more questionable to the eyes of the law than gathering for worship.

At approximately the same time, Ignatius of Antioch wrote to the church in Smyrna a letter saying that, without the bishop, there should be no baptisms, Communion celebrations, or agapes. From that point on, and with increased frequency, we find passages referring to the agape. The anonymous *To Diognetus* refers to Christians having a "common table" (8.5). The *Martyrdom of Perpetua and Felicitas* says that the martyrs turned their last meal into an agape: "In that last meal, which they call the free meal, they were partaking as far as they could, not of a free supper, but of an agape" (5.4; ANF 3:704). However, the clearest early description of an agape comes from Tertullian, near the end of the second century:

> A great to-do is made about the modest supper room of the Christians. Our feast explains itself by its name: The Greeks call it *agape*: affection. Whatever the meal costs is really a gain, because our pious spending for the good things of the feast benefits the needy. This is not true with you. In your banquets parasites sell themselves for a belly-feast in order to aspire to glory, satisfying their sinful desires and leading to all sorts of disgraceful treatment. With us, however, as with God himself, a peculiar respect is shown to the lowly. If the object of our feast is good, consider that there are even further regulations. Because it is an act of religious service, there can be no vileness or immodesty. The participants, before reclining, first taste prayer to

God. They eat as much as needed to satisfy hunger. They drink as much as befits the chaste. They say it is enough, since they remember that even during the night they have to worship God. They talk as those who know that the Lord is listening. After they wash their hands and the lights are brought in, each is asked to stand up and sing, as he can, a hymn to God, either one from the holy Scriptures or one of his own composing. This is a proof of how much we have drunk. As the feast began with prayer, so with prayer it is closed. We go from the supper, not like troops of mischief-makers or a band of vagabonds. We do not break out into sinful acts, but we have as much care for our modesty and chastity as if we had been at a school of virtue rather than a banquet. (*Apol.* 39; ANF 3:47)

The *Apostolic Tradition* of Hippolytus includes another description of the agape. While Tertullian's description is addressed to pagans with the purpose of explaining to them what Christians do, this document is intended to be read by Christians, giving them directions for the celebration of the agape. Hippolytus is concerned on the one hand over the need to establish order in such meals, which by their very nature could prove disorderly, and on the other hand he also wishes to make it clear that, although bread and wine have an important place in the agape, this should not be confused with Communion. As to the first, Hippolytus says that the bishop should preside over the agape, and how this is to be done. As to the second, in a somewhat confusing passage, Hippolytus seems to distinguish among three sorts of bread. The first of these, which is not the bread to be eaten in the agape, is bread over which a thanksgiving has been pronounced. (At this point one should remember that in the Last Supper Jesus took bread and "gave thanks." This is the origin of the word "Eucharist," which simply means giving thanks, but became a synonym for Communion. As early as the time of Justin [*1 Apol.* 46; ANF 1:185], Communion was already called the "Eucharist.") Second, there is bread that the bishop "blesses" in the agape, and which Hippolytus clearly distinguishes from the bread over which thanks have been given—the "eucharistized" bread. After blessing this second bread, each of the participants is to take a piece of it and eat it before the rest of the meal. Third is a bread over which what is pronounced is not a blessing but an exorcism. This seems to have been the bread that was given to the catechumens and others who had not yet been baptized. Several Eastern churches still retain echoes of this custom.

Hippolytus adds that while prayers are offered over what is to be eaten and drunk, all except those leading the prayers should be silent. While eating, there is also to be silence, without discussions, and all people paying attention to what the bishop is teaching, or answering his questions. If the bishop is not present and a presbyter or a deacon is there, the same order is to be followed.

If there are only laypeople, the meal will not include the blessed bread, for the blessing of the bread requires ordination. Hippolytus adds that if for some reason—apparently mostly for lack of room—it is not possible for the person offering the agape to invite others to eat in the banquet, people may take food to eat at home. These instructions are to be applied particularly to elderly widows, who may go to the house of the person offering the meal and then eat at home. This would seem to indicate that the agape was a way of helping the needy. In other words, the meal that takes place at Communion should be reflected in the practice of those who have more resources to share with the needy by means of the agape (*Ap. Trad.* 26).

Still on the subject of the agape, one must note that, on occasion, the ancient practice of celebrating Communion at the tombs of martyrs on the anniversary of their deaths was transformed so that now, rather than Communion, it was an agape. Over the centuries, this would lead to the pilgrimages that still take place in many towns in Europe.

Finally, on the subject of the impact of worship on daily life, and particularly in view of the pandemic that began in 2019—whose consequences would be felt for years—in times of plague Christians became known for their attitude in support of the sick and needy. Among many testimonies to that effect, one may quote a letter that Dionysius of Alexandria wrote to the faithful in that city, preserved in a quote by Eusebius of Caesarea:

> Truly the best of our brothers and sisters died in this way, including some presbyters and deacons and people who had the highest reputation. This form of death, showing great piety and faith, lacked nothing of being martyrdom.
> They took the bodies of the saints in their open hands and bosoms. They closed their eyes and mouths. They bore them away on their shoulders and laid them out. They clung to them and embraced them. They prepared them suitably, washing and dressing them. And after a little they were treated the same way, for survivors were constantly following those who had gone before.
> But with the heathen everything was very different. They deserted those who began to be sick. They fled from their dearest friends. They cast them out into the streets when they were half dead, and left the dead like refuse, unburied. They shunned any participation or fellowship with death. And yet, with all their precautions, it was not easy for them to escape. (*Church Hist.* 7.22.8–10; NPNF2 1:307)

(At the time of this writing we quote this passage in the midst of a pandemic in which we know that for some of us the best way to serve our neighbors is to stay physically distant, in order to avoid spreading the disease, while others are called to serve them more directly. Clearly, love of neighbors must always take into account the circumstances of each particular situation.)

THE END OF AN ERA

We now come to the end of this second period in our narrative. It was slightly over two hundred years, but during that time the church changed noticeably. What was originally mostly a movement among Jews and God-fearers, convinced that God's promises had been fulfilled in Jesus, had now become a vast organization present throughout the Roman Empire. Its Hebrew roots could still be seen, particularly in its Scriptures, mostly taken from Judaism. Such roots could also be seen in the worship of a God who requires both justice and love. But at the same time, that church, though grounded in Hebrew traditions, saw Judaism as one of its main rivals. In consequence, while affirming those ancient roots, the church was becoming ever more distant and antagonistic to the actual faith of Israel.

Even though it already covered most of the Roman Empire, and had extended far beyond the imperial borders, by the end of this period the church was still facing enormous difficulties. Most notable among them was persecution. Under the leadership first of Diocletian and then of his successors, beginning in 303 CE, the most terrible of all persecutions of that time was unleashed on Christians. This was followed by a series of decrees threatening prison, torture, and death, first on Christian clergy, and then on all believers. Christians had ample reason to call this the "Great Persecution." Under its terror, many denied their faith when threatened with torture or death.

In such circumstances, worship was one of the main means that the church had for affirming and strengthening Christian identity, for in worship believers could see themselves as a unique people that, despite pressing circumstances, trusted in the power and final victory of their Lord. This community, rather than reacting in hatred, saw itself as a priestly people, praying for the emperor and for all those who persecuted it, and still hoping against all hope for a better world. Hardly could they ever have imagined what would happen ten years after the beginning of the Great Persecution!

PART III

From Constantine to the Invasions

12

New Circumstances

Early in the fourth century, beginning in 303 CE, the church had been suffering under the Great Persecution. There were numerous martyrs; tortures were ever more cruel; the buildings where Christians used to meet had been confiscated and sometimes destroyed. Diocletian, the emperor whose effort to restore the ancient glories of Rome had a measure of success, was convinced that the restoration he sought required the destruction of the church.

In order to make sure that the order he had created would persevere, Diocletian developed a system in which there were four rulers or emperors—two of them with the title of "Augustus," and two others under them with the title of "Caesar." Convinced that his work was complete, Diocletian abdicated in 305, but this did not put an end to persecution. In 311, for reasons that are not altogether clear, Gallerius, one of the four emperors, decreed the end of persecution in his territories. This had limited effect. The four who were supposed to be the orderly successors of Diocletian soon began vying for power in a series of wars and maneuvers in which Constantine and Licinius finally were the victors, with the former ruling the western areas of the empire, and the latter the eastern.

In February 313 Constantine and Licinius, meeting in Milan, came to a decision that would change the history of the church for centuries, putting an end to persecution and ordering the return of the properties of churches and believers that had been confiscated. It is unnecessary to discuss here the details of that edict, of which there is more than one version. In general, what was decided was freedom of religion for all, but particularly for Christians. Nor is it necessary to discuss the reasons why the two emperors made such a move. To this day, historians debate whether that decision was the result of the conviction that persecution was more costly than beneficial, whether it had to do mostly with political calculation, or if there was a measure of religious conviction on the part of one or both emperors. Since shortly after the meeting in Milan the two emperors were again at war, with Constantine becoming the sole emperor, it was he who implemented the decisions made in Milan. Although some churches consider him a saint, one must not forget that for a long time Constantine's family had been worshipers of the Unconquered Sun, that Constantine himself rendered homage both to Jesus Christ and to the Sun, that he kept the priestly titles that he held within the ancient religion, that he was extremely cruel with his own son when this seemed expedient, and that only on his deathbed was he finally baptized.

The process that began with Constantine and Licinius in 313 CE eventually—in 380 CE—led to an edict issued in Thessalonica by Emperor Theodosius making Christianity the official religion of the empire, declaring that those who were not in communion with bishops Damasus of Rome and Peter of Alexandria were not to be allowed to call themselves "catholic Christians," and that all others were fools and demented people who should simply be called "heretics," whose "conventicles" could not be called "churches." The only other religion allowed to conduct public worship was Judaism.

In less than a century, between 313 and 380, a religion that until then had been forbidden became the dominant religion of the empire. The ancient religions persisted mostly in the hinterlands, and therefore they came to be known as "pagan"—meaning the religion of the *pagani*, the rude and uncultured. The ancient religions also persisted among some in the old Roman aristocracy, who saw the abandonment of the ancient gods as the reason for the decadence of the aristocracy itself and of the entire Roman Empire. During the period to which we now turn, some continued claiming that the abandonment of the ancient gods was the cause of the calamities, disorder, and invasions that the empire suffered. When Constantine created a new capital where Byzantium earlier stood, and named it "Constantinople" in his own honor, he gave it its own senate and a new aristocracy. The aristocracy of the old capital saw this as a threat to their power and their religious traditions. For some time the old Roman Senate insisted on keeping the images of the ancient gods in their meeting place. Several defenders of the ancient religions wrote criticisms of Christianity that help us understand the reasons for their opposition to it. When in the year 361 Julian came to occupy the imperial throne, he made a strong effort to restore the ancient religions, but this ended with his death in 363—although pretenders to the throne would still appear who would declare themselves defenders of the gods. When the Visigoths sacked Rome in 410, Augustine found it necessary to write against those who claimed that the old city had fallen because it had abandoned the gods that made it great. The result was his vast work titled *The City of God*.

In summary, although paganism did not disappear entirely or immediately, beginning with the edict issued at Milan the number of Christians grew rapidly. Knowing exactly the number of believers at the time of the edict is impossible. The most optimistic calculations suggest that in some eastern regions of the empire, where Christians were more numerous, they may well have been about 15 percent of the population. Possibly there were similar situations in some areas in North Africa. But throughout the West, as well as in vast areas of the East, Christians were still a small minority.

Constantine's support developed and grew slowly, and always with a measure of ambiguity. A typical example is the anecdote about the time when he was walking around ancient Byzantium, marking what would be the city walls of Constantinople. People began wondering about his dreams for the city, for he seemed to be walking far and wide. When finally someone asked him how far he intended to go, Constantine answered, "I shall walk as far as I am led by the one who goes before me." Christians who followed as part of the imperial entourage understood this as a reference to Christ, while the pagan priests who were also marching with Constantine took it as a reference to one of their gods.

Throughout his reign, Constantine increased the concessions and advantages that he gave to the church, such as the use of the imperial post and the exemption of Christian clergy from military service. Partially at the request of his mother, Helena, he ordered the building of great churches to which we refer later. On this point several of his successors emulated him. Among the emperor's advisers were several Christian bishops—notably Hosius of Cordova. Since Constantine hoped that the church would become the cement unifying his empire, when the church in Alexandria was divided over Arianism, he sent Hosius to mediate the matter. When Hosius reported that a reconciliation between the two parties seemed unattainable, Constantine ordered that a great council of bishops should gather to decide on this and other matters. This was the Council of Nicaea in 325, the first of a long series of councils commonly known as "ecumenical." On their way to Nicaea, bishops traveled at imperial expense.

All these measures, and many others of a similar nature, made it quite clear that Constantine favored the church—although he himself was not baptized until he was ready to die, apparently because he did not wish to place himself under the authority of bishops, as other Christians did. However, although the emperor himself was not immediately baptized, his clear inclination in favor of Christianity led many to join the church. This began a process that, with the brief exception of the reign of Julian, continued uninterrupted in such a way that by the end of that fourth century, practically all the population had been baptized—the main exception being Jews. The consequences of this process were soon to be noted, particularly in the preparation of candidates for baptism—to which we return in chapter 14.

The great Christian basilicas that Constantine, his family, and his successors ordered built seemed to require a more elaborate form of worship, as we see throughout part 3 of this book. That more elaborate worship also led to an ever more active participation by those who conducted it—clergy and choirs—and a more passive role for most Christians.

Constantine's interest in the Arian question set a sad precedent, encouraging several of his successors to try to make decisions on matters of doctrine, with the result that theology quite frequently was entangled in political issues. This is not our particular interest here, but one must note that this also impacted worship, for those who led it knew that whatever was said, sung, or done in worship could easily be tied up with politics.

A good example is the hymn we now know as the *Gloria Patri*. By affirming that glory belongs equally to the Father, the Son, and the Holy Spirit, and that this is "as it was in the beginning," a strong anti-Arian statement was being made. The Arians claimed that only the Father is God in the strict sense, and that both the Son and the Holy Spirit are creatures of the Father. Therefore, instead of saying, "Glory be to the Father, to the Son, and to the Holy Spirit," they would say, "Glory be to the Father, *through* the Son and the Holy Spirit," thus indicating that the glory is only the Father's, and that the Son and the Holy Spirit do not have divine and eternal glory. In the complicated politics of the time, sometimes a ruler strongly supported one faction in the struggle, and pressured or even persecuted those who held another view. In consequence, in a service all were very attentive to see what was said in singing the *Gloria Patri*. In Antioch, Bishop Leontius, when coming to the singing of the *Gloria Patri*, would suddenly begin coughing and not recover until he came to the final "forever." All knew that this was a mere subterfuge to avoid being involved in theological debates and the possible consequences that could bring.

Now that persecution had ended, martyrdom, which many had considered the highest degree of devotion, was no longer an option. In response to this new situation, and to a degree as a substitute for the high vocation of martyrdom, many devout people, women as well as men, found refuge in deserted places in order to lead there a life of devotion and discipline. The areas where this movement was strongest were the deserts of Egypt and Syria. These "deserts" were not areas absolutely dry and covered with sand, but rather inhospitable zones of arid and rocky soil, and therefore incapable of supporting a large population, but where the ascetic life of these fugitives from the rest of society could be sustained through hard and constant labor. A veritable exodus to the desert took place beginning in the fourth century. It became a refuge for solitary hermits, male as well as female, who fled from the comfortable life of the city and from society at large in order to practice their devotion more fully. Progressively, the most distinguished and famous of these hermits were surrounded by others who settled nearby seeking their teaching and guidance. Eventually, especially in Syria and Egypt, this led to communities of monastics who embraced what came to be called the "cenobitic" life—that is, life in community. This was particularly appreciated because it gave an opportunity to practice both discipline and love, and it eventually became the main form of monastic life as we know it today.

This emphasis on communal life also made a difference for the groups of women who earlier had devoted themselves to the service of the church and the community, and who, taking the title of "widows" or "virgins," were committed to a life of celibacy and were supported in their ministry by the church. Now that this other alternative was available for women who wished to lead a devout life, many of them went to the desert, where there were also monastic communities for women. Still there were in many cities groups of women—in many cases, well-to-do women—devoted to prayer and study. Much later, the functions and responsibilities that widows and virgins had met earlier would become the purview of a new order or group of "deaconesses"—whose duties and authority were very different from those of male deacons.

Several of the most distinguished bishops that we shall study in part 3 of this book—Augustine, Basil, and many others—adapted monastic life so that it could take place in their own residences in the cities, where the bishops were accompanied by other members of the clergy.

Economic motives also prompted the flight to the desert. Poor peasants, overburdened by taxes and obligations that they could not meet, joined monastic communities even though they themselves were not yet Christians. There, before being accepted into the community, they were taught the rudiments of the faith, given the opportunity to practice Christian living, and in many ways prepared for full participation in the monastic community. Significantly, while people often speak of the "fathers of the desert" or the "monks of the desert," there is no doubt that—at least in some areas of Egypt—the number of women devoted to monastic life far exceeded the number of men.

The new freedom that the church now enjoyed allowed its intellectual leaders to have time for study, reflection, and writing, with the result that the fourth century and the first years of the fifth produced several of the main luminaries in the history of Christianity—Ambrose, Jerome, Augustine, and several others in the West, as well as Athanasius, Basil, Gregory of Nazianzen, and others in the East. The Christian pulpit reached its peak during this time with John Chrysostom in Constantinople, Augustine in North Africa, and Leo the Great in Rome. Making use of a library that to a large extent Origen had compiled, Eusebius of Caesarea wrote the first church history, thanks to which we know much of what books like this one can say today.

Relations between church and civil authorities were not always easy or cordial, for several of the great figures we have just mentioned—Ambrose, Athanasius, Basil, and Chrysostom—had severe clashes with governmental authorities. A number of valiant bishops suffered exile and even death because they refused to ignore the prevailing injustices in society, or because they held doctrines different from those of the emperor ruling at the moment. Large numbers of people began requesting baptism and to join the church. This brought enormous changes in the catechetical system developed in earlier centuries, as well as in practices regarding baptism. Worship, still centering on Communion, became ever more elaborate, now led by bishops and clergy whose very titles gave them prestige in society. New hymns and musical styles were created for worship. Great churches were built in the main cities and in the most sacred places of Christian origins. In brief, those relatively few years following the decision of the emperors in Milan had enormous consequences—positive and negative—for the life of the church.

One of the consequences of the new situation is that we now have much more material about the church in the fourth century than we have from the previous three centuries. Up to this point, our analysis of existing texts has been almost exhaustive—the main exception being part of the enormous literary production of Origen. But beginning in the fourth century, an exhaustive approach becomes impossible, and we have to select what seems most relevant among the many materials available.

In the chapters that follow, continuing the basic structure of the earlier parts of this book, we deal first with preaching, offering at least a few examples from that time (chapter 13). Then we move on to baptism and preparation for it (chapter 14), to Communion and the ceremonies surrounding it (chapter 15), and finally end this part with a chapter (16) on the Christian calendar, meeting places, and a number of worship and devotional practices beyond preaching, baptism, and Communion.

13

Preaching

Early in the fifth century, Rufinus, after translating Eusebius's *Church History* from Greek into Latin, wrote an appendix bringing that history up to his time. There one finds an interesting note regarding Libanius, one of the most distinguished professors of rhetoric in the fourth century, who was a profoundly devout pagan. According to Rufinus, when Libanius had come to a ripe old age and was facing death he was asked who among his disciples should be his successor in his famous school of rhetoric. Libanius answered, "John, were it not that Christians have stolen him" (Rufinus, *Church Hist.* 6.3). This "John" to whom Libanius was referring is today known by the name given to him by his admirers after his death, John "Chrysostom"—that is, John the golden-mouther or of golden speech—often considered the greatest Christian preacher of all time.

Rufinus's anecdote may not be historically true, but it certainly points to one of the main factors shaping Christian preaching during the fourth century and early in the fifth: the use of Greco-Roman rhetoric. Chrysostom studied in the famous school that Libanius headed in Antioch. Earlier there had been few Christian writers and speakers who knew classical rhetoric, and most of these had studied it before their conversion to Christianity. Such was the case with Tertullian and Cyprian. The main exception was Origen, who grew up in a Christian home and therefore was already a believer when he began his studies. But Origen himself was more interested in philosophy than in rhetoric. His literary studies, rather than leading to rhetorical analysis of texts, were used for their allegorical interpretation, similar to the manner in which pagans interpreted classical Greek or Roman literature. The main reason few Christians studied rhetoric was that these studies dealt with the classical texts referring mostly to the ancient gods, their myths, and their miracles.

199

In times of persecution, many believers saw in such studies a concession to the idolatry of the surrounding culture. Only upon reaching the fourth century, once persecution has subsided, did the church at large begin seeing true value in rhetoric, and to consider the possibility of studying that discipline and the ancient texts that served as its basis while at the same time retaining Christian monotheism and rejecting the gods.

Chrysostom's case is typical. Born and raised in a pious home, after completing his basic studies he went to study with Libanius, the most famous professor of rhetoric in the area, even though Chrysostom knew that Libanius was a fervent devotee and defender of the Greek gods—not of the Roman gods, for Libanius was convinced that the Romans were ignorant "barbarians." Chrysostom's case is not the only one; there are many similar stories. Another of the great preachers we study here is Basil of Caesarea, known as "the Great," who lived a few decades before Chrysostom. He was also born in a Christian home. In contrast to Chrysostom, during his early years Basil was not interested in asceticism, preaching, or theology. He had decided to devote his life to administration and civil service. Among his professors were some of the most famous teachers of his time, for after completing his studies in his native Caesarea of Cappadocia he went to study first in Constantinople and later in Athens. Upon returning to Caesarea after his studies, he became quite successful in the practice of law and in rhetoric until his sister Macrina pointed him in a different direction, leading to an ascetic life, to the episcopacy of Caesarea, and to involvement in the intense theological controversies of his time.

What was taking place in the Greek-speaking East had its counterpart in the Latin-speaking West. The most distinguished Latin preachers of the fourth and fifth centuries, Ambrose, Augustine, and Leo, were all accomplished in rhetoric. Ambrose had followed a career in the civil administration of the empire when—much against his will—he was elected bishop of Milan. He then applied to his preaching the rhetoric that before had served him in civil service. Augustine, although raised by his Christian mother, Monica, had doubts about his mother's faith, and particularly about the value of Scripture, when he went to hear Ambrose preach. What Augustine says about his experience there is significant—first because his words show the impact that Ambrose had on the young Augustine, but also because they show how classical rhetoric was used to communicate a message to a more educated public. As Augustine tells the story, he did not go to hear Ambrose in order to learn anything about what he preached, but rather because Ambrose was a famous speaker. Augustine, as a professor of rhetoric, thought he could learn something from Ambrose that he could apply to his own work. But slowly his attitude changed, as Augustine himself says:

> I did not take the trouble to learn what he spoke about. I only wanted
> to know how he said it. (I had only empty concerns left to me, for I
> had despaired of any way that a human being might come to You.)
> However, along with the words which I prized there also came into
> my mind the things about which I did not care. I could not separate
> them. And while I opened my heart to admit "how skillfully he spoke,"
> there also entered with it, gradually, "and how truly he spoke." (*Con-
> fessions* 5.14.24; NPNF1 1:88)

In brief, Augustine, like Ambrose and several of his contemporaries, was a
lover of rhetoric, in which he saw valuable resources for Christian preaching.
For generations, rhetoric had been a subject of enthusiastic interest among the
more educated elites. Some people attended the courts as a pastime, just to listen to the arguments presented. Therefore, when making use of the rhetorical
practices and canons of the time, those famous preachers of the fourth and fifth
centuries found in them a way of relating the message preached to the interests
and tastes of their listeners. At the same time, however, there was always the
danger that rhetoric would become merely a series of instruments in order to
attract the attention of an audience, with little interest in the communication
of truth. Sometime after his experience with Ambrose, Augustine declared that
"the day arrived when I was actually to be released from the professorship of
rhetoric. I already intended to end my career. Now it was done. You delivered
my tongue in the same way you had earlier delivered my heart" (*Confessions*
9.4.7; NPNF1 1:131). Even after writing these words, Augustine continued
making repeated use of his knowledge of rhetoric. But his words, which also
echoed in several of the great preachers of that time, pointed to the need of
employing rhetoric, not to impress or to entertain an audience, but rather to
awaken its interest in the truth of what was being said. Augustine tried here to
follow Ambrose's example, whose expert use of rhetoric was a means to make
certain that his audience would listen to the truths he proclaimed.

Thus, the great preachers of the fourth and fifth centuries, while accomplished in rhetoric, were also firmly anchored in the Scriptures they were interpreting. This is why the vast majority of the sermons from that time that have
survived may well be called "expository sermons." On the other hand, these
are not mostly expository sermons in the sense of being content with explaining what Scripture says, for they also relate their preaching to the concrete
conditions and concerns of their audience and of the surrounding society.

The number of sermons we have from that time is enormous, particularly compared to the previous periods. The only large collection of homilies
or sermons that we have from those early years are those of Origen. With
important exceptions, most of his homilies are actually theological lectures
addressing the intellectual elite. In contrast, we have hundreds of sermons

from the centuries we are now studying. Most of them are the work of the most famous preachers of the time, but some also survive from those less famous. In a way, the very fame of those great preachers of the fourth and fifth centuries poses difficulties for today's historians, for there were people writing sermons and circulating them under the names of those famous preachers. Thus, while there is a vast number of homilies of whose authors there is no doubt, there are also others whose authorship is still a matter of debate among scholars. This is why, while we can assert that we have more than seven hundred homilies from Chrysostom, giving an exact number is impossible.

Another difficulty we have in approaching these sermons is that, since we have not been shaped by the same rhetorical tastes and their language is not ours, we frequently do not see these sermons' beauty. Sometimes the original text has cadences that cannot be repeated in translation. The same is true with many concatenations and plays on words that cannot be translated.

There is also the matter of the relationship between these written sermons and what was actually said from the pulpit. In some cases it would seem that we have a text that the preacher wrote before approaching the pulpit, at which point he may have added extemporaneous comments. In some other cases what we have are shorthand notes that someone took down. Some seem to have been written or corrected by the preacher himself after the actual preaching. In any case, the texts of most of the homilies that we have from people such as Basil, Chrysostom, Ambrose, Augustine, and Leo the Great were read and approved by those who had preached them.

Given the vast number of preachers and sermons from that time that we have, the best way to show the nature of preaching in the fourth and fifth centuries is to focus attention on some of the most important preachers and some of their sermons or homilies. Therefore, in the rest of this chapter we deal first with two of the great preachers in the Greek-speaking East—Basil the Great and John Chrysostom—and then turn to three figures in the Latin-speaking West—Ambrose, Augustine, and Leo the Great.

BASIL OF CAESAREA

As we have said, Basil grew up in a Christian home. After beginning a successful career in the fields of law and rhetoric, he turned to a monastic life. Eventually he became bishop of the city of his birth, Caesarea of Cappadocia. As a bishop, he was a staunch defender of the Nicene cause against the Arians. This led him to conflicts with the authorities that we cannot discuss here. The most notable homilies we have from him are a series of nine on the six days of creation, and another series on the Psalms—at least thirteen authentic ones, and

others that may or may not be his. To this should be added other homilies in
defense of orthodox faith, several on special occasions such as the anniversary
of a martyr's death, and others on diverse subjects. However, the best known
among his homilies are those that he preached at the time of the great famine
that struck Cappadocia and by the year 268 was causing many deaths while also
laying bare the economic injustices of that society.

As an example of Basil's preaching, we may take one of his homilies having
to do with the famine, based on the parable of the Rich Fool in Luke 12:16–
21. Basil begins his sermon by explaining that, while need is a fertile ground
for certain temptations, opulence also leads to other temptations. The question that the rich man in the parable asks himself, "What shall I do?," is the
same that a poor man asks himself. Regarding that question, Basil then asks,

> Who would not feel pity for a person so tormented? He is destroyed
> by abundance, worthy of compassion because of all he has, but even
> more worthy of compassion for what he desires, for his lands do not
> do him any good, but rather produce wailing; they bring him no
> abundance of fruit, but rather an abundance of concerns, pains and a
> terrible problem. (*Destruam horrea mea* 1; PG 31:264)

The poor man also asks himself the same question: "What shall I do?" But
when asking this question he is not thinking about an abundance of goods,
like the rich man with many barns, but rather about not having what is absolutely necessary. At this point Basil describes the situation of many among the
poor at that time of drought and failed crops who came to the place where
they had to sell their own children into slavery in order to be able to feed the
rest of the family:

> Finally, he looks at the children, thinking about taking them to the
> market and thus finding a way to stop death. He struggles between
> the need of hunger and his fatherly love. Hunger looms threaten-
> ing with a horrible death. But fatherly love calls him to die with his
> children. Again and again he makes a decision, and again and again he
> changes his mind. Finally he yields, overcome by need and by absolute
> scarcity. Now, what does he think? "Which of them shall I sell first?
> Which one would be more attractive to the seller of wheat? Do I take
> the eldest? If I do so I betray his primogeniture. Then, the youngest?
> I feel sorry for him, for his few years, that still does not know calam-
> ity. . . . Oh, oh, what a problem! What am I to do? Who will it be?
> On which of them shall I fall? I must have the soul of an animal! How
> can I deny my own nature? If I keep all of them, I will see all of them
> suffering. If I sell one, how will I be able to look at those I keep? . . .
> How shall I live at home without one of them? How would I dare set
> the table with the result of such a payment?" (*Destruam horrea mea* 4;
> PG 31:268–70)

Basil goes on to declare that the rich fool is wrong in thinking that he is only keeping what belongs to him. Such a miser is like one who arrives first at the theater and on that basis claims all the room that was actually prepared for others. Addressing then the rich, he says, "The bread you have belongs to the hungry, and that cape that you keep in your closet belongs to the naked, and the sandals that are rotting with you belong to the unshod, and the money you have hidden away belongs to the needy" (*Destruam horrea mea* 7; PG 31:277).

Even though we may imagine Basil thundering such words, in fact he did not have a strong voice, as later his friend and colleague Gregory of Nazianzen would recall. Sometimes when he was preaching he found it necessary to stop and ask people to be quiet so they could hear him. But what Basil preached resounded in his actions. We have a letter he wrote some four years after the beginning of the famine, addressing the provincial governor in defense of his action creating a refuge for the homeless, sick, and poor. As Basil describes that place, people found assistance and shelter there, and the poor were trained. The refuge itself included several buildings and grew to such an extent that it came to be known as the city of the poor until, after Basil's death, it was given the name of Basiliades in honor of its founder. More than a century later, historian Sozomenus could say that it still existed, and was famous as a refuge for the poor.

JOHN CHRYSOSTOM

The early life of John Chrysostom has already been outlined. Practically all his life was spent first in Antioch and then in Constantinople. After some time leading a monastic life, he was ordained in 386 and began preaching in Antioch. His fame as a preacher was such that in 397, when the bishop of Constantinople died, the emperor had Chrysostom kidnapped and carried to Constantinople, where in 398 he was made a bishop much against his will. From that point on, and until his death, he was involved in political struggles that he did not seek, but that he did not know how to avoid. His firm and clear preaching earned him repeated exiles, and he died in exile in 407. Three decades later his remains were taken back to Constantinople amid a solemn procession. Only in the following century, the sixth, did somebody give him the name by which he is known today: "Chrysostom"—mouth or speech of gold.

Among Chrysostom's homilies are a number of series dealing with various subjects. Probably the best known are the series *On the Statues, to the People of Antioch*. In that city there was a riot protesting taxes, and in the tumult, statues of Emperor Theodosius and his family were thrown down and destroyed. All feared that the emperor would order a massacre in the city. Panic reigned. In that situation, Chrysostom preached a series of homilies in which, while consoling the people, he also sought to provide them with guidance. There are also numerous homilies of Chrysostom on religious dates such as Christmas, Epiphany, Good Friday, and Easter Sunday.

However, the vast majority of the more than seven hundred homilies of Chrysostom that are still in existence are fairly detailed expositions of entire books of the Bible. The most extensive of these are two collections of homilies on Genesis that are in fact a commentary on the entire text of that book in sixty-seven homilies. There are also homilies on about a third of the Psalms, and several on Isaiah. Although this shows that he was interested in the Old Testament, most of his homilies are commentaries on the New Testament. His ninety homilies on the Gospel of Matthew are the oldest commentary on that book that we have. The same is true of his fifty-five homilies on the book of Acts. To this should be added seventy-four on Corinthians, twenty-four on Ephesians, fifteen on Philippians, twelve on Colossians, sixteen on Thessalonians, thirty-four on the pastoral Epistles, three on Philemon, and thirty-four on Hebrews. There is also a *Commentary on Galatians* that may well be an adaptation of another series of homilies.

Given such a wealth of sources, choosing one or two pieces that may represent the whole is practically impossible. Somewhat arbitrarily, we have chosen homily number 12 in the series about Matthew, which deals with Jesus' baptism. Chrysostom begins the sermon by commenting on the reason Jesus wished to be baptized by John. Chrysostom's words show that his Christology follows the lines of the Antioch school, with its emphasis on the humanity of Christ—although, naturally, without denying his divinity:

> The judge comes to be baptized with the subjects of the Lord, with the criminals who will be judged. Do not be bothered by this, for in these humiliations his exaltation is most manifest. He is the one who agreed to be born of the Virgin, to come in our nature, to be beaten with rods and crucified, and to suffer all the rest that he suffered: why do you marvel that he also agreed to be baptized, and to come to his servant [John the Baptist] hidden among the rest? Amazement should lie in this one thing: that being God, he would be made human. All the rest follows in the course of reason. (*Hom. on Matthew* 12.1; NPNF1 10:75)

Chrysostom then moves on to an apparent digression explaining why the Jews did not believe in Jesus and thought John to be superior to him. Then he asks himself why the heavens open at the baptism of Jesus. He answers, "So you would know that this is also done at your baptism. God is calling you to your country on high, and persuading you to have nothing to do with earth" (*Hom. on Matthew* 12.3; NPNF1 10:77). The descent of the Spirit as a dove is a sign of peace and hope, as was the dove in the story of Noah and the ark—in which we have an example of the typological interpretation that characterized the of Antioch school. Furthermore, this passage also gives Chrysostom opportunity for another theological digression in which he affirms the full divinity of the Holy Spirit, which some denied.

Having completed this exposition, Chrysostom moves to a practical application of what he has just said, inviting his hearers to "show forth a life worthy of the love of Him who calls you, and of your citizenship in that world. Having crucified this present world to yourself, show that you live with all strictness as citizens of the heavenly city" (*Hom. on Matthew* 12.5; NPNF1 10:78). In explaining the nature of that life, Chrysostom stresses a theme that appears in many of his sermons: the proper use of wealth and the rights of the needy. To take this into account is important not only for one's own salvation but also to make the Christian witness believable. Commenting on believers who are constantly trying to become wealthier, Chrysostom says,

> When unbelievers see that those who have participated in such great mysteries are serious about these earthly matters, how much more will they cling to them themselves. Therefore we are heaping much fire upon our heads. When we, who ought to teach them to despise everything that is visible, do ourselves urge them to lust after them, how is it possible for us to be saved, since we shall have to give account for the perdition of others? (*Hom. on Matthew* 12.5; NPNF1 10:79)

This sermon was preached in Antioch, where some among the most wealthy in the city severely criticized it. When Chrysostom was moved to Constantinople and began preaching in the great Cathedral of St. Sophia, his preaching resulted in mortal hatred from people in high places. As in any center of political power, the city was full of conspiracies, hatred, and envy. The powerful bishop of Alexandria, Theophilus, conspired against his colleague in Constantinople—a city adorned with palatial residences bespeaking enormous fortunes, but also teeming with impoverished multitudes who had come to the city because life had become impossible in their own lands, but now found that the opulence of the city was not for them. Chrysostom began a thorough program of reformation not only of the clergy but also of the city's social order, calling on the rich to leave aside their vanity and to respond to the needs of the poor. So that people could hear him better, rather than speak from the bishop's cathedra—a chair at one end of the cathedral where only the privileged could hear him clearly—he decided to preach from a pulpit near the center of the nave. Frequently he was accused of being against the rich, to which Chrysostom responded that he was actually in their favor, for he was trying to free them from the eternal fire awaiting them. At any rate, one may well imagine the response of Empress Eudoxia, who went to church surrounded by luxury, gold, and precious stones, on hearing words such as these:

> Would you like to appear beautiful and attractive? Be content with the way the creator made you. Why do you add to this bits of gold, as if you wished to amend God's creation? Clothe yourself with alms; clothe yourself with kindness; clothe yourself with modesty and humbleness. These are all more precious than gold. These make the attractive even more beautiful. These are able to make even the unattractive to be attractive. . . .
>
> That Egyptian woman of old was adorned. Joseph also was adorned. Which of them was more beautiful? When she was in the palace, and he was in the prison, he was naked, but clothed in the garments of chastity; she was clothed, but more unseemly than if she had been naked, because she lacked modesty. When you have adorned yourself excessively, O woman, you have become more unseemly than if you were naked, because you have stripped yourself of what would make you beautiful. . . . Why do you adorn yourself? Tell me: is it to please your husband? Then do it at home. But here the reverse is the case. . . . So you should put aside all your ornaments when you go to the market or to the church. Do not please your husband by the means that harlots use. Use those means which wives are free to employ. (*Homilies on Colossians* 10; NPNF1 13:308)

Words such as these, often repeated from the pulpit, would not be pleasing to the empress. Therefore it was not difficult for Chrysostom's enemies to create a series of incidents and misunderstandings that eventually led the famous preacher to death in exile.

Once again, as we saw in the case of Basil the Great, we have in Chrysostom an example of a preacher who bases what he says on the careful study and exposition of the biblical text, but at the same time is able to carry that text to its most difficult applications in his own context.

AMBROSE OF MILAN

The story of Augustine being led to conversion by Ambrose's preaching is one of many witnesses that we have regarding his eloquence and effectiveness. Ambrose's hymns—mentioned later—are proof of his literary ability. Unfortunately, a limited number of his sermons have survived, and therefore it is difficult to study his style of preaching. He compiled most of his sermons into biblical commentaries behind which one may still discover traces of the preaching style. Such is the case, for instance, of his *Commentary on Luke*, which was originally a series of sermons but is now a commentary of more traditional style. Furthermore, a good part of Ambrose's literary production is actually a series of translations from Greek—particularly from Basil—frequently sprinkled with his own commentaries.

This being said, we can still select one of his homilies that bears his personal imprint. The theme of this particular homily is the episode of Naboth's vineyard, which appears in 1 Kings 21. In contrast to most of the preaching of Basil and Chrysostom, Ambrose begins his sermon taking for granted that the congregation already knows the biblical narrative on which he will be speaking:

> The story of Naboth happened a long time ago, but it still happens every day. What rich man does not constantly covet what is not his? Which of them does not try to take from the poor their small possessions and invade the inheritance of their ancestors? Who is content with what is his? Is there a rich person whose covetousness is not inflamed by another's property? Therefore, there has been not only one Ahab; what is worse, every day more of them are born, and their seed is never extinguished. If one dies, more are born. . . . Nor is Naboth the only poor man killed. Every day his sacrifice is renewed. Every day the poor are killed. Overwhelmed by fear, the poor abandon their lands and flee with their children, who are a gauge of their love. Their wives follow, weeping, as though they were accompanying their husbands to the grave. (*On Naboth the Israelite* 1.1; PL 14:731)

In this sermon Ambrose is particularly addressing the rich in his congregation. He knows them well, for before being a bishop he ruled the province as its governor, and he constantly rubbed shoulders with the same potentates whom he now criticizes. He knows that they are inclined to think that they are better than the less fortunate, and therefore almost at the very beginning of his homily he says that "in their nature, there is no distinction among people either in birth or in death. All are equally begotten by nature, and likewise does nature receive all of them in their tombs" (*On Naboth the Israelite* 2; PL 14:732). God knows that the rich not only consider themselves fortunate, but are also ruled by their own goods. That is why Ambrose tells them,

> You probably think that in this life you have an abundance of things. O rich man, you do not know how poor you are, how needy you are because you think you are rich! The more you have the more you want. And if you get everything, you will still be poor. Greed burns in you, and its fire cannot be put out with profits. . . . Naboth did not desire the possessions of the rich man. But the king felt that he himself was poor because he did not have the vineyard of the poor man, his neighbor. Who is poorer, the one who was content with what he had or the other, who desired what was not his? Naboth is poor in property, but Ahab is poor in his heart. The desires of the rich

mean they do not know how to be poor. The greatest wealth is not enough to fill the heart of the greedy. (*On Naboth the Israelite* 1.4–5; PL 14:732–33)

At this point Ambrose turns to the biblical text itself, comparing the condition and attitudes of the king and of Naboth. The king who thinks that he is rich is actually miserable, for he will always feel in need of what he does not have. Naboth, who suffers the king's injustice, is actually rich with those things that really count: a clear conscience and love for others.

This is followed by a long disquisition in which Ambrose turns his attention to another story in Luke, that of the rich man who did not know what to do with all his grain and decided to build greater granaries. Although the words are different, much of what Ambrose says here agrees with what we have seen Basil say on the same passages. Furthermore, Ambrose even includes a searing description of the pain of a father who finds himself forced to sell his child so that his family can subsist. Clearly much of Ambrose's preaching is inspired by Basil's. For this reason, many scholars say that Ambrose, who was a wise manager of the church and faithful defender of truth and justice against the abuses of Emperor Theodosius, and who was certainly one of the greatest writers of his time, was not as original in his exegesis and biblical interpretation as were Basil and others in the Greek-speaking East. This, however, does not make him a lesser preacher, for he seeks to base what he says on what he can find in Scripture, often supporting it with other parallel passages—in this case, the story of the rich man who thinks he can solve his difficulties by building bigger barns.

Certainly, Ambrose does not lag behind the other preachers of his time when it comes to being able to apply the biblical text directly and clearly to the lives of those who hear him. At the end of this particular homily he addresses the rich among his audience and tells them that they deceive themselves if they simply seek to become richer and to aggrandize themselves, repeating what he said earlier: "The wantonness of the rich doesn't know how to be poor. The greatest wealth is not enough to fill the heart of the greedy" (*On Naboth the Israelite* 14.60; PL 14:755).

AUGUSTINE OF HIPPO

Much could be said about Augustine of Hippo—commonly known simply as St. Augustine. In the entire Latin-speaking ancient church, no one can compare to him as a theologian, as a writer, as a philosopher of history, or as a teacher of later generations. Even to this day, aside from the apostle

Paul, no other theologian has had a greater influence in the entire Western church—Catholic as well as Protestant. All the pages of this book could barely touch the spiritual anxieties; the intellectual doubts through which he passed on the way to faith; his debates with Manicheans, Donatists, Pelagians, and many others; the impact of his letters and sermons circulating throughout the Latin-speaking world; his far-reaching vision of the designs and work of God in history; and much more. Fortunately, here we deal only with a single aspect of his immense work, his preaching.

Even this task is too much to ask in these few pages. Among his sermons is an outstanding series of *Expositions on the Book of Psalms*, which is the only ancient commentary on the entire book of Psalms that we still have. Several similar series are not quite as significant. Even leaving aside those large collections of sermons, we have more than five hundred other sermons by Augustine—although one must point out that a vast number of sermons traditionally attributed to him may or may not be his. In general, his sermons are briefer than Chrysostom's. They are elegant but not with the preciousness of Chrysostom, who sought to reflect the cadences of the purest Attic Greek. Some of his sermons deal with the polemics already mentioned. However, most of them focus on the significance of Scripture and its teachings for the actual life of believers. In some cases, we have collections dealing with a single book of the Bible. However, most of his sermons—probably the most interesting—were preached on a particular occasion or a special date in the Christian calendar. Some sermons also deal with the life and work of a particular person whose memory was celebrated on that day—Peter, Paul, John the Baptist, and some of the martyrs. But in general his sermons—as those of many of his contemporaries—reflect the dates and locations celebrated and commemorated during the Christian year—Epiphany, Lent, Good Friday, Easter Sunday, and so on.

Once again, since examining all Augustine's preaching is impossible, we shall take as an example a brief sermon that he preached on the feast of the Ascension—number 263. This particular sermon has been selected partly because of its brevity, partly because it shows some important points of theology that were preached at the time, and partly because Augustine used images that his audience would understand clearly, even at the risk of scandalizing some of the more pious among them.

At the beginning of the sermon, Augustine places his preaching within the context of the period after Easter:

> We celebrated the resurrection of Jesus on Easter Sunday itself, and today we celebrate his ascension. For us, these two days are feasts because he rose from the dead in order to show that we too shall rise. And he ascended into heaven in order to protect us from there. Jesus is our Lord and Savior whether he hangs from a cross or reigns

in heaven. . . . It was necessary for him to come in a hidden fashion in order to be judged. Who would have dared to judge him if he had appeared in his full majesty? . . . But had he not died, then death would not have died. His victory was in overcoming the devil. The devil actually rejoiced when he seduced and delivered to death the first man. . . . but the death of the second man [the second Adam] broke the chains that had bound the first. The resurrection and ascension of our Lord Jesus Christ crowns the victory. (*Sermon* 263.1; PL 38:1209–10)

In these lines we see a clear expression of an understanding of the work of Christ that was typical in antiquity and remained dominant in much of the Eastern church, and later was generally marginalized or even forgotten in the West. Here Jesus is not presented primarily as a payment for human sin—on which Augustine would certainly agree—but rather as the conqueror of the devil. The human problem is not only that we owe God because of our sin, but also and above all that, by reason of that very sin, we have been enslaved to Satan and have no power to free ourselves. Remarkably, the victory of Jesus does not come through an ostentatious manifestation of his unlimited power, but rather through a combination of humility and weakness on the one hand and power and authority on the other. Augustine expresses it as follows:

His name was that of a lion, but he was sacrificed as a lamb. A lion in his strength, a lamb in his innocence. An invincible lion and a meek lamb. And this lamb, dying, with his own death destroyed the lion that was accosting us, seeking for prey—for the devil also is called a lion, not because he is strong, but because he is ferocious. (*Sermon* 263.1; PL 38:1210)

Augustine continues exploring the theme of Christ's victory through death and dares to use some images that today some might find surprising:

A lion against the lion; a lamb against the judges. Upon Christ's death, the devil rejoiced. But with that very death Christ conquered the devil. The devil ate the bait in the rat trap. He was satisfied with death, king of death, and this made him rejoice. But it was a bait. The cross of the Lord was the devil's rat trap, and the death of the Lord was the bait by which he was trapped. (*Sermon* 263.1; PL 38:1210)

On the basis of this victory of Jesus through his incarnation, death, and resurrection, Augustine then moves to the ascension itself:

Since he ascended without ceasing to be one of us, we now are with him in heaven—even though what we are promised has not yet been fulfilled in our body. He has already been exalted above the heavens. . . . We are not to lose hope of definitively living with the angels

> in heaven. This is why our union is signified by speaking of him as our head and of us as his body. When he ascends to heaven, we are not separated from him. If he has come down from heaven, it was not to close it to us, but rather he seems to be calling: "Be my members if you wish to come up to heaven." (*Sermon* 263.2; PL 38:1210)

This union of believers with Christ, and therefore the presence of believers with him in heaven, suggests to Augustine a short argument in which he declares that, since Scripture affirms that husband and wife are a single flesh, and since the church is the bride of Christ, thanks to being united with him, the groom of the church, in a way we are already with him in heaven.

Finally, Augustine refers to the forty days during which Jesus, after his resurrection, ate and drank with his disciples, and contrasts these with the other forty days he fasted in the desert. This parallelism suggests that those who now, so to speak, fast while living in the midst of a hostile world and of their own temptations are also preparing for the day that will no longer be of fasting, but of celebration. Augustine concludes, "let us fast to the vanities of the present age and let us feast on the future age. . . . Let us be nourished with the hope from above" (*Sermon* 263.4; PL 38:1212).

This brief sermon may serve as an example of Augustine's preaching. Several points should be noted: First, Augustine establishes a relationship between the various stages in the life of Jesus and their reflection in the Christian year. Second, when discussing the work of Christ, the emphasis is not on his being a payment to God—which this sermon does not even mention—but rather on the victory of Jesus Christ over the devil and over death. Third is the strong emphasis on the bond between the faithful and the risen and ascended Lord. Fourth, the moral dimensions of what is required now of believers are a result of the life and work of Jesus himself; that is, ethics is solidly grounded on theology. Finally, one must note the simplicity and clarity of the images that Augustine employs, even to the point of referring to the cross as a rat trap that captures the devil with the bait of Jesus' death.

LEO THE GREAT

Before closing the present chapter, we must look at another preacher who lived near the end of the period that we are considering, and who may well be considered its high point in preaching as well as a bridge with the time that would follow. This was Leo, bishop of Rome from 442 to 461, today appropriately known as "Leo the Great." His contribution to the field of theology is undeniable, for his *Dogmatic Epistle*—usually called "Leo's Tome"—was one of the most important documents leading to the christological definition of the Council of Chalcedon in 451. The most famous incident in his distinguished career took place in 452, when Attila and the Huns, after overrunning and sacking the north of Italy, were preparing to attack the city of Rome, which was practically defenseless. Leo and a delegation from the city went to meet with Attila. No one knows exactly what the conversation was or what Leo told him, but without any further explanation Attila decided to withdraw his troops. Precisely because of these great achievements, Leo's preaching is often eclipsed. Yet he was not only a great preacher but also had a clear understanding of the function of the homily within the whole of worship.

Leo's understanding of the purpose of preaching appears repeatedly in his homilies. Thus, preaching on Epiphany, he begins by summarizing what all already know, the story of the star, the Magi and their gifts, the actions of Herod and the massacre of the children; but then Leo moves on to say,

> Today we must fulfill our ministry of the word to draw your attention in such a way that with the aid of the Spirit of God, and following the paths of reason, we may come to understand what this feast means for the faithful of all times. We must not come to the conclusion that what is told here is so extraordinary that, following the order of time, we simply praise it as something that happened long ago. (*Sermon* 38.1; PL 54:250)

On another occasion, now preaching on the passion of the Lord, Leo explains what he believes to be his task in preaching:

> We have come to the Feast of the Lord's passion, for which we have longed. Indeed, the whole world may well desire it. But we cannot keep silent even in the midst of our spiritual joys. Though it is difficult to speak often on the same topic and do so worthily and appropriately, yet the priest is not free to withhold from the people instruction by means of a sermon on this great mystery of God's mercy. The subject itself is unspeakable. Therefore the priest has some comfort, for what is said cannot completely fail when what is said can never be enough. (*Sermon* 62.1; NPNF2 12:173)

Guided by this vision of the task of preaching, Leo's sermons do not shine for their erudition, nor do they express profound exegetical studies—even though such studies are certainly behind his own preaching. They are both simple and elegant. Leo knew classical Latin rhetoric, and he mastered its resources in many ways, particularly in the cadence of some of his paragraphs. On the basis of the same vision, his sermons always take into account their liturgical context: in the case of particular feasts or observances, they relate to the meaning of those occasions, and they connect the biblical text with the Communion that would follow the homily. One can well say that Leo's homily prepares for Communion, and the Communion that follows it is a practice or reflection of what was announced in the homily.

This connection between preaching and sacraments may be seen, for instance, in his homilies on the passion. In one of them he says,

> The renunciation of the devil and the affirmation of belief in God, the passing from the old state into newness of life, the casting off of the earthly image and putting on of the heavenly form—all this is a form of dying and rising again, whereby the one who is received by Christ and receives Christ is not the same after as before coming to the font, because the body of the regenerate becomes the flesh of the Crucified. . . .
>
> Partaking of the body and blood of Christ does nothing less than transform us into that which we receive, so that in everything, in the spirit as well as in the flesh, we take with us this one in whom we died, in whom we were buried and in whom we have risen. . . . He, with the Father and the Holy Spirit, lives and reigns forever and ever. Amen. (*Sermon* 63.6–7; NPNF2 12:177)

Another homily, now on the transfiguration of Jesus, shows how Leo intertwines his preaching with matters of great theological significance. In this case, we see him using the story of the transfiguration in order to expound, on the one hand, the doctrine of the two natures in Christ and their perfect union, and on the other, Trinitarian doctrine. As to the first, Leo declares that the story of the transfiguration "invites us to understand a great mystery." The transfiguration took place to show Christ's divine nature in his human flesh,

> so that they would acknowledge him as the only-begotten Son of God and as the Son of Man, since one of these without the other would not have been sufficient for salvation. It was equally dangerous to believe that our Lord Jesus Christ was only God, and not human, as to think that he was not God, but only human. Both truths had to be confessed: that in him true divinity was joined with humanity, and true humanity with divinity. (*Sermon* 51.1; NPNF2 12:162)

This doctrine of the two natures of Christ is important not only from the dogmatic or theological point of view, but also in practice: "it was necessary for the faith of the apostles that, having risen to the glory to confess his divinity, would not then imagine that the humiliations of human nature were unworthy of an impassible God" (*Sermon* 51.2; NPNF2 12:162).

As to the second, Trinitarian doctrine, Leo points to the voice from heaven that announces that Jesus is "my beloved Son." This witness from on high serves to prove both the union of the divine persons and their distinction:

When the Father said: "This is my beloved Son, in whom I am well-pleased. Listen to him!" is he not saying clearly: "This is my Son, who from me receives and with me has an eternal being"? For the begetter is not before the begotten, nor is the begotten after the begetter. This is my Son. We are not divided in divinity. We are not divided in power. We are not distinct in eternity. This is my Son, not adopted, but true; not created from another source, but begotten of me. He was not made like me from another nature, but born equal to me of my nature. "This is my Son," "through whom all things were made. Without him nothing was made. He does what I do, and whatever I do he also does, for he is inseparably joined with me." (*Sermon* 52.6; NPNF2 12:164)

At the end of the homily, Leo takes all of this to the practical dimensions of Christian life, calling those who hear him to be ready to "suffer for justice" and also to be certain that they will "receive the promised reward." This can be done because we must constantly hear the words of pleasure that the Father pronounced over the incarnate Son.

The five preachers whom we have discussed in the present chapter were not the only great preachers of that time, which many rightfully consider the golden age of Christian homiletics. In brief, what distinguishes these and the many other great preachers who were their contemporaries are their careful exposition of Scripture, their ability to relate doctrine with life, the elegant simplicity of many of their sermons, and the connection they show between the biblical text on the one hand and the rest of worship on the other—baptism, Communion, and special dates such as Christmas, Epiphany, Lent, and more.

14

Surrounding Baptism

THE CATECHUMENATE

In part 2, dealing with the period before Constantine, we saw the importance of the catechumenate in preparation for baptism. In most cases this preparation took at least three years, during which leaders from among the baptized believers guided the catechumens in the study of doctrine and the practice of Christian living. This system continued and became even more necessary after Constantine's conversion, when ever-growing multitudes requested baptism. This led almost all the great teachers of the church to produce works discussing both the methodology in catechetical teaching and its content. On the methodology itself, Gregory of Nyssa wrote,

> The cure must be adapted to the kind of disease. You will not overcome by the same methods the polytheism of the Greek and the unbelief of the Jew regarding the Only-begotten God. As to those who have wandered into heresy, the same arguments will not be effective in overcoming various erroneous beliefs about the tenets of the faith. (*Great Catechism* prologue; NPNF2 5:474)

Several decades later, now no longer in Cappadocia, as Gregory, but now in North Africa, Augustine received a request from a Carthaginian deacon by the name of Deogratias, who asked the famous teacher to give him advice as to how he was to instruct those who were under his guidance. In response to the request, Augustine wrote a treatise titled *On Catechizing the Uninstructed*. Augustine summarizes the concerns of Deogratias: "You confess and complain that often, when you are teaching for a long period of time, you have become profitless and distasteful, even to yourself. The learner must feel the same way" (*On Catechizing* 1.1; NPNF1 3:283).

To begin with, Augustine tells Deogratias that he should not be too concerned with this, for he himself has had the same experience. Probably this is not due to the inability of the teacher, but rather to his desire that all who hear will learn truly important matters, and that these matters are much higher than can be expressed. Augustine begins his response by presenting a general picture of the purpose of the instruction to be imparted to catechumens, and then summarizing the content of that instruction itself. This is not the place to analyze that summary of doctrine, but what Augustine says about the purpose of instruction itself must be noted. According to him, the goal of a teacher should not be to have catechumens learn every detail or to memorize the Bible, but rather that they have a wide vision of the entire history leading from creation to the present, all of it pointing to the final goal of Christian life, which is love. Augustine explains completion of the instruction of catechists:

> The lesson is complete when each person is catechized, for example, on what is written: "In the beginning God created the heaven and the earth," and from there to the present times of the church. It is not necessary for them to learn all the details, or to commit to memory the entire Pentateuch through Acts. We should not lecture on all these details or expound them. There is not time for that, and there is no need. (*On Catechizing* 3.5; NPNF1 3:285)

As we have seen, by this time it was customary for the bishop to be responsible for the last weeks of instruction of catechumens before the baptism, which normally took place on Easter Sunday. This final period of instruction would become increasingly uniform, eventually resulting in the forty days that we know as Lent. However, that uniformity took some time to develop. For instance, according to Ambrose, in the church of Milan catechumens were to begin their final instruction on Epiphany (January 6), and at that point they were marked as candidates for baptism by the sign of the cross. Elsewhere the process was different, but there was always a special moment in which, with rites such as the sign of the cross on the forehead, exorcisms, and blessings, the catechumens who were in the final steps of preparation for baptism were marked as such. Normally, before entering this last step in the catechumenate, the person had to go through an exam or scrutiny to determine readiness for baptism. The Galician pilgrim Egeria (*Diary of a Pilgrimage*, trans. George E. Gingras [ACW 38; New York: Newman Press, 1970]) says that in Jerusalem those who were to be baptized had to appear before the bishop and the presbyters several weeks before Easter Sunday, each accompanied by a sponsor—what today we call a godfather or godmother. (Egeria literally says that males are to be accompanied by their "fathers," and females by their "mothers," but most historians agree that this actually refers to those who had accompanied them during the catechumenate.) There, before the bishop and the elders, the life of the candidate was scrutinized, and those who were considered unworthy were rejected. The rest would continue in the process of preparation for baptism and were now called *competentes* among Latin-speaking Christians and *phōtizomenoi* (those in the process of illumination) among Greek-speaking believers.

As to the content of the teaching itself during that period, we have several contemporary witnesses. The most valuable among them is a series of lectures by Cyril of Jerusalem. These lectures are not addressed to people who know nothing about the faith, but rather to catechumens who for years have attended the service of the Word and who have also been under the guidance of other believers who have instructed them on matters of doctrine and the sort of life Christians are to lead. Addressing these believers, Cyril notes the long path they have traveled, seemingly referring also to the beginning of spring and to the rites by which the catechumens were declared to be almost ready for baptism—rites that, at least in Jerusalem, seem to have included a procession with torches:

> Already there is an odor of blessedness upon you, who are soon to be enlightened. Already you are gathering the spiritual flowers to weave heavenly crowns. Already the fragrance of the Holy Spirit has breathed upon you. Already you have gathered in the vestibule of the King's palace. May you be led in also by the King! For blossoms have now appeared upon the trees; may the fruit also be found perfect! Thus far there has been an entering of your names, a call to service; you have been given torches for the bridal train. You have a longing for heavenly citizenship, a good purpose, and the hope which that brings. (*Catechetical Lectures* prologue, 1; NPNF2 7:1)

Cyril also makes it clear that the teachings he is about to impart are not for all, but only for those who are or are about to be baptized:

> These Catechetical Lectures are for those who are to be enlightened. You may lend them to candidates for baptism and to believers who are already baptized so they may read them. But you are not to give them to catechumens or to any others who are not Christians. You shall answer to the Lord for this. And if you make a copy, write this at the beginning, as in the sight of the Lord. (*Catechetical Lectures* prologue, 17; NPNF2 7:7)

According to Cyril, this time before Easter Sunday, as these people prepare for baptism, should be a time of confession, and therefore those who hear him should acknowledge their sin and be constant in attending the lectures to learn what they would be told, for these "are spoken not only for your ears but so that by faith you may seal them up in your memory" (*Catechetical Lectures* 1; NPNF2 7:7). Continuing with that subject, the second lecture deals mostly with repentance and the forgiveness of sins, as well as with temptations. The third finally broaches the subject of baptism, and the fourth opens a series of three lectures dealing with some of the main points of Christian doctrine—particularly the one God, the heresies that believers will have to face, and why such views are to be rejected. In the seventh lecture Cyril begins an exposition of the Nicene Creed. This series on the creed ends with lecture 18. In view of what has been explained earlier regarding the giving and returning of the creed, the purpose of these lectures was for catechumens to be able to learn, affirm, and "return" the creed to the bishop before their baptism. This was done in preparation for baptism itself, where once again—now more formally—they would be asked to confess their faith on the basis of the creed. Therefore, this other lecture (19) was delivered shortly before Easter Sunday—probably in the evening of Good Friday or early on Saturday. The rest of the lectures would be delivered after baptism, and they would explain to the baptized the meaning and significance of what had happened during the rite. We return to this topic when dealing with baptism itself.

The catechumenate reached its apex during the period we are now studying, when the great teachers who have been mentioned and many others had the time and resources to prepare their catechetical lectures, and when large numbers seeking baptism attended them. At the same time, two new factors were being introduced that led to the decline and eventually the practical disappearance of the catechumenate. The first was simply the church's inability to absorb and adequately prepare the growing number of people asking to join it. During the second and third centuries, the church was growing rapidly, but not as rapidly as in the fourth, and therefore it was still possible to select from among its members people who could be charged with teaching the catechumens, and to train them for that task. The task of these teachers with the catechumens included, if at all possible, visiting them at home and at work, and in general guiding their daily life, particularly when they faced difficult moral decisions. During much of the fourth century this continued thanks to a generation that had been shaped through a strict catechetical formation when the church was still persecuted or at least threatened with persecution. However, as the fourth century advanced, and more and more people wished to join the church, giving them instruction and guidance with the same continuity and intensity was no longer possible. When, in the 380s, Christianity became the religion of the empire, the church was flooded with people seeking baptism, and under the pressure of that flood the catechetical system had to give way. The second factor leading to the decline of the catechumenate was the custom of baptizing the infant children of Christian parents. As we have seen, the baptism of infants was probably practiced at least as early as the last decades of the second century, and certainly by the third. Now such baptisms became increasingly common. When an adult decided to join the church, it was possible to require a period of learning before being baptized. Such training could obviously not be required of infants. When children baptized as infants grew up, it was more difficult to require that they go through a process of catechetical instruction. One consequence of this situation in the West was the development of confirmation, which eventually some considered a sacrament.

Although this carries us far beyond the limits of our study, a word seems appropriate about the origins of what some churches consider the "sacrament of confirmation." As we have seen, from a very early time it was customary, when neophytes emerged from the waters of baptism, to anoint them and call for the presence of the Holy Spirit over them. This anointing and the laying on of hands that went with it were normally the prerogative of the bishop. In the third century, amid the controversies regarding whether heretics who abandoned their heresy and wished to return to the church were to be rebaptized or not, the notion developed that, while any baptism with water and in the name of the Trinity was valid, no matter who administered it, the anointing that followed baptism, with invocation of the Spirit, is the bishop's prerogative. Those who thought that converted heretics should not be rebaptized insisted that they should go before the bishop so that he could perform the anointing that usually followed baptism itself. Thus, already by the third century the tendency began developing to separate baptism from this other action of anointing the baptized, laying hands on them, and invoking the presence of the Holy Spirit over them. Later, in 366, Hilary of Poitiers seems to refer to baptism and to the laying on of hands and invocation of the Holy Spirit as two separate sacraments. Similar phrases appear in Cyril of Jerusalem and others.

In a synod gathered in Spain early in the fourth century, it was decided that people who had been baptized by a layman or a deacon because of urgent need should go to the bishop as soon as possible to have the baptism completed by the laying on of hands. The reference to an "urgent need" is a result of the notion that had become common in the West, that every child had to be baptized as soon as possible, especially if in danger of death, for otherwise he or she could not be saved. Within the new circumstances that were developing, the tendency to separate baptism from the anointing and the laying on of hands became a way to make certain that those who had been baptized as infants would have a later occasion when they would be required to reaffirm

their faith and to learn at least part of what adult catechumens did while preparing for baptism. Therefore, while in an earlier time baptism had sufficed
to allow someone to attend Communion, in the Western church the notion
emerged that access to Communion should be forbidden to those who had not
yet received the anointing and laying on of hands that came to be called "confirmation." Because of this development—which took place mostly beyond the
chronological limits of our study—the Roman Catholic Church began forbidding children to participate in Communion until they had passed through
a catechetical process and confirmed their faith and commitment that other
adults had made for them at the time of their baptism. Then, after this act
of confirmation, they would finally be allowed their first Communion. Over
against this, the Eastern churches continued—and still continue—the ancient
custom of offering both the anointing and Communion to the newly baptized,
no matter what age. This also meant that in the Western church it became
customary for the bishop to officiate at a confirmation, while in the Eastern
churches, where baptism was still conjoined with the anointing and the laying
on of hands, a priest could baptize and anoint a person at the same time.

BAPTISMAL RITES

Although this may surprise us today, in ancient times catechumens usually
were told little about what would happen in their baptism—or in Communion, when they would finally be allowed to take part in it. This is why Cyril
includes at the beginning of his lectures a warning that his writings should
not be circulated among those who were not already baptized or at least are
catechumens about to be baptized. Egeria mentions the same practice when
she says that, after their baptism, the neophytes gathered in the Church of
the Resurrection (in Western tradition, the Church of the Holy Sepulcher) to
have the bishop explain to them the meaning of the sacraments. She adds that
many other people who were already baptized also came to these explanations, but that anyone who was not baptized was prohibited from attending.
During the first week after their baptism, those recently baptized and still
in the process of receiving instruction about baptism and Communion were
generally known as "infants," and they were distinguished from the rest of the
congregation in that they still wore the white robes that they began wearing
upon emerging from the baptismal waters. The custom of spending the next
week instructing these infants seems to have been rather universal. While at
one end of the Mediterranean, Cyril devoted five lectures to this purpose,
hundreds of miles away, in what is now Tunisia, Augustine was telling the
recently baptized,

These days after the passion of our Lord, when we sing alleluia to God, are for us a time of feasting and rejoicing. This continues on to Pentecost, the day on which the promised Holy Spirit came from heaven. Within those days, the seven or eight where we are now, are dedicated to the sacraments that the newly born have received. Those who until now were *competentes* are now infants. . . . They are called infants because those that earlier were born to the world now have been born to Christ. (*Sermon* 228.1)

What Egeria says about teaching after baptism exactly agrees with what we see in Cyril's lectures. Among those lectures, those to be delivered after baptism are commonly called the "mystagogical" lectures, for they have to do with the "mysteries" (sacraments) of baptism and Communion. In them Cyril explains to the recently baptized the meaning of the rites that they have undergone. His words at the beginning of the first of these mystagogical lectures—number 19 in the entire series—clearly state the context and purpose of what Cyril is about to say:

O true-born and dearly beloved children of the church, I have long wanted to teach you about these spiritual and heavenly Mysteries. I knew, however, that seeing is far more persuasive than hearing. I waited for this time so that I would find you more open to the influence of my words because of your present experience, and I might now lead you by the hand into the brighter and more fragrant meadow of the paradise now before us. This is especially possible because you have been made fit to receive the more sacred Mysteries after you were found worthy of divine and life-giving baptism. It remains to set before you a table of the more perfect instruction. Therefore, let us now teach you these things exactly, so that you may know what are the effects wrought upon you on that evening of your baptism. (*Catechetical Lectures* 19.1; NPNF2 7:144)

This is important for us, for these lectures are among the most complete documents in which the process of baptism is described. They guide us in our attempt to make a similar description—although always with the caveat that there are multiple signs that these rites were not the same everywhere, and therefore the witness of other authors is also important.

Cyril begins by reminding his audience that when they entered the building where they were to be baptized they were told to face west and then, extending their hand as if they were repulsing Satan, they would say, "I renounce thee, Satan." In so doing, they were telling Satan, "We fear your power no longer; for Christ has overthrown it. Christ became a partaker with me of flesh and blood so that he might by death destroy death, and I might not be subject to bondage for ever" (*Catechetical Lectures* 19.4; NPNF2 7:145). Likewise, they renounced not only the devil but also his works and his pomp. Chrysostom seems to show a different practice, for he places the renunciations on Good Friday at three o'clock in the afternoon, the hour of the crucifixion. Also, while Cyril and others say that the renunciations take place while people are standing, Chrysostom and Theodore of Mopsuestia say that the candidates should be kneeling. Here too, after the renunciations, candidates are to turn to the east and proclaim their faith in Jesus Christ.

Cyril continues his narrative telling the recently baptized that they then disrobed, imitating Christ, who went naked to the cross. This nakedness of those preparing to receive baptism reflects the original innocence of Adam, who was naked in the garden and was not ashamed. Now that they were nude, the candidates were anointed from head to foot with the "oil of exorcism." (There are other references to this oil, at least beginning in the third century. It was a receptacle that had been blessed before employing it to anoint the person.) This anointing was a sign that the baptized had been cut off from the old olive tree and grafted into the good tree of Israel.

After this anointing, they were finally taken to the water just as Christ was taken from the cross to the tomb. The candidates for baptism were asked, one more time, whether they believed in the Father, the Son, and the Holy Spirit, and they were submerged three times, as a symbol of the time that Jesus spent under the earth. Chrysostom and Theodore seem to differ from Cyril in another detail here, for according to them the person performing the baptism should use the passive voice (not "I baptize you," but "You are baptized") as a sign that it is God, and not this person, who actually baptizes. Cyril continues his narrative saying that as they were being submerged in the water they were dying in order to be born again, so that "at the exact same moment you were both dying and being born; and that water of salvation was at once your grave and your mother" (*Catechetical Lectures* 20.4; NPNF2 7:148). This leads Cyril to consider what happens in baptism:

> O strange and unimaginable thing! We did not really die. We were not really buried. We were not really crucified and raised again. Our imitation was as a type, and our salvation is a reality. Christ was actually crucified, and actually buried, and truly rose again. And all these things he has freely bestowed upon us, so that we, sharing his sufferings by imitation, might gain salvation in reality. O surpassing loving-kindness! Christ received nails in his undefiled hands and feet, and suffered anguish; while on me, without pain or toil, by the fellowship of his suffering, he freely bestows salvation. (*Catechetical Lectures* 20.5; NPNF2 7:148)

Baptism was then followed by another anointing, which now made the believers "Christians"—that is, "anointed ones." This anointing, with perfumed oil from another receptacle that had been blessed separately, was now applied to the forehead, the ears, the nose, and the breast. Cyril explains the meaning of each of these, saying that the anointing on the forehead is a sign that one now belongs to Christ, anointing the ears makes them capable to listen to the teachings of the mysteries, being anointed on the nose is a reminder that we are to be a pleasant perfume before the Lord, and anointing the breast strengthens the believer with the "breastplate of justice."

At this point, baptism is complete, and Cyril now moves to what took place when those newly baptized were able to partake of Communion the very first time. This is similar to what Hippolytus says, and we already discussed the issue in chapter 10. Still, practices were not always the same everywhere. For instance, from Ambrose (*On the Sacraments* 6) we learn that in Milan it was customary to wash the feet of the newly baptized as they were received into the Communion service. This practice continued in Milan for several centuries.

Not all the lectures and explanations that the recently baptized received while they were "infants" were the same as Cyril's. What seems to have been a common characteristic was their concern for giving the neophytes not only an intellectual understanding of the significance of baptism and Communion, but also a deeper existential experience. This may be seen in Augustine's sermons addressing the "infants" in Hippo. In one of those sermons, preached on an Easter day, and therefore when the "infants" had just shared in Communion for the first time, Augustine deals with various elements of the baptismal rite (fasting, exorcism, baptism itself, and anointing):

> By these means [the bread and the wine] the Lord wished to give us his body and blood, which he poured out for the remission of our sins. If you have received it worthily, now you are what you have received. Thus, the apostle says: "We are many; but only one bread, one body." Behold what the sacrament of the table has shown: "We are many; but only one bread, one body." This bread tells you that you must love unity. Was this bread made of only one grain? Were there not many grains of wheat? Before they became bread they were separate. They were joined by means of water after being crushed. Unless it is crushed and kneaded with water, it would never become what we call bread. The same has happened to you: through the humiliation of fasting and the rite of exorcism you have been crushed. Then came baptism, and you were kneaded with water to become bread. But there is still the fire, without which there can be no bread. What is the meaning of the fire, the anointing with oil? Since oil feeds fire, it is a sign of the Holy Spirit. . . . Be alert, and remember that in Pentecost the Holy Spirit will come. And see how he will come: in tongues of fire. He inspires love. He should make us burn for God and despise the world. He will burn our straw and purify our hearts as if of gold.

After water comes the Holy Spirit, which is fire, and you become
bread, which is the body of Christ. And thus in a way unity is shown.
(*Sermon* 227; BAC 447:285–86)

THE MEANING OF BAPTISM

During this period, while the number of baptisms increased, the images
expressing their significance and meaning also multiplied. This may be clearly
seen in a sermon that Gregory of Nazianzen preached on Epiphany in the
year 381—which celebrated not only the story of the Magi but also the miracle in Cana and the baptism of the Lord. This third element in the celebration
of Epiphany leads Gregory to turn his attention to baptism:

> We call it: the gift, the grace, baptism, unction, illumination, the
> clothing of immortality, the bath of regeneration, the seal, and every-
> thing that is honorable. We call it the gift, because it is given to us in
> return for nothing on our part; grace, because it is conferred even on
> debtors; baptism, because sin is buried with it in the water; unction, as
> priestly and royal, for that is who was anointed; illumination, because
> of its splendor; clothing of immortality, because it hides our shame;
> the bath, because it washes us; the seal, because it preserves us, and is
> also the sign of dominion. (*Oration* 40.4; NPNF2 7:360)

Cyril of Jerusalem also uses similar images, indicating that baptism is "a ransom of captives, a remission of offences, a death of sin, a new birth of the soul;
a garment of light, a holy indissoluble seal, a chariot to heaven, the delight
of paradise, a welcome into the kingdom, the gift of adoption" (*Catechetical
Lecture* procatechesis, 16; NPNF2 7:5).

Even this list of images does not suffice to reflect all that is said during the
fourth century regarding baptism. The most common image, which Gregory
does not mention here but Cyril does, relates baptism to the new birth of
which Jesus speaks in John 3. This image of baptism in connection with the
new birth appears repeatedly throughout this period, but always with strong
words relating it to death to the old life, newness of life, and the hope of resurrection. Commenting on Romans 6:3–7, Theodore of Mopsuestia declares
that we are baptized in imitation of Jesus' death and resurrection, so that our
hope of a new life and a final resurrection is constantly based on the memory
of Jesus' death and resurrection, and also of our own death to the old self in
baptism. Only because in baptism we have shared in the death of Jesus will we
in the final day share in his resurrection. In other words, the new birth is not
just an experience of moving to a higher level of life, but also the experience
of dying to the former life and its values.

In his sermons, Chrysostom frequently uses the image of baptism as a marriage. In marriage, as it was understood then, the bride left her family in order to join her husband's family. Likewise, says Chrysostom, when one is baptized, one leaves the former common humanity and joins a new family whose head is Christ. This is another way of expressing what we have already found from New Testament times: humanity is like a body whose head is Adam, and the church is a new humanity whose head is Christ. This emphasis on baptism, not as a personal experience but rather as becoming part of a new reality, was beginning to disappear in the West, while most of the main theologians of the East still stressed it. One of them was Theodore of Mopsuestia, who says that what happens in baptism is that one becomes a member of this body whose head is Christ—and that, precisely because Christ took human nature, now humans, by being joined to him through baptism, can partake of the divine nature. Theodore expresses this saying that, by the power of the Holy Spirit, all who are baptized become a single body whose head is Christ. This is similar to what Cyril says of baptism as being grafted into the true olive tree.

Several authors speak of baptism as a "seal." This image is taken mostly from the seal that was used to mark a property—including slaves. There is a certain parallelism between this and the image of the baptized as part of the new humanity whose head is Christ. On renouncing Satan and all his works, and turning eastward to proclaim themselves servants of Christ, those who were about to be baptized, who had already been exorcised, now declared themselves to be servants or slaves, no longer of Satan, but of Christ. Theodore of Mopsuestia speaks at length of baptism as a liberation from the yoke of Satan. He and many others speak of the anointing that takes place upon emerging from the baptismal waters as a seal of possession, the mark of Christ. The slave who used to bear the mark of Satan now bears the seal of Christ. All of this reflects an emphasis on Christ as conqueror of Satan that would soon begin disappearing in Western theology, but would continue being central in much Eastern theology as well as in the worship of the entire church. Some interpreted the anointing of the entire body before entering the waters as similar to the anointing of athletes' bodies before going into the arena, saying that one who renounced Satan and entered the waters of baptism did so as an athlete who was about to face a powerful enemy. although always supported by an even more powerful Lord.

In a way, this image of baptism as a seal counteracted some of the deficiencies of the image of baptism as a washing. If what happens during baptism is that one is cleansed of all previous sin, there is always the problem of sins committed after baptism. The emphasis in the Western church on the image of baptism as a washing resulted in a constant preoccupation with sins committed after baptism, and eventually led to the development of the penitential system. In the East, although baptism was certainly seen also as a washing from sin, the emphasis was more on baptism as a seal of possession claiming that the baptized person now belonged to Christ, and therefore giving the person strength to face not only previous sins but also the many temptations and sins that would follow baptism. Thus, Gregory of Nazianzen tells his audience,

> If you have been fortified with the seal; if you have secured yourself with the best and strongest of all aids, then you have been signed both in body and soul with the unction with which Israel was of old signed with blood so that the firstborn were guarded that night. Therefore, what can happen to you? What has been done for you? (*Oration* 40.15; NPNF2 7:364)

In order to explain this, Gregory takes as an example a sheep in a flock. A sheep that does not have its owner's mark can easily be stolen. But a sheep with that mark can sleep peacefully knowing to whom it belongs. Therefore, "If you lose all things, or they are taken from you violently: money, possessions, thrones, distinctions, and everything else that belongs to this earthly turmoil; you will still be able to lay down your life in safety" (*Oration* 40.15; NPNF2 7:364). In one of his homilies exhorting his audience not to postpone baptism, Basil the Great says practically the same as his friend Gregory of Nazianzen, also taking the sheep in the flock as an example of the power of baptism's seal, and also relating baptism to the seal of the blood of a lamb on the houses of the children of Israel in Egypt.

This takes us to the relationship between baptism and Passover, when the angel of the Lord passed over the firstborn of Israel. Basil himself, in the homily to which we have just referred, declares that Israel could not be free from sorrow without crossing the sea into the desert, and that the same is true of those who now are listening to Basil's preaching, for without crossing the waters of baptism they cannot escape from the tyranny of Satan. This typological interpretation, relating the exodus from Egypt to liberation from the slavery of the evil one, is a common theme among writers and preachers in the fourth century. Cyril of Jerusalem says it quite strongly: "If the lamb under Moses drove the destroyer far away, then did not much more the Lamb of God, who takes away the sin of the world, deliver us from our sins?" (*Catechetical Lectures* 13.3; NPNF2 7:82). Later, in the first of his mystagogical lectures, Cyril would explain this more fully:

> Now turn from the old to the new; from the figure to the reality. There we have Moses sent from God to Egypt; here Christ is sent forth from his Father into the world. There, Moses was sent so that he might lead an afflicted people out of Egypt; here Christ is sent so that he might rescue those who are oppressed in the world under

sin. There, the blood of a lamb was the spell against the destroyer; here, the blood of the Lamb without blemish, Jesus Christ, is made the charm to scare evil spirits. There, the tyrant was pursuing that ancient people even to the sea; and here, the daring and shameless spirit, the author of evil, was following you even to the very streams of salvation. The tyrant of old was drowned in the sea; and this present one disappears in the waters of salvation. (*Catechetical Lectures* 19.3; NPNF2 7:144–45)

This typology relating the history of Israel and its liberation from Egypt to baptism led to a theme that first appears in the fourth century, and from that point on became common in discussions regarding the nature of baptism. That theme is the relation between circumcision and baptism. John Chrysostom, in one of many passages showing his anti-Jewish prejudice, calls his congregation not to be like the Jews, whose circumcision was contaminated because they joined sinful people, but rather, "since we are circumcised through baptism, let us keep watch over our behavior" (*Homily* 45.17). Basil makes the same connection, now using it as a reason not to postpone baptism. If the Jews did not postpone circumcision, neither should Christians postpone their baptism.

In considering the use of this typology of circumcision as a way to understand baptism, two points should be considered: The first is that circumcision was an act whereby the newly born was acknowledged and added as part of the people of Israel. The same was true about baptism from an early date. Baptism was not simply a matter of the salvation of the person being baptized, for by means of that water the person was added to this people of God, to this body of Christ that is the church. Thus, the image of baptism as a new circumcision served to stress the corporate rather than individualistic nature of Christian faith. The second point regarding thinking about the circumcision as a type or figure of baptism is that, as may be seen in the words of Basil, this typology was employed in order to oppose the practice of delaying baptism— particularly rejecting "clinical" baptism, which took place on one's deathbed, but also affirming the baptism of newly born infants. From that point on, many people would use the relationship between baptism and circumcision as an argument favoring infant baptism.

All of this was connected with another theme that appeared earlier, but becomes common and in some cases even dominant among authors in the fourth century: baptism as necessary for salvation. Cyril of Jerusalem puts it starkly: "If any are not baptized they do not have salvation. The only exception is the martyrs, and they would receive the kingdom even if they were not baptized" (*Catechetical Lectures* 3.10; NPNF2 7:16). Following the same line of typological relationship between baptism and circumcision, Basil declares that just as the children of Israel could not be free without crossing the sea, so today can believers escape from the tyranny of the devil only by going through the waters. This notion led to what were often called "emergency" baptisms: if somebody, either recently born or already an adult, was in danger of dying without being baptized, baptism was immediately administered.

The notion that baptism is necessary for salvation leads directly to the matter of when and how baptism is valid. We have seen that the validity of the baptism of heretics was debated in the third century, particularly in the dispute between Cyprian of Carthage and Stephen of Rome. In the fifth century the problem emerged again, although now not so much in connection with the baptism of heretics, but rather in connection with the character of the person who administers baptism. If a baptism's validity depends on the sanctity of the one administering it, how can believers trust that they have been truly baptized? Gregory of Nazianzen declares that what is important in baptism is God's grace, so the virtue or holiness of the person administering it has no connection with the validity of baptism itself. The same reasoning was used to support the preference of some to pronounce the baptismal formula in the passive voice, not "I baptize you," but rather "You are baptized"—that is, baptism is not my work in baptizing you, but God's work.

All this consideration led to the conclusion that baptism is valid whenever it is done with water and in the name of the Trinity. An extreme consequence of such a view is seen in an anecdote—probably apocryphal—that Rufinus tells about Athanasius. According to that anecdote, Bishop Alexander of Alexandria had invited some clergymen to dine with him by the sea. Looking out the window, he saw some children playing on the shore and baptizing one another. Offended by what he saw, Alexander called the children to him. Although at first the children denied that they had been doing this, eventually they confessed and explained their actions. Alexander decided that this baptism was valid, and was so impressed by those children that he recruited them for the clergy. One of them was Athanasius, who later became secretary to Alexander and eventually his successor. Even though the story is probably untrue, the very fact that Rufinus wrote it shows the possible extremes following from the notion that the validity of baptism does not depend on who administers it, as long as it is done with water and in the name of the Trinity.

However, such extremes should not hide the value of a good understanding of baptism. In the early church, baptism was necessary, not primarily because it was a rite that in some magical form guaranteed the forgiveness of sin, but rather because it was through baptism that a believer would join the church. And it was only as part of the church, of the body of Christ, that one could enjoy the benefits of his death and resurrection.

15

Surrounding Communion

FIXED FORMULAE AND SPLENDID CEREMONIES

The new social and political circumstances in which the church now found itself led to increasingly complex and fixed ceremonies that sought to express the glory of God with all the riches, the art, and the pomp the world could afford. Now present at the service were the most distinguished personalities of society—in the imperial capitals, the emperor and his entourage; in provincial capitals, the governor and his officials; and so on. Such people had to be surrounded with expected protocols. But it was inconceivable that mere mortals would be received with more ceremony or more honor than God: no gesture, salutation, or particular attention awarded the powerful figures present should eclipse the glory of God. Soon, not only in Constantinople and in Rome, but in every large city, the pomp surrounding official ceremonies left its imprint on Christian worship—particularly on Communion.

What was true regarding the aristocracy and government officials was also true among the more educated spheres of society. In earlier times, when the church gathered in a private home, at the cemetery, or in the best of cases in a former residence that had been remodeled for this purpose, very few highly educated people were in worship, and they did not attend in order to hear beautiful and well-pronounced words but because they believed in the gospel of Jesus Christ and came to celebrate it jointly with their sisters and brothers. Conditions had changed. Now among the multitudes attending church there were experts in literature and rhetoric who would immediately notice any error in grammar or diction—and some who were ready to point out any possible error.

In his treatise *On Catechizing the Uninstructed*, Augustine deals with the difficulties emerging from the various levels of education within a congregation, and then recommends humility to those who belong to schools of grammar or are professional orators, so that they may pay due attention to what is being said, "and learn not to despise individuals whom they may discover keeping themselves free from vices of conduct more carefully than from faults of language." Such intellectuals must also learn not "to compare with a pure heart the practice of pure speech." And then, apparently remembering his own experience when he went to hear Ambrose, Augustine declares that "ideas are to be preferred to words, just as the soul is preferred to the body" (*On Catechizing the Uninstructed* 9.13; NPNF1 3:291).

Such instructions, which could be applied in the more private sessions of catechesis, would be difficult to apply in worship itself, where highly educated people would be together with the uneducated. As a means of overcoming the difficulties of such a situation, fixed formulae and phrases that could be learned and generally understood became ever more common, particularly in the most important parts of the Communion service, as well as the prayers after the offertory, when the bread and wine were consecrated for sacramental use. Even later one notices a constant process in which more and more formulae and even gestures are repeated and become fixed.

This was not entirely new. In the *Apostolic Tradition* of Hippolytus, on which we based much of our discussion of Communion in the late second century, an entire dialogue at the beginning of Communion by then seems to have become fairly common, and is still used to this day. This dialogue begins, "The Lord be with you," and ends, "It is meet and right so to do." Similar dialogues, with the same structure but with different words, would become increasingly common throughout the fourth and fifth centuries, although there would still be regional variations. For instance, in Rome the dialogue began with the words "The Lord be with you"; in North Africa the words were "Peace be with you"; and in the area around Constantinople they were "Peace be with all of you." Later, other variants would appear, as in the case of Spain during the early Middle Ages: "The Lord be always with you." Therefore, while there was uniformity as to the practice of beginning the dialogue with a salutation, the words themselves varied, and such differences lasted for centuries. On the other hand, the similitude among these various forms attests to the antiquity, if not of the words themselves, certainly of their general tenor.

A similar development may be seen in other prayers offered during Communion. Earlier, when describing such prayers, Hippolytus makes it clear that he does not expect the prayers he writes to be more than a model for others to follow:

It is not, to be sure, necessary for anyone to recite the exact words that we have prescribed, by learning to say them by heart in his thanksgiving to God; but let each one pray according to his ability. If, indeed, he is able to pray competently with an elevated prayer, it is well. But even if he is only moderately able to pray and give praise, no one may forbid him; only let him pray sound in the faith. (*Ap. Trad.* 10)

Although Hippolytus suggested such freedom in the third century, by the fourth there was a strong current seeking uniformity, eventually resulting in carefully crafted, fixed formulae and prayers. This process was partly due to the concerns that Augustine expressed, reflecting a situation in which, particularly in lesser cities, bishops were uneducated people whose use of language left much to be desired. For such people to use their own language ran against the desire to make worship ever more elegant and refined. As a way to avoid what seemed to be crass mistakes or uncouth conduct, worship leaders had to be told exactly what they should say and do. Thus, while the "service of the Word" still left room for great homilies and the originality of people like Chrysostom, Augustine, and many others, the "service of the Table" was becoming increasingly uniform.

This movement toward uniformity was also aided by improved communications and the influence of major population centers. The new order that began in Constantine's time included, among many other benefits, bishops' right to the use of imperial post. The end of persecution made possible constant visits from one city to another, and from one region to another. Such correspondence and visits would inspire some to imitate what they saw in other churches, and sometimes to cast aside what they had been doing and replace it with something that seemed better. This would particularly be the case for churches in minor cities, which sought to replicate what was said and done in the great capital cities. In the East, there were differences between Alexandria and Antioch. In Alexandria, the Copts—descendants of the ancient Egyptians—preserved some of the traditional practices of the region, and still do. Those practices expanded southward, so that the traditional order of worship in the church of Ethiopia now reflects some of the practices and emphases of the ancient Alexandrine rite. Meanwhile, other liturgical practices developed in Antioch that then expanded not only to the neighboring areas of the Roman Empire that spoke Greek but also eastward, to Armenia and beyond, wherever Syrian influence reached. The Latin-speaking West had two great centers: Rome and Milan. Each of them developed its own liturgical practices. Rome's influence grew, and the Roman rite became dominant. However, there were variations in the West, proudly maintained in various areas: the Gallican in southern Gaul, the Milanese or Ambrosian in the area of that city, and a form in Spain that later was termed "Mozarabic." The Second Vatican

Council of the Roman Catholic Church in the last century permitted the constant celebration of the Gallican Mass in one church in Lyon, the Mozarabic Mass in one chapel of the Cathedral of Toledo, and the Ambrosian Mass in the churches of Milan. With a few other exceptions, all Catholic churches use the Roman Mass. The history of the relationship of these various forms of the Mass remains a complicated subject of ongoing study.

In the western areas of Europe—which are what most interest us here, for that is where most of the churches we know today have their roots—Greek continued as the main language of worship at least through the fourth century, although by the third century Latin seems to have been in general use in some areas, particularly in places distant from the capital and from its intellectual elites. The church in Rome was born speaking Greek and continued using that language until approximately the year 380—although already by the third century many of the church's writings and lapidary inscriptions were in Latin, and Greek would never disappear entirely. Most likely the passage from one language to another was slow and often incomplete. Just as some Hebrew or Aramaic words were never translated, but are used even today—for instance, "amen" and "hallelujah"—Greek persisted in some words, phrases, and formulae. The most notable case is the very name given to Communion, "Eucharist," which is mostly a transliteration of the Greek word meaning "thanksgiving." For a long time, a part of Rome's Christian population apparently preferred Greek to Latin, which was one of the factors leading to present-day use of the Greek phrase *Kyrie eleison* ("Lord, have mercy"). The persistence of Greek in Rome was such that as late as the thirteenth century Greek was still used jointly with Latin for reciting the Creed and other canticles and formulae.

Still, despite such lingering differences, some of which persist today, there was a clear movement toward uniformity. This meant that most of the service of Communion—particularly its very core, the anaphora or prayer of consecration—was fixed into what came to be known as the "canon of the Mass" (with "canon" meaning regulation). As time went by, phrases such as "the Roman canon of the Mass" became common to include all that was done following the directives of Rome, from the introductory dialogue to the final doxology. Naturally, there was also resistance to strict uniformity, particularly noticeable in the provinces of North Africa, where Latin-speaking Christianity had first emerged—long before it did in Rome. There were repeated synods in North Africa seeking to make worship more uniform. The most notable gathered in 393 in Hippo, where Augustine was bishop, and decreed that any change in the prayer of consecration of Communion could only be done after "consulting the instructor brothers" (Mansi 3:922). This decision seems in response to Augustine's concern over the poor use of language mentioned earlier. In any case, the need to insist on this decree in repeated later synods would seem to indicate that it was not generally heeded.

This discussion suffices to give a general idea of the process leading from multiplicity to a uniform inflexibility against which many would protest during the Middle Ages, at the time of the Reformation, and even later. However, what marked liturgical development toward the end of this period is not only uniformity but also a pompous ostentation vying with civil ceremonies such as those in imperial and royal courts. While this tendency marked the entire period, it was most noticeable in the Greek-speaking East, which featured a long tradition of ostentation by the aristocracy, civil officials, and above all the imperial court.

Such ostentation was shown in part by the number of people leading worship. It was expected that worship would begin with a long procession of people with various functions in the service, followed by the bishop or the person who would preside over the service, accompanied by a crucifer—the person carrying the cross—and another carrying the Gospel with stately ceremony and pomp. Other clergy or church dignitaries, as well as a choir, then followed.

Although much discussion has taken place on the nature of Christian music during the early centuries—of which, in truth, little is known—by the time we are now studying, the hymns sung in church were sufficiently complex to require a choir or at least cantors directing them. Some songs were repeated often enough so that the congregation could learn and sing them. Some of these are still sung in churches today, Catholic as well as Protestant, such as the *Sanctus*, "Holy, Holy, Holy, Lord God Almighty," the *Gloria Patri*, "Glory Be to the Father, and to the Son, and to the Holy Spirit," and the *Gloria in excelsis*, "Glory to God in the highest."

Much of what was sung in churches was still the Psalms—although apparently with more elaborate music than earlier. In singing the Psalms, one option was to divide the congregation in two groups, one responding to the other, and another option was to have a cantor who would sing the text of the psalm, stopping at appropriate places to allow the congregation to respond by singing a brief antiphon that was repeated at each pause. Sometimes that antiphon was drawn from the psalm itself, and sometimes it came from another source—for instance, the *Gloria Patri*. Like the rest of the service, music also became more elaborate during the course of the fourth century, and particularly thereafter. It eventually reached a point where it was difficult for the congregation to join in song. By then, even antiphonal singing was done by two groups within the choir responding to one another.

The consequence was to create a growing chasm between the congregation and those who led in worship, increasing not only the musical, cultural, and aesthetic distance, but also the physical distance, since the choir was placed between the altar and the congregation. While this separation of the congregation and clergy was already visible in formal worship during the fourth century, the real consequences of the distancing became more obvious after the fifth century. During the time we are studying now, on some occasions singing was shown to be a powerful force of unity between clergy leaders and their lay followers. One of the best-known stories—often repeated, probably with some exaggeration—concerns the time when Empress Justina ordered that troops surround a basilica in Milan and take possession of it so that it could be dedicated to Arian worship. Ambrose, the bishop of the city at the time, staunchly resisted, refusing to yield the basilica. Entrenched inside the building, Ambrose referred to the psalm that had been sung earlier, and applied it to the troops invading the church (*Epistle* 20.20; NPNF2 10:422).

Having mentioned this anecdote, this is probably the best place to refer to Ambrosian chant and to Ambrose as an author of hymns. As to the first, the name of "Ambrosian" is given to a vast number of hymns and to a musical style that for a long time were connected with worship in Milan. In truth, there is no reason to credit Ambrose with this musical style, which apparently appeared after the famous bishop's death. Ambrose did compose hymns, although it is impossible to say much about the music that would accompany them, beyond the apparent fact that it was simpler and easier to sing than earlier music. Among the many hymns that tradition attributes to Ambrose, only four are considered authentic by most scholars. Among these, the best known is "*Veni redemptor gentium*" ("Savior of Nations, Come").

Another indication of the importance of singing not only for the clergy but also for all the people comes from the report of Egeria, the pilgrim who visited the Holy Land four years before the incident between Ambrose and Justina, and sent a report to her sisters in Galicia. In that document, she speaks repeatedly of the people's emotion and enthusiasm as they joined their bishop, the clergy, nuns, and monks in singing psalms and other hymns. In a word, toward the end of the fourth century, singing, though becoming more elaborate, was still an activity in which the entire congregation could share. Mostly after the fifth century, such singing would become the exclusive domain of clergy, choirs, and cantors.

The increasing luxury and ostentation in ceremonies may also be seen in the artifacts employed in worship. A good example is the chalice for Communion. Quite likely, what Jesus used was a cup made of clay or at best of glass;

indications are that in the first century some Jews used glass cups for their ritual meals. Slightly over a hundred years before the opening of the period we are now studying, Tertullian seems to be referring to the Communion cup when he speaks of cups—perhaps glass cups—bearing an image that brings to mind the parable of the Lost Sheep. Also, in one of the murals in the catacombs, among several loaves of bread appears a transparent cup with a red liquid that seems to be wine—which certainly suggests that this was a glass cup. Shortly before the time we are studying, in 303 CE, the church in Cirta, in what now is Algeria, had six silver chalices and two of gold.

The move toward more valuable chalices continued through the fourth and fifth centuries. In the fourth, when the Goths defeated the Romans at Adrianapolis and a large number of captives were to be ransomed, Ambrose was criticized because he melted the church's sacred vessels to pay the ransom. He responded,

> Although we did not do this without good reason, we have continually followed our action with confessing that we indeed did this, and adding again and again that it was far better to preserve people than gold for the Lord. He who sent the apostles without gold also brought together the churches without gold. The church has gold, not to store it up, but to use it, and to spend it on those in need. (*On the Duties of the Clergy* 2.28.137; NPNF2 10:64)

In the following century, John Chrysostom complained that many rich people in his own congregation had become rich by exploiting the poor and then thought that their sin would be forgiven because they were giving the church chalices made with the gold that they had amassed by plundering the weak.

Besides chalices and other artifacts of gold or silver, frequently adorned with precious or semiprecious stones, there were also golden altars encrusted with precious stones. In chapter 16 we shall see more of the costly altar that Constantine gave to the Cathedral of St. Peter in Rome. The veneration of martyrs became practically a form of worship—despite the official teaching of the church—and in order to keep the remains or other relics of the martyrs and saints, precious reliquaries were made, often of gold and silver, and adorned with precious stones. In brief, luxurious ostentation was not limited to the ceremonies themselves, but extended to all that had something to do with them—including buildings, as we shall see in chapter 16.

In summary, what we see in the centuries we are studying is not yet what would take place later, beginning with innovations particularly in the fifth century. But there already was a clear tendency to more elaborate worship, with ceremonies whose very complexity risked obscuring their meaning.

THE GREAT LITURGICAL FAMILIES
IN EAST AND WEST

The influence of the great centers of power, population, and prestige—Antioch, Alexandria, and Rome—gave rise to what today are called "liturgical families" or rites. In the West these are further divided into the four we mentioned earlier in this chapter. North Africa, centered in Carthage, clearly had a church with differing practices. As elsewhere, also in North Africa there was a movement toward uniformity. This process was cut short with the invasion of North Africa by the Vandals in the first half of the fifth century. Justinian's attempt to reconquer it a century later only led to greater weakness, and the rapid sweep of the Muslim Arabs ended that church's history.

At first glance these various liturgies are very similar among themselves—particularly from the perspective of Protestants who are not used to elaborate rites—but when studying them more carefully one can see that each of the four major families resulting from the four centers has its own characteristics. Since here it is not possible—and probably not of interest to most readers—to describe each of these liturgical families in detail, a brief word about them should suffice.

The Communion service in all these various families begins with a form of the dialogue that appears already in the *Apostolic Tradition* of Hippolytus—a dialogue that begins with the words "The Lord be with you," and ends with "It is meet and right." (Earlier in this chapter we noted that, even though the dialogue is essentially the same, there were already slightly different words.)

In the East it was customary to go directly from this dialogue to the Great Prayer of Thanksgiving or eucharistic prayer, while in Rome—but not in Milan—a "preface" was included relating the celebration of Communion with the particular day in the liturgical year. After that preface a hymn was sung or recited: "Holy, Holy, Holy, Lord God Almighty," known in the West as the *Sanctus*, and in the East as the "Hymn of Victory." (This hymn reminds us that the church understood its worship as joining the heavenly worship of "angels and archangels, and all the company of heaven," and as a rehearsal for a time when those now worshiping would join that heavenly worship.) In the Roman rite, after the *Sanctus* came a series of prayers for the church and its leaders, as well as for all believers and the entire world—in other words, what we have already discussed as the "prayer of the people." This was followed by the words of institution of the Lord's Supper. In the East, after retelling the institution of the Supper, a prayer was added—the epiclesis—asking the Father to have the Holy Spirit descend upon the bread and the wine so that the consecration that the church had made would be confirmed and rendered effective by the Spirit. This is possibly the most important difference between the two traditions, because asking for the Holy Spirit to descend upon the elements consecrated by the priest left no doubt that the one who ultimately consecrates the elements for Communion is not the priest—and not his words—but the Holy Spirit.

While there were other differences, what is remarkable when one looks from today's perspective is not these variations, but rather the relative uniformity of all that was said and done. Even though the order of prayers and songs may have changed from one tradition to another, many of the formulae were the same and would be perfectly familiar to believers from other areas.

THEOLOGICAL EMPHASES

We have already seen (chapter 9) that, while the churches in various areas agreed on much theologically, there were also some differences in what each of them emphasized. What has just been said about the importance of the invocation of the Holy Spirit in Communion is an indication of such differences, for—particularly beginning in the fourth century—the Eastern church had a tendency to stress the work and significance of the Holy Spirit much more than its Western counterpart. At the same time, the Western church was increasingly emphasizing the importance of the priest and the power that he had been given through ordination by the bishop. The time came when it seemed that asking for the Holy Spirit to come and ratify what the priest had already declared diminished the priest's authority as well as that of the entire ecclesiastical hierarchy.

The differences mentioned in chapter 9 regarding baptism may also be seen within the context of Communion—particularly since we are now dealing with a later time frame. If we compare some of the eucharistic prayers remaining from that time, we see that those representing the West carry different emphases than their Eastern counterparts, and that among the latter significant differences are also present between the practices in Alexandria and those based in Antioch or Asia Minor.

In chapter 9 we sketched three basic types of theology reflected in baptism. The first of these, typical of the Western and Latin-speaking areas of the empire, understood that the human tragedy from which we must be freed is the debt that we owe God because of sin. From that perspective, what would be stressed throughout the entire corpus of theology—but in this case clearly in eucharistic prayers—would be our awesome debt and the grace of God in forgiving it through the merits of Christ. Such a theology bears the imprint of the famed Roman legal system. During the period we are now studying, this type of theology was still in process of formation—but it may already be noticed in the context of Communion in the emphases on the elements being offered as a sacrifice to God, asking God to accept the sacrifice and because of it to have mercy on those who offer it. Were we to move further beyond the chronological limits of this history, we would note that this emphasis became even stronger after a series of invasions by peoples whose social and legal order was based on a system of debts, rewards, and indemnification. But during the time we are now discussing, what we have are mostly signs of this emphasis in the manner in which Communion is understood, as a bloodless sacrifice whose merit is transferred to those who offer it and who partake of it. An example of this is the prayer of consecration that Ambrose has left us, which includes words such as, "We offer you this immaculate victim, a reasonable sacrifice, an unbloody victim" (*On the Sacraments* 4.27; FoC 44:206).

Long before this emphasis in the West on sin as a debt and the work of Christ as payment for it appeared, in the East, particularly in Alexandria and its environs, a different theological focus had emerged that sought to speak of God using images and words taken from the dominant philosophy of the time. This second type of theology understood the human tragedy to be our ignorance and lack of understanding regarding spiritual realities. From that region, and precisely from the time we are now studying, we have a strange book of prayers or *Euchologion* by Bishop Serapion of Thmuis, who lived in the mid-fourth century. Whether the book itself is entirely the work of Serapion, or rather a collection of materials that he compiled, is impossible to know. At any rate, the prayer over Communion in this book has a distinctive Alexandrine flavor, with its emphasis on philosophy and the human need for enlightenment. After the customary dialogue leading to the prayer of consecration, Serapion's prayer says,

> It is proper and necessary to praise you, O, uncreated Father of your only-begotten Jesus Christ, . . . We praise you, uncreated God, inscrutable, indescribable and incomprehensible for every created being. We praise you, who have revealed yourself to us by the only-begotten. . . . We laud you, invisible Father, who gave us immortality, who are the fountain of life, light, grace and truth. . . .
>
> Give us your Spirit of light to know you, the only true God, and to know your messenger, Jesus Christ. (trans. V. Martín Pindado and J. M. Sánchez Caro, *La gran oración eucarística* [Madrid: La Muralla, 1969], 185)

Naturally, the prayer is much longer and includes the narrative of the institution of the Supper. But the lines quoted, and several others similar to them, full as they are of philosophical words, clearly show an Alexandrine influence.

If we then turn our attention to the region of Syria and Asia Minor, we note a third type of theology that stresses the history of the relationship between

God and humanity from the very beginning of creation; then with the people of Israel; and finally, in Jesus Christ, with the church. In that relationship, the human problem is not so much a debt—as in the emerging Western theology—nor a lack of enlightenment or understanding—as in the theology that characterized the region around Alexandria—but rather a bondage to the powers of evil. These powers must be defeated for humanity to be free and enjoy true communion with God. This may be seen in the very extensive eucharistic prayer in the *Apostolic Constitutions*. Immediately after the introductory dialogue to which we have referred repeatedly, a prayer is raised that begins by praising God's creative power. Following a few lines about the eternal attributes of God, the emphasis is on creation, in which, through the Only-begotten, God has made all things. Because God has made them and tended to them, all things are worthy of attention. The prayer then moves on to the creation of celestial beings—cherubim, seraphim, and others—and to the creation of all that exists in the visible world: heaven and earth, light and darkness, work and rest, the sun and the moon, and the "choir of the stars." God is praised for creating water, air, fire, and land; as all sorts of animals, domestic and wild; trees with their flowers and seeds; and everything else. This continues until finally the prayer praises God, because, besides having created the entire universe, God created the human being as if it were another world within the larger world that God had made. Then follows the story of the garden and the fall, with the result that humans now have to gain their sustenance with toil and sweat. Even in this situation, it was God who made humankind multiply. Next comes a review of several passages of the Old Testament, including Abel's sacrifice and Cain's fratricide; the destruction of Sodom; the calling of Abraham; the story of Isaac, Jacob, and Joseph; slavery in Egypt; the flight from that slavery; and the time in the desert until reaching Jordan. The prayer is interrupted with the *Sanctus*, and then continues with the saving work of God through natural law, written law, the words of the prophets, the actions of angels, until finally reaching Jesus Christ, who came to reconcile the world with God and to free humanity from the threatening wrath. The prayer includes a summary of Jesus' life from his birth until he was betrayed to Pilate. It then explains the reason for the sufferings in terms of victory over the powers of evil, death, and the devil:

> He was delivered to Pilate the governor, and He who was the judge was judged. He who was the savior was condemned. He who was impassible was nailed to the cross. He who was by nature immortal died. He who is the giver of life was buried, so that he might free from suffering and death those for whose sake he came, so that he might break the bonds of the devil and deliver humanity from his deceit. He arose from the dead the third day; and after he had continued with his

disciples forty days, he was taken up into the heavens and he is seated at the right hand of You, his God and Father. (*Apostolic Constitutions* 8.12; ANF 7:489)

Today, many centuries later, all of these voices tell us, first, that it is possible to gather around a single table—not our table, but the Lord's—despite our theological differences, and in a way thanks to them, for these differences witness to the wide scope of God's grace.

Second, these voices tell us that we must not forget that our worship joins that of the heavenly host, and that therefore it is a foretaste of when we shall be counted among that host. Among the many passages we could quote in this direction, the words of Cyril of Jerusalem at the end of his *Catechetical Lectures* stand out. There, after reviewing the introductory dialogue that has repeatedly been mentioned, Cyril says,

> After this we make mention of heaven and earth and sea; of sun and moon; of stars and all the creation, rational and irrational, visible and invisible. We mention angels and archangels, virtues, dominions, principalities, powers and thrones. We add the cherubim with many faces, in effect repeating that call of David's "Magnify the Lord with me." We make mention also of the seraphim, whom Isaiah, in the Spirit, saw standing around the throne of God. With two of their wings they veiled their faces; with two their feet, while with two they flew. They cried: "Holy, holy, holy is the Lord of sabaoth." The reason we recite this confession, which was delivered to us by the Seraphim, is so that we may be partakers with the heavenly hosts in their hymn of praise. (*Catechetical Lectures* 23.6; NPNF2 7:154)

Finally, those voices tell us that no matter how we seek to adorn our worship with beautiful-sounding words and impressive ceremonies, in fact there can be no greater adornment to our worship than the incredible truth that our Lord—crucified, risen, and exalted—offers himself to us in a meal that nourishes us as the body of his that we are. Centuries have passed, and worship has evolved; but throughout the centuries what makes us one is the conviction placed in us by none other than the Holy Spirit that God was in Christ reconciling the world unto himself.

16

Times, Places, and Practices

THE TIMES: THE CALENDAR

Two important dates were added to the calendar during the fourth century: Christmas and Ascension Day. Both celebrate events that appear in the New Testament as well as in the most ancient Christian writings, and about which Christians have been preaching throughout history, but until this time there was not a date set apart for them in the calendar.

The first authors who emphasized Jesus' birth—for instance, Ignatius of Antioch early in the second century—did it as a way to counteract the Docetic teachings of people such as Marcion and the Gnostics. Since these teachings considered matter either evil or inferior, they rejected the notion that Jesus could have a physical body. Such doctrines were what led Ignatius to insist that Jesus was truly born. For the same reason, the Old Roman Symbol, the oldest form of what we now call the Apostles' Creed, affirmed that Jesus "was born of the Virgin Mary." Yet even though believers were certain that Jesus had been born, there was no special date to celebrate that birth. The reason is that, while the date of Jesus' passion may be more or less established on the basis of its relation to the Jewish Passover, this is not the case with his birth. Therefore, while some celebrated Jesus' birth on one date, others celebrated it on another, and some do not seem to have had a day for such a celebration at all. In general, Eastern churches were inclined to celebrate the birth of Jesus on or near January 6. Scholars do not agree as to why that date was selected. We do know that in Egypt there were some Gnostics—the followers of Basilides—who celebrated Jesus' baptism on that date. (For them the baptism of Jesus was particularly important because they believed that at that point the divinity came to dwell in Jesus.) In order to counteract such views, orthodox Christians in Egypt began celebrating on that date not only the baptism of Jesus, as these Gnostics did, but also his birth, as a way to emphasize at the same time both his humanity and his divinity. For reasons that are still unclear, on that date Egyptian Christians also commemorated the miracle at the wedding in Cana. Perhaps this was done because that miracle showed the authority of Jesus to transform water, and thus to give power to baptismal water. Another possibility is that the miracle in Cana manifested Jesus' divine power to the disciples; the dove and the words from heaven showed his divinity to the Jews; and the Magi, whose arrival some celebrated on this date, proclaimed his divinity to the Gentiles—although one should note that the story of the Magi seems to have been of greater interest to Christians in the West than in the East. Finally, others believe that January 6 was chosen in order to counteract pagan celebrations on that date that had to do with water.

While these developments were taking place in the Eastern churches, in the West the tradition was developed that the birth of Christ should be placed on December 25. Also in this case the date was quite possibly chosen in order to take the place of existing pagan traditions and festivities. Some suggest that the choice of this day was based on the date of the crucifixion, on March 25. Since God does everything in order, and nothing should be incomplete, this would mean that Jesus was conceived on the same date, March 25. Nine months after March 25 is December 25, and therefore that seemed to be the best day to celebrate the birth of Jesus. Although some documents seem to support this theory, they are late and most likely are an attempt to justify a posteriori what was already being done. At any rate, following a complicated process of scholarly research that reminds us of a detective novel, it can be proven that by the year 335, Western Christians—or at least those in Rome—considered December 25 as the date when the birth of the Lord should be celebrated.

In summary, while in the West the birth of Christ was celebrated on December 25, in the East it was celebrated on January 6. These conditions prevailed during the first half of the fourth century. Inexplicably, this divergence, which could have created serious difficulties similar to those that divided Christians over the date of Easter, was resolved without major conflicts. Both in the East and in the West, December 25 came to be the date to celebrate Jesus' birth, and January 6 became the date of Epiphany, commemorating the revelation of Jesus' divine nature disclosed at his baptism, the visit of the Magi, and the miracle at Cana. This date was so well received that on December 25, 386, preaching in Antioch, John Chrysostom rejoiced, declaring, "It is only ten years since we learned of this celebration," but it was "as if we had been given it from the very beginning" (*Homily on the Date of the Birth of Christ*; PG 61:737).

As time passed, just as a period of special preparation for Easter had developed into Lent, a similar period of preparation for Christmas and Epiphany developed into Advent.

The case of Ascension Day is somewhat different. Once the date of the resurrection of Jesus is established, it suffices to count forty days to reach the date of the ascension. Until the middle of the fourth century, the various lists that we have regarding great Christian festivities and services do not mention Ascension as one of them. Near the end of the same century, we find references to it in both Gregory of Nyssa and John Chrysostom. Approximately at the same time, Egeria reports that on the fortieth day after the resurrection, there were in Jerusalem special vigils, and the bishop and the priests preached on subjects related both to the place and the occasion. Slightly later, in a homily Augustine declared,

> The glorification of the Lord came to fulfillment with his resurrection and ascension. We celebrated his resurrection on Easter Sunday, and we celebrate his ascension today. Both are feast days for us, for he rose from the dead in order to prove our resurrection, and ascended in order to protect us from on high. Therefore, our Lord and savior is Jesus Christ, who first hung from the cross and is now seated in heaven. (*Sermon* 263.1; PL 38:1209)

In the fifth century, Socrates Scholasticus, while discussing a different subject, said in passing that in one of the suburbs of Constantinople—Elaea— "from ancient times the custom was for the whole population annually to assemble for the celebration of our Savior's ascension" (*Church Hist.* 7.26; NPNF2 2:168).

While these feasts were being added to the Christian calendar, that calendar itself was becoming more complicated due to the ancient custom of gathering at the tombs of martyrs on the anniversary of their death to celebrate Communion, and thus to signal that those martyrs are part of the same church. Until the fourth century such observances were necessarily local, for each place gathered to celebrate the death of its own martyrs. But beginning in the fourth century, as more interchange took place among churches, the names of those martyrs and the dates of death were also exchanged, so that the number of special dates grew exponentially. This also included names of martyrs who never existed, and false tombs or relics. A good example is the case of Saints Gervasius and Protasius, whose relics Ambrose claimed to have discovered and who soon became venerated not only in Milan but also in North Africa. There were also frequent cases in which an ancient god or goddess was, so to speak, "baptized" with the name of a saint, who then became an object of devotion for the former worshipers of the pagan deity. Through the centuries the result was that the originally Christocentric nature of the Christian calendar was eclipsed, and the devotion of many, rather than addressing the Triune God or Christ, turned to the most popular saints in a particular place. That devotion to local figures weakened the unity of the church, for each region came to have its favorite saints—and each occupation or human condition soon also had its own patron saint.

THE PLACES: THE BASILICAS

When persecution ended, all confiscated properties were returned to the churches, and therefore Christians immediately had places to gather. However, quite soon construction began on new buildings devoted to worship that were much larger and more ornate than those of an earlier time. This was necessary due to the growing numbers of people joining the church and made possible thanks to the direct support of people of means—among them, Emperor Constantine and his mother, Helena, as well as several of their successors.

A certain style of building constructed then for worship is called a "basilica." Although the architectural style of these basilicas comes from various sources and influences, the name itself comes from the Greek word for "king." The reason is that originally a basilica was simply a large government building. But after Constantine and the vast church buildings that resulted from the new circumstances, the word "basilica" came to mean a certain type of church that was dominant in ecclesiastical architecture for several centuries.

Essentially, a basilica was a rectangular building whose main nave was generally oriented from east to west, with the entrance to the west, so that worshipers would be facing east—although Constantine seems to have preferred the opposite orientation, with worshipers facing west. This main nave was then divided lengthwise by parallel rows of columns. Most commonly a basilica would have two such rows, thus dividing the nave into three long sections. However, more rows of columns were added later, so that some basilicas had up to seven parallel naves. In some cases, particularly in the West but also elsewhere, near the end of the main nave there was a cross-vault or transept running from north to south, thus giving the entire basilica the shape of a cross.

At one end of the basilica, after going through an atrium, one reached the entry doors. Commonly there would be a door for each of the several naves into which the basilica was divided, so that if a basilica had two rows of columns and therefore three naves, it would also have three entry doors, one next to another on the far side of the building. At the other extreme there was a curved niche, the apse, with a concave roof. There the altar stood, and normally the high members of the clergy would sit there. Originally, most altars were wooden, but some were also made with precious materials. The basilica of St. Peter in Rome, whose construction began in 333—and was not the same building as today—had an altar donated by Constantine made out of silver with an encrustation of gold and four hundred precious stones, weighing over 350 pounds.

Between the apse and the main part of the nave there was a pulpit—or sometimes two. This was set up high so that people could see and hear the preacher from afar. In the naves themselves, men and women would sit or stand in different areas. Normally most people would remain standing during the service, although there were also places where those needing to sit could do so. Most commonly the men were on the right and the women on the left, but this varied from place to place.

Since the basilica was often the see of a bishop, a special chair in the apse was set for him. Because of this chair, or *cathedra*, eventually churches where a bishop presided came to be known as "cathedrals."

Since the great nave was divided into at least three narrow and long naves, the central one was not only the widest but also the highest, resulting in walls above the central nave with room for windows that allowed light into the building. This in turn made it possible to decorate the walls and ceilings with pictures representing biblical scenes, episodes in the life of important figures in the history of the church, and sometimes the image of the person who had provided the funds for the building itself. Much of this art was in mosaic—an art form that would soon flourish in the Byzantine Empire.

The magnificence of those basilicas is described in detail in the panegyric of Eusebius of Caesarea about the new church in Tyre. Eusebius places his speech within its historical context, reminding the hearers of the destruction of the old church during the persecution, a church that stood on this very ground. He declares that this is "the sight that we had all desired and prayed for. There were feasts of dedication in the cities and consecrations of the newly built houses of prayer. Bishops assembled; foreigners came from abroad" (*Church Hist.* 10.3.1; NPNF2 1:270). Speaking of the new church, he says that its glory will far surpass its predecessor's. Eusebius then praises Paulinus, the bishop of Tyre, for his planning and building this new church:

> Since a much larger space was enclosed, the fortified outer court—with a wall completely surrounding it—serves as a very secure bulwark for the entire building. And he elevated and spread out a vestibule toward the rays of the rising sun. It is so lofty that even those far outside the sacred enclosure have a full view of those within. Thus the eyes of strangers to the faith will almost be turned to the entrances. No one can pass by without being impressed by the memory of the former desolation and of the present incredible transformation. . . .

He has surrounded and adorned it [the sanctuary] with four transverse cloisters, making a quadrangular space with pillars rising on every side. These he has joined with lattice-work screens of wood which rise to a suitable height. He has left an open space in the middle, so the sky can be seen, and the free air bright in the rays of the sun. Here he has put symbols of sacred purification, placing fountains opposite the temple which give an abundance of water, so that those who come into the sanctuary may purify themselves. This is the first stopping-point of those who enter. In addition, it furnishes a beautiful and splendid scene to everyone, and it is a fitting station for those who still need elementary instruction.

Beyond this beautiful area there are open entrances into the temple with many other vestibules inside. There are three doors on one side, also facing the rays of the sun. The one in the middle is adorned with plates of bronze, embossed and iron bound. This door is much higher and wider than the other two, so it almost looks as though the others are guards as for a queen. In the same way, arranging the number of vestibules for the corridors on each side of the temple, he has made above them openings to let more light into the building. These he has adorned with very fine carving in wood. But the royal house he has furnished with more beautiful and splendid materials. He has been unstintingly liberal in his spending. . . .

When he had completed the temple, he furnished it with lofty thrones in honor of those who preside. There are also seats arranged in proper order throughout the whole building. Finally, placed in the middle is the holy of holies, the altar. So that it might be inaccessible to the multitude, it is enclosed with wooden lattice-work, with beautiful artistic carving. It presents a wonderful sight to the beholders. He did not even neglect the pavement, for it is adorned with beautiful marble of every variety. (*Church Hist.* 10.4.37–45; NPNF2 1:375)

As one may well imagine, such basilicas had a profound impact on worship itself, which soon began developing ceremonies, vestments, choirs, and other elements that seemed more worthy of the majesty of the buildings themselves. The latticework around the altar shows the increasing separation of the clergy from the people. When there were hundreds of people in the congregation, many of them at some distance from the altar, clerical vestments gained importance, for people needed to know who was a bishop, who were priests, who were deacons, and so forth. What each person wore, how they covered their head, and other such signs made those distinctions clear. The Sunday service, particularly Communion, became a drama taking place in this new scene, and the vestments distinguished the roles and functions of each actor. This was an enormous change from earlier times, when Christians gathered in private homes, or perhaps in a residence turned into a place of worship. Naturally, back then it was unnecessary to have special vestments to know who was who.

This is probably the best place for an additional word regarding the development of liturgical vestments. The origin of vestments that became universal until the Protestant Reformation harkens back to the dress that ancient Romans wore. Briefly stated, originally these were not special clothes one wore to lead worship but simply the normal clothing worn by most of the population. As the clothing evolved that laypeople and the clergy wore, the garments did so in different directions. During the time that we are now studying, mostly the fourth and fifth centuries, what clergy wore was still generally very similar to what most people wore. Later, partly under the influence of the invaders, fashion would change for the common people (for instance, trousers developing and becoming more typical). Meanwhile, garb for the clergy developed along its own lines but always reflecting ancient Roman customs. Already by this time, since bishops and the high clergy enjoyed ever-growing social prestige, their vestments became more luxurious, while still similar to what the laity wore. By the end of this period, strong words emerged warning against inappropriately ostentatious vestments. In 424 Bishop Innocent of Rome chastised his colleagues in Gaul, telling them that, although the clergy is to be distinguished from the people at large, this difference ought not to be in clothing but rather in doctrine; not in what one wears but in one's relations and conversations; not in ostentation but in mental purity. Roughly from the same time, almost in passing, a sermon of Augustine tells us that he dressed just as all the others who lived with him. But the words that Innocent addressed to the bishops in Gaul show that there was indeed an inclination to ostentation.

This evolution producing more elaborate services was particularly noticeable in the East, partly in emulation of the imperial court. In the West, invasions and other disruptions affected every aspect of life, so that splendor in worship was not as noticeable as in the East. Later in the Middle Ages, though, when a new Germanic empire ruled the West, a magnificence similar to that of Eastern worship would develop.

THE PLACES: OTHER BUILDINGS

Besides new churches, numerous baptisteries were built. To understand the significance of these buildings, remember that people were normally baptized naked, and therefore not in the presence of the entire congregation. The congregation itself would be waiting for the newly baptized—the "infants"—to join them and take Communion for the first time. We have already seen that the church in Dura-Europos had a special room for baptisms. Now that sumptuous churches were being built, it was normal to place next to them another structure where baptisms would take place. The buildings themselves and the pools within them varied in shape. Particularly in the West, but also elsewhere, quite often the building or the pool itself was octagonal in shape, with a dome held up by eight columns. This was a reference to baptism as the entrance into the "eighth day" of creation, that is, eternity. Other baptisteries and pools were round, or had the shape of a cross or of a coffin.

Although infant baptism was becoming ever more frequent, at least until the eighth century baptisteries were designed to allow for the baptism of adults by immersion. For a long time, baptism was normally by immersion— of infants as well as of adults. This custom disappeared in the West around the twelfth century but continued in the East. In the West, the old baptisteries were replaced by a baptismal font, normally at the church entrance.

Besides the basilicas that were constructed in the main cities and sacred places, particularly in the Holy Land, and the baptisteries accompanying them, other churches were built following other architectural patterns, particularly some in the shape of a cross. Numerous monuments were also raised in honor of the martyrs or of an important event. These were called *martyria*, or *martyrium* in the singular.

The most notable of these buildings was the *martyrium* built at Constantine's command on the site of the resurrection of Jesus—the Holy Sepulcher. Eusebius quotes the letter that Constantine wrote Bishop Macarius of Jerusalem with instructions for this particular building: "that not only the church itself may surpass all others in beauty, but that the details of the building may be such that they excel the most beautiful structure in any city in the empire" (*Life of Constantine* 3.31; NPNF2 1:528). Then Eusebius describes the building itself: marble columns without equal, with all sorts of decorations; a wide pavement of polished stone, surrounded on three sides by extensive porticos; facing the sepulcher, a great and tall church with a floor of marble of various colors; a lead-covered roof under which there were decorations; and space "as vast as the sea." Three decorated doors provided access to the building, in which there was a high altar surrounded by columns honoring the apostles, each with a silver capital.

THE PRACTICES

One of the main consequences of the new order and the end of persecutions was the surge of monasticism, to which we have already referred. Acknowledging the presence of women in monastic life is important. One must also note that this undercut the traditional ways in which women participated in the life of the congregation. As we have seen, from an early date the church supported widows in need. These women were given various functions, particularly in care, teaching, and providing spiritual direction for other women. Soon women who were not widows devoted themselves to a similar celibate life, and therefore we find references to the "widows and virgins" who were commissioned to work for the church. But with the presence of monastic houses where such women could live and gain their sustenance, the former order of "widows and virgins" began losing ground. Their place was occupied partly by aristocratic women who were able to use their resources to lead a life of prayer, contemplation, and good works, and partly by women in convents.

In general, the monastic movement was a way in which the ancient practice of sharing goods and meeting the needs of the poor was continued. The church at large no longer paid much attention to that ancient practice, while in monastic life goods were shared, and usually private property was forbidden. Communal monastic life was organized following a "rule," of which there were many—although eventually the Rule of St. Benedict became the most widely followed in the West.

Earlier customs involving Christians setting aside certain fixed times for prayer—so that although they were apart they were all praying at the same time—became the pattern that monastics followed in their prayer life. The vast numbers of people who now came to the church no longer felt compelled to keep those hours, which the laity progressively ignored. However, among monastics—men and women—the custom of having certain determined times for prayer became an essential element in their devotional life. Basil the Great was one of many distinguished persons who outlined programs for prayer in monasteries. What he proposed, and many followed, was that there be eight daily times of prayer: upon rising in the morning, at the hours of terce, sext, and none, at the end of the day, upon going to bed, at midnight, and before dawn. If any were working at some distance from the monastic chapel and were not able to return for a particular hour of prayer, they were to stop what they were doing and pray at the same time as the rest of the community prayed in the chapel. Life was governed by bells that indicated the schedule. In this life of devotion shaped by such fixed hours of prayer, the Psalms had a particular place, as did thanksgiving, confession, petition, and a significant emphasis on meditation. The *Rule* establishing these practices was translated from Greek into Latin in 397 and became very influential in the development of Western monasticism.

In short, what happened was that, while the number of believers in Christ increased enormously, the level of commitment soon divided them into two categories: a relatively smaller number followed the high and difficult demands of monastic life, while the rest simply participated in the rites of the church.

Significantly, almost all monastics were laypeople—that is, they were not ordained. Therefore, Communion, which required an ordained presbyter to celebrate, was not the most common form of worship in monasteries. Each monastic community made arrangements to be able to celebrate Communion. In some cases a monk was ordained for this purpose, and in others a local priest served as a chaplain and visited regularly in order to celebrate Communion. Studying the development of Christian worship after this period requires keeping in mind the ever more marked difference between the laity at large and the monastics.

Another notable development during the fourth century is the growing devotion to the martyrs and the annual celebrations at their tombs. For a long time, Christians had venerated those among them who had witnessed to their faith with their blood. As early as the second century, in the *Martyrdom of Polycarp*, Christians in Smyrna rejoiced that after the death of their bishop they were able to gather his bones, which for them were "more precious than the most exquisite jewels and more purified than gold. And they deposited them in an appropriate place" (*Martyrdom of Polycarp* 18; ANF 1:43).

This interest in celebrating the martyrs' witness on the anniversary of their death, often gathering at their tombs to share Communion, continued throughout the history of the ancient church, although there were repeated statements that the martyrs were not to be worshiped but were given particular honor and respect for the witness they had given.

Even so, during the fourth and fifth centuries, with the peace of the church and improvement in communication, the number of martyrs whom any particular church had heard about rapidly increased. As in the case of Ambrose and the supposed bones of Gervasius and Protasius, legends of doubtful origin were bolstered by the even more doubtful declaration that some bones were actual relics of the martyrs.

All this took place amid voices of protest and others defending the practice. In 406 a certain Vigilantius, who had been part of and left Jerome's monastic community in Bethlehem, produced a treatise in which, as Jerome quotes him, he asked, "Why do you not only pay such honor, not to say adoration, to the thing, whatever it may be, that you carry about in a little bottle and worship?" And again, in the same book, "Why do you kiss and adore a bit of powder wrapped up in a cloth?" Further, in the same volume, "Under the cloak of religion we see what is all but a heathen ceremony introduced into the churches" (*Ag. Vigiliantius* 4; NPNF2 6:418).

Jerome responded saying that he did not worship the martyrs but simply admired and venerated them for their great faith, and that therefore this was not idolatry. Perhaps both were right. Jerome was correct that martyrs and their relics were not to be worshiped but just respected, for only God is worthy of worship. But Vigilantius was also right, for much popular religiosity surrounding the apostles, martyrs, and other great figures amounted to worship, and this would take the place of the worship of God. Cyril of Jerusalem, the scholarly bishop whose *Catechetical Lectures* we have repeatedly quoted, believed that the relics of saints could produce miracles, and even cloth that had touched the body of a martyr had miraculous powers. Ambrose, the illustrious and highly educated bishop of Milan, believed that his brother Satyrus had been saved in a shipwreck thanks to a piece of consecrated bread that he carried around his neck.

During those years of the fourth century and early in the fifth, this stress on relics combined with a certain level of peace and security to produce all sorts of pilgrimages. Since most martyrs were buried beyond the city limits, when the date of their martyrdom approached people would plan pilgrimages to their tombs. Naturally, since some of the supposed martyrs were in fact ancient local gods who had been more or less Christianized, these pilgrimages were very similar to the pagan customs that they had supplanted. Because of the end of persecutions, longer-distance travel was also possible. Egeria's pilgrimage is unique because she left a written testimonial of what she saw, but pilgrimage to the Holy Land was not exceptional. Pilgrims visited other places in Egypt, Syria, and Rome. In such places, pilgrims took part in worship, as we saw Egeria do in Jerusalem and elsewhere. They also collected supposed relics that they took back to their homes, where these became objects of devotion. Partly in response to such abuses, in 426, toward the end of the time we are now studying, the Code of Theodosius prohibited tampering with tombs or moving the remains of the dead. But even so, the traffic in relics continued and even grew throughout the Middle Ages.

PART IV

After the Invasions

17

A New Era

THE INVASIONS

The cradle of Christianity—the Holy Land—was near the eastern reaches of the Roman Empire. Out of that land, in a story too vast to even outline here, Christianity expanded eastward, to the point that by the eighth century—or even before—it had reached China. The history that we have followed up to this point is mostly our own history, that of Christianity within the borders of the Roman Empire. Beginning in the fourth century, but particularly during the fifth, a series of invasions led to the eventual disappearance of the Western Roman Empire and the survival of the Eastern Roman Empire, with its capital in Constantinople—usually called the Byzantine Empire, since Byzantium was the ancient name for Constantinople. That Byzantine Empire would last for another thousand years, until Constantinople fell to the Turks in 1453.

The Western regions of the Roman Empire included most of Western Europe and the north coast of Africa west of Egypt. Toward the north and the east, the traditional borders were the rivers Danube and Rhine. Although sometimes the Roman legions established outposts beyond those borders, such outposts did not last long and therefore had less impact on the cultures that emerged there. Most of the rest of Europe, east of the Rhine and north of the Danube, was less densely populated than the areas closer to the Mediterranean basin. Forests occupied much of the area, in which there were no major cities. There were certainly settlements whose life was based mostly on fishing and mining, but none of them was comparable to the Greek or Roman cities.

The Romans called all these people who lived beyond the great rivers "barbarians." Most among them were Germanic, which included various peoples such as the Visigoths, the Ostrogoths, the Vandals, the Franks, the Lombards, the Alemanni, and the Saxons. For a long time many of these various peoples had made incursions into imperial lands. At the beginning, these invasions were mostly in search of booty and slaves, and therefore did not lead to the establishment of barbarians within Roman territory. Slowly, but progressively, the situation was changing in various ways: first of all, the Romans themselves frequently imported mercenary troops from among the "barbarians." Some of them had even become the core of the imperial guard, and therefore many settled within Roman territory. Second, these peoples themselves were strongly pressed by a migratory wave that had begun centuries earlier in Mongolia and that now was being felt in the European Northeast. This led the Germanic people, threatened as they were by invaders from the east, to develop warrior societies in order to defend their traditional territories. Even so, many of the inhabitants of those planes north of the Danube and east of the Rhine were forced to move into the Roman Empire. Furthermore, the riches and comforts of the Roman Empire were highly desired by many among these barbarian neighbors. Pushed from the east and pulled from the west, many Germanic peoples settled within Roman territory, frequently invited by the Romans themselves in order to use them as buffers against further invasions. However, such immigrants did not always receive what they had been promised, so the Romans repeatedly found the need to suppress rebellions in the areas where Germanic peoples had settled. The most important case, which became a landmark in Roman history, was that of the Visigoths, who had settled within the borders of the Roman Empire at the invitation of Emperor Valens. When they did not receive what they had been promised, they rebelled. In the great battle of Hadrianopolis in 378, the Visigoths crushed the imperial troops and killed the emperor himself. Then they sacked the Balkans and, marching along the shores of the Adriatic Sea, they invaded Italy. In 410 they took and sacked Rome—an event of such importance that it is frequently used to mark the end of antiquity and the beginning of the Middle Ages. From Rome the Visigoths continued northward, proceeding along the south of what now is France and finally settling in Spain. There they established a Visigothic kingdom that persisted until the Arab invasions in 711. Meanwhile, the Franks had crossed the Rhine and taken much of what today is France. The Vandals crossed the same river, marched through France and Spain, crossed the Strait of Gibraltar, and conquered the ancient Roman territories in North Africa. They then sailed back to Sicily, and in 455 they too sacked Rome.

Although these repeated invasions produced great damage to crops, and sacked monasteries and other cultural centers, their purpose was not to destroy the empire, but rather to settle within it and to enjoy the advantages of its civilization. For this reason, even though soon various Germanic chieftains called themselves kings, for a long time they considered themselves subjects of the empire, rendering at least verbal homage to their rulers. Even after the last western emperor was officially deposed in 476, some Germanic kings still considered themselves part of an empire whose capital was now in Constantinople. When, more than three hundred years later, in 800, the papacy gave the title of "emperor" to Charlemagne, he was the ruler of one of the ancient kingdoms resulting from the Germanic invasions—the kingdom of the Franks.

When they crossed the Roman borders, most of these invading peoples brought with them the paganism of their ancestors. Those who were already Christian, mainly the Goths and Vandals, were Arian—that is, they did not accept the Trinitarian doctrine as it had been defined in the councils of Nicaea (325) and Constantinople (381). The reason was that when Christianity entered the lands of the Goths, Arianism was politically dominant in Constantinople, and this was the form of Christianity that the Goths—and later the Vandals—adopted. Therefore, a consequence of these invasions was that Arianism, which had never been strong in the West, now became an important issue there.

Saying much in detail about worship in the Germanic Arian churches is impossible. Most of the languages did not have a written form. The main exception was Gothic, which had been reduced to writing by Bishop Ulphilas—usually credited with taking Christianity to the area—in order to translate the Bible into their language. (Of note, Ulphilas did not translate some biblical books because he was afraid that their frequent description of wars and battles would exacerbate the bellicosity of the Goths.) With little written record, it is difficult to know the shape that worship took in the Germanic churches after the invasions. The lack of written languages would mean wide use of short, fixed formulae, but not extensive written prayers. Those formulae seem to have existed for some time. In a writing falsely attributed to Augustine (*Collation against Pascentius*; PL 33:1162), we are told that in Africa it was not only the Vandals, but even the Romans themselves who, instead of saying in Latin *Domine miserere* (Lord have mercy), said in Vandalic, *Sihora armen*.

It was not only the lack of a written language, but also the social and cultural structures that developed after the invasions that eventually led to the use of Latin as the main liturgical language throughout the former Western Roman Empire. (We say "main" liturgical language because for centuries in some areas, particularly in Rome itself, Greek was also used with some frequency.) The conquerors were a minority in the land they had conquered. Thanks to their military might, they became an aristocracy that others must honor and obey. But that minority did not have the cultural requirements necessary to administer the lands it had conquered. In most cases, not only did they not know how to read, but it was actually impossible to write in their own language. Thus, that aristocracy of power surrounded itself with a Latin-speaking bureaucracy—a bureaucracy recruited among the con-quered—that was necessary for the proper management of their lands. Also, Latin was the only language in which the leaders of the different Germanic kingdoms could communicate, which had two consequences that would lead to the same result: First, much of the economic and cultural management of the new Germanic kingdoms was left in the hands of people who spoke Latin and had been educated in that culture. Second, the new conquering aristocracy had great interest in learning about the land and culture of the conquered—particularly that their children would learn them also. Eventu-ally, jointly with the language and culture they also absorbed the religion of the conquered.

Even apart from religious considerations, the consequences of this process remain noticeable today in that almost all the Roman lands conquered by the invaders now speak Romance languages—that is, languages derived mostly from Latin. The most noticeable exceptions are some lands along the banks of the Rhine, England, and North Africa. What happened in North Africa was that both Latin and Vandal disappeared as a result of the Arab conquests.

Apparently one of the main reasons that Germanic Arians often clung to Arianism was that it became an affirmation for many of their own national and cultural inheritance. Shortly after the invasions themselves, in 496, the king of the Franks, Clovis, who had been a pagan, was baptized into the Nicene faith. Eventually the descendants of all the invaders—including those who had been Arians—accepted the same faith, although the process took centuries. In that process, the final turning point seems to have been the conversion of the Visigothic king of Spain in 589.

For all these reasons, almost immediately after the invasions Latin had become the lingua franca for business administration and liturgy among both the Arians and the Nicene.

However, this predominance of Latin also had strange consequences. The destruction of the ancient empire, jointly with the dominance of people speaking various Germanic languages, led to an evolution such that soon Latin—which had once been lingua franca of the entire area, and was still the only language in which scholars and traders from different areas could communicate—was no longer anyone's native language. As time passed, con-gregations could understand less and less of what was being said in worship, and consequently the rift grew between the learned and the clergy on the one hand and the majority population on the other.

Another factor was the growing importance of monastic life, which also left its imprint on the manner in which all believers understood faith and devotion. There were now two styles or levels of Christian obedience. Much of what earlier had been expected of all the faithful now became the practice of monastics, while less was required of the people at large. The sharing of goods so that everyone's needs were met, which had been the ideal and often the practice of earlier Christians, now became the hallmark of the monastic life. What used to be the priesthood of all believers as part of the priestly people of God, and was expressed in the prayer of the faithful, now became the particular task of monastic communities, which devoted long hours to intercession for the rest of the population, which in turn simply laid its former priestly tasks on the shoulders of monastics. Beginning in the sixth century, the Rule of St. Benedict, which followed older practices by including eight periods of prayer every twenty-four hours, spread throughout the Latin-speaking West. Besides prayer, much of the common worship in convents and monasteries was devoted to reading the Psalms. At first in a few monastic houses, but eventually in practically all of them, the study of Scripture and other religious books—and often also copying them—became one of the main tasks of residents.

As we shall see, the catechumenate continued losing importance until it eventually disappeared, and what eventually took its place for the most devout was the novitiate in a monastery or convent. In some monastic communities people entered the novitiate who had only a rudimentary knowledge of Christian faith.

Eventually this entire process led to the disappearance of the old prayer of the faithful, which reflected the vision of the church as a priestly people, so that baptism itself made a believer part of the holy priesthood of God. The prayer of the faithful continued in both East and West into the sixth century, when it generally disappeared from Western liturgies. Sometimes there was a similar prayer after the homily, which now implied that the people were no longer part of the holy priesthood, but rather those who respond to the teachings and expectations of the priesthood. As time passed, the priestly prayer of the people completely disappeared except in some special prayers for Holy Week, particularly Wednesday and Friday. The Wednesday prayer disappeared in the eighth century. Thus, during the rest of the Middle Ages and until a fairly recent date, the only significant vestige of the ancient prayer of the faithful was a series of particular prayers for Good Friday.

THE IMPACT OF THE INVASIONS ON WORSHIP: PREACHING

In each part of this study we have not sought to mention all worship practices but rather to focus on the most important. Likewise, but even more so, here we cannot follow every liturgical development after the invasions. Therefore, as in previous sections, here we deal particularly with preaching, then move on to baptism and preparation for it, followed by Communion, and finally we address the places of worship and devout practices.

There is no doubt that, after the great preachers whom we discussed in the previous section—Basil, Chrysostom, Ambrose, Augustine, and Leo—the period we are now starting lacks any comparable luminary, partly due to the general decline of letters after the invasions, and partly to the degree to which Communion eclipsed preaching. From the earliest times, worship had included both preaching—in the "service of the Word"—and Communion—the "service of the Table." In short, during the first part of worship the essentials of Christian life and faith were explained and commended, and this gave meaning to the second part, which focused on Communion. Likewise, this second part was designed to show and practice the life and faith explained verbally in the first. Words explained action, and action applied the words; the homily presented Communion, and Communion put the homily in practice.

Beginning toward the end of the fifth century, the nature of the homily changed drastically. Preaching remained, but now under a different form and with different tones. In the East, many sermons became philosophical and theological disquisitions over complex questions of Christology that supposedly had been resolved by the Council of Chalcedon in 451, but in fact continued under debate for centuries. Within that context, homilies frequently used the Bible only as an arsenal of arguments against adversaries. In the West, mostly as a result of the lack of education on the part of the clergy, so that many had difficulty with reading and with Latin, homilies were generally devoted to setting the rules and practices of the church or—as a response to the often reigning chaos—to moral teachings and threats of punishment to those who did not follow the teachings. The Scriptures that were supposed to be the main subject of preaching were often reduced to a prop supporting the rules set by the church. In East and West preaching lost the vibrant and lively tone that had characterized it in times of Augustine, Chrysostom, and Leo.

There were distinguished preachers, but they didn't reach the level of their predecessors. In the West, the most famous was Gregory the Great, who was bishop of Rome from 590 until his death in 604. There is no doubt that Gregory was convinced that preaching was important, especially since the decline of the catechumenate left people with no more than a very superficial understanding of Christianity. But from the point of view of style, and as literature, his sermons do not have the elegance and order of those of Chrysostom or Augustine. Clearly, Gregory understood that expounding Scripture in preaching was necessary, and therefore most of his homilies that have survived deal with the book of Ezekiel, and the rest with the Gospels. But in truth Gregory was more significant for his abilities in administering and organizing society—and thereby restoring some of the lost order—than as a preacher. While he considered preaching an important responsibility, his own emphasis on miracles that supposedly had taken place in connection with Communion stressed the significance of Communion over preaching.

THE IMPACT OF THE INVASIONS ON WORSHIP: BAPTISM

The new era also brought about changes in baptism. Such changes are particularly noticeable in two areas: the preparation for baptism and its administration.

Regarding the first, one immediately notes the decline of the catechumenate. Already in the fourth century, shortly after Constantine, the catechumenate began facing difficulties as ever larger numbers wished to join the church and there were not enough believers sufficiently prepared to lead in their catechesis. At least until the middle of the fifth century, the church was still able to offer substantial catechesis, as may be seen in the abundant catechetical documents of the time—among them the *Catechetical Lectures* of Cyril of Jerusalem, which were one of our main sources for dealing with this subject in part 3.

Particularly after the invasions, the catechumenate began its rapid decline. This was partly due to the increasingly common practice of baptizing recently born infants, which obviously made it impossible to catechize them before baptism. During the period immediately after Constantine, the lack of catechesis resulting from this factor had partially been supplied by the instruction that took place in the service of the Word, with its extensive Bible readings and homilies explaining the meaning of the text itself as well as its relevance for daily life. At that point, whoever had been baptized as a child at least had the opportunity to learn the rudiments of the Christian faith by listening to the biblical readings and the homiletic exposition.

After the invasions it became necessary to catechize enormous multitudes who spoke various languages, and in general did not understand the language of the catechists. As a result, the catechumenate was abbreviated. Traditionally, it was expected to last two or three years. In 305—and therefore a few years before Constantine, a synod in Elvira, on the outskirts of what today is Granada, had ordered that the catechumenate should last two years. Slightly over two centuries later, in 506, a synod gathered in what now is France reduced that time to eighty days. And less than a century later Gregory the Great gave instructions that it should last forty days—which often coincided with Lent.

Another factor undermining the significance of the catechumenate was that many of the invaders and their descendants retained much pagan religiosity and customs. The constant support of the state and society to the church gave the impression that there was little difference between being a Christian and being part of civil society, so that people who had grown up in the general culture and society did not have to change much in their perspectives and actions, nor to learn much about Christianity before receiving baptism—and even after it.

Earlier chapters showed that administration of baptism also evolved. From a very early time it was expected that baptism was to be done by immersion and preferably in running water. Even then, using water in a pool was allowed, as was also—in cases of extreme scarcity of water—baptizing by simply pouring water over the head three times. Later, as the notion developed that in order to be saved one had to be baptized, "clinical baptisms"—that is, baptisms given on a deathbed—became more common. Since in that case immersion was not possible, the person baptized had water poured over the head three times. Thus was Constantine baptized. We have already encountered some debates regarding the validity of such baptism, but eventually it was generally accepted.

Likewise, as the conclusion was generally reached that baptism was necessary for salvation, infant baptism—especially of those who seemed to be in peril of death—became ever more common, perhaps a sort of clinical baptism similar to what was done earlier with adults.

Note that, except in the case of the very frail, all baptisms, of children as well of us adults, were still normally by immersion. Naturally, in a society that expected everyone to be a believer, the baptism of adults became rare, and usually was administered to someone from other lands, or to Jewish converts to Christianity. Later, whole contingents of "barbarians" defeated by Christians were forced to receive baptism. Such was the case when Charlemagne defeated the Saxons. Such adults, as well as healthy infants, were baptized by a triple immersion—that is, they were submerged three times in the name of the Father, the Son, and the Holy Spirit.

Baptism by aspersion did not become the common practice of the church until much later—and even then only in the Western church, for Eastern churches such as the Greek, the Russian, and others continued baptizing children by immersion. Apparently, the first area where aspersion became the common practice was the frigid European north. If, as it was then thought, baptism was necessary for salvation, it could not be postponed because of inclement weather. A weak newborn or a sick person in danger of death had to be baptized immediately, no matter how cold the temperature might be. In such cases it was obviously not wise to break the ice and dip the person in the water under it, and therefore the practice of an aspersion as suggested much earlier by the *Didache* became common. However, baptism by immersion continued as the common practice in Rome at least until the twelfth century, and even to this day is still the norm in the Eastern churches.

Finally, still on the subject of baptism, there was another notable change. In the ancient church the most common and preferred practice was to baptize all the catechumens who were ready on the same day, Easter Sunday. If for any reason some who were ready for baptism could not receive it on that day, they were baptized on Pentecost. But now, since supposedly baptism was absolutely necessary for salvation, and somehow erased all sin committed before it, it was necessary to baptize people—particularly those in danger of death—as soon as possible. This resulted in setting aside the relationship between baptism and the resurrection of Jesus—a relationship that did not need much emphasis or explanation when baptism was received on Resurrection Sunday, and after a period of preparation culminating with fasting on Good Friday. The connection between baptism and the crossing of the Red Sea and of the Jordan was equally eclipsed. Now it was customary to offer baptism any day and any time, frequently separating it from the celebration of Communion, from congregational worship, and with no reference to baptism as the act of joining the people of God.

THE IMPACT OF THE INVASIONS ON WORSHIP: COMMUNION

Long before the period we are studying, some of the most illustrious leaders of the church—Ambrose, for instance—believed that the consecrated eucharistic bread had miraculous powers. Now, as the choir sang hymns that the congregation often did not understand and liturgy was ever more elaborate and mysterious, the celebration of Communion—the Mass—began to be regarded as an almost magical moment in which a person with special powers produced a miracle. This miracle was such that in order to approach and take Communion a very rigorous preparation was necessary, and therefore it became increasingly common to be satisfied with merely being present when the miracle took place. Eventually, as people understood Latin less and less, the celebration of the Mass in that language was surrounded by even deeper mystery. As is well known, it was against all this, which had reached an extreme, that the Protestant reformers of the sixteenth century protested—a protest that eventually found echoes in the Roman Catholic Church in the documents of the Second Vatican Council in the twentieth century.

The emphasis on Communion as a miraculous event that took place through the words of the priest increased the clergy's authority and made preaching less important. This was particularly the case in the Western church, for the Roman Mass generally omitted—or did not stress—the epiclesis, the prayer asking the Holy Spirit to bless the consecrated elements. The most important function of the priest became the consecration of bread and wine in Communion. While one had to be ordained to perform such consecration, this was not necessary for preaching. In a word, the pastor, whose function had earlier been partly similar to the prophets and rabbis of earlier times, became more a priest than a prophet, and more an officiant than a preacher. His authority was no longer that of a teacher but rather that of a representative of higher authorities. His gestures and vestments gained importance, while his homilies lost it. With the passing of time, there were occasions when the homily completely disappeared, and its place was taken by parish announcements, explaining church rules, and a few words promoting moral standards.

By this time the Eucharist had clearly become the center of worship—and for some people practically its totality. However, Communion at that time differed in many ways from what it had been in earlier times. First, the ancient service of the Word had essentially disappeared. Second, Latin had now become the language of the church and therefore was the language to be used in the liturgy. It was now a dead language that scholars employed to communicate across language barriers, but was not anybody's mother tongue. This meant that people attending worship did not understand much of what was being said. They came, even though they did not understand, because what happened there was the very center of their faith. They did not come to partake in Communion, but rather to look upon it. Communion became increasingly fearful. People were afraid of touching the consecrated elements and were convinced that in order to take Communion a high degree of purity was necessary. In such circumstances, the distance between clergy and laity became ever more pronounced, for the priest not only celebrated but also partook of the sacrament, and the laity simply witnessed and admired. This came to such a point that in 1215 the Fourth Lateran Council had to decree that all believers must take Communion at least once a year, preferably on Easter. The seeds of the tragic situation that this decree sought to correct had been sown much earlier, in the changes that took place beginning in the fifth century.

The situation was aggravated by the increasing importance in the Christian calendar and in popular faith of the saints and the person of Mary. While earlier there had been a few dates when the life of a distinguished martyr was commemorated, now there was a detailed daily calendar where the commemoration of saints left little room for the central themes of Christian faith.

PLACES AND PRACTICES

In chapter 16, when discussing the places of worship in the times immediately following Constantine, we referred to basilicas and other buildings devoted to worship. In describing those basilicas, we spoke mostly of their interior, with their elaborate decorations and symbolism. We also said something about the distribution of the various leaders and participants in worship within the building. In all their splendor, the basilicas of the fourth century were still places for the people to gather for worship. In this sense they were a continuation of the ancient houses that had been adapted to be places of worship, such as the one in Dura-Europos. At first, the invasions of the fourth and fifth centuries—and others that followed—hampered the continuation of that tradition in the West, although not in the East. Witness to this is the great Cathedral of St. Sophia in Constantinople—now Istanbul—which was built by Justinian in the sixth century (and whose name did not mean that it was dedicated to a saint named Sophia, but rather that it was consecrated to Jesus Christ, the holy Wisdom [in Greek, *Sophia*] of God).

When the kings and potentates of the new Germanic kingdoms began building their own churches, in what today we call the Romanesque style, these became, jointly with castles and palaces, the main buildings in European cities. Still those Romanesque churches were built as a place to meet for worship. The decorations and symbols were mostly inside the building. And if that space inside was not as splendorous as later Gothic cathedrals, this was not for lack of interest, but rather for lack of light, for Romanesque construction, for structural reasons, did not allow for great windows adorning the nave. Then came the greatest contribution of Western Christianity to ecclesiastical and architectonic style, the Gothic cathedrals. When today we approach those cathedrals seeing them from the outside and compare them with the ancient Romanesque constructions, we immediately note that their splendor is not only in the interior, but also outside, in façades, gates, towers, and gargoyles. While earlier churches were built mostly to be seen from inside, now they were being built also to be seen from outside. This was due not only to new methods of construction but also to significant demographic and theological developments.

The most ancient churches had been built in times when the population at large was not Christian, and therefore they were above all a place for believers to meet. After the conversion of the Germanic peoples both to Christianity and to the Nicene faith, the distinction between civil society and the community of the church disappeared. Except for Jews, all the population was at least nominally Christian. Now the church building was no longer primarily a place for believers to meet but the place to which the entire community looked in aspiration to eternity.

Demographically, the great Gothic cathedrals—as well as the smaller churches imitating them in other places—had become like great reliquaries in which the consecrated bread was kept and cherished—bread that was literally, according to the theology of the time, the very body of Christ. It was a time when relics of martyrs and saints—most of them of dubious authenticity—enjoyed high veneration. A bone of a martyr, a piece of St. Martin's cape, a nail from the cross of Christ, or a few drops of milk from the Virgin were considered worthy of beautiful reliquaries of gold and silver encrusted with precious stones. Likewise, but even more so, the consecrated host, now become the very body of Christ sacrificed for believers, reserved in the tabernacle where it was preserved after the Mass, and the always burning lamp announcing its presence, was encased in the enormous reliquary that was the entire building, whose splendor witnessed to the inestimable value of the consecrated bread that was kept in it.

Having said all this, while there may be reason to deplore or at least question much of the liturgical development of those times, we must at least mention their most important contributions to Christian worship. The first of these is Gregorian chant. Although named after Pope Gregory the Great, who reigned from 590 to 604, and even though some of its early adumbrations may have been Gregory's contemporary, it was only much later, in the ninth century, that it was first called "Gregorian," apparently in an effort to attribute it to a distinguished figure in antiquity. It is plain chant that has only a melodic line—a monody—and normally no musical accompaniment. Its origins may be traced to several musical traditions, some of which have already been mentioned earlier, combining Hebrew and Greek elements with the plain chant that for a long time had been used in order to help the projection of the voice. Although such chant was common in the cathedrals, great churches, and monasteries, in the village churches worship was less elaborate. At any rate, Gregorian chant became the most common form of liturgical music in the West and was employed not only for the Mass itself but also for the singing of Psalms and other texts in monastic houses. There is no doubt that Gregorian chant is one of the main sources of all Western music, sacred as well as secular.

The other main contribution of those difficult times to worship is much more important, for it is no less than the very preservation of Scripture.

Today we have very few manuscripts dating from before the invasions and their tragic consequences. The Bible has come to us mostly through a long chain of believers, mostly monastics, with whose theology we might not agree. However, by copying and recopying Scripture these monastics have bequeathed it to us, and with it have also left us a legacy of high respect for the written Word of God.

Therefore, no matter how dark those times may seem to us, they left lights that still illumine our days.

18

Epilogue

Today's Worship between Yesterday and Tomorrow

Throughout this historical survey we have seen the church worship the same God and with the same principles, but in changing situations that have resulted also in changes in worship itself. At first glance, it is easy to look at these changes as a process of decay, as if a pristine worship in the primitive church, pure and inspiring, had then followed a process of constant loss with a few attempts at reformation and restoration. Were that the case, all we would need would be to restore Christian worship as it was conducted during the time of Judeo-Christianity. Some groups today claim to be restoring that early worship by simply adding a few Hebrew phrases or some other element taken from practices in the synagogue. But in truth the matter is much more complex. For one thing, in the New Testament itself we already see difficulties and disagreements regarding worship. And even more, if worship is a dialogue between the people and God, this means that the circumstances of each time and church or congregation must be reflected in worship. Thus, the easy solution of trying to restore primitive Christian worship, besides being impossible, would lead to a form of worship completely disconnected from the circumstances of the worshiping church.

A second solution that might appeal to some is trying to find which of those periods in the past is most like ours, and then take it as a paradigm for the renewal of our worship. However, this also is excessively simplistic, for it takes for granted a uniformity that does not exist in the church today, worshiping as it does in various places, cultures, and conditions. This supposed solution is not really feasible.

Thus, our task here is not to seek the restoration of primitive Christian worship or to find some other period worthy of wholesale imitation. The task is to reflect on what we may learn from each of those periods that may be a help or a warning within our present context. Given the diversity within the church today, it is quite possible that different communities of faith may find different lessons and warnings in various periods.

Therefore, by way of suggestions, in this last chapter we shall simply summarize some of the characteristics of each period and consider ways in which they may be helpful to today's church. As we do this, an initial step in a process of reflection may be to ask how our present circumstances are similar or different than those that existed in each of the four periods into which we have divided our narrative. On the basis of that reflection, we may then consider what lessons we may learn from the experience of each of those past times. This is not a simple matter, for it is not just a question of determining which of the four periods is most like ours, but rather of considering what elements, circumstances, and forms of worship in each of those past periods seem more relevant to our present situation, and then exploring ways of applying what we have learned to our present-day worship.

THE FIRST PERIOD: JUDEO-CHRISTIANITY

At first, it may well seem that the conditions of the church during the period of Judeo-Christianity were completely different from what we now know or have known, for in our faith communities the presence of Jewish people who have embraced Christianity is minimal. But if we look deeper into our own history and our present situation, we see many points of contact and similarities between our circumstances and those of early Christianity.

Since the nineteenth century was the great period of expansion of Protestant Christianity, many of us, being heirs to the legacy of that period, learned our worship practices at a time when we still thought that the West would forever be the center of Christianity. This was Christendom, and the rest of the world was the "mission field"—some even called it "Heathendom." We also took for granted that Protestantism was eminently rational and modern, and tended to transmit such views to those in other lands who joined our faith. When modernity, with its rampant rationalism, came to the intellectual foreground in the West, Roman Catholicism resisted it. The *Syllabus of Errors* issued by Pius IX is a stark summary of all that conservative Catholicism believed to be wrong in modernity. Taking the opposite tack, many Protestant leaders, theologians, and entire denominations embraced modernity. The debates in the early twentieth century between Catholics and Protestants were in many ways a debate about modernity. Worship in the vernacular became a hallmark of Protestantism. As a result, even the most conservative Protestant churches were proud of worship services that people could understand. Being able to understand everything became a goal of modern Protestant worship. Many also ridiculed the mysterious and almost magical worship of Roman Catholicism, in a language that worshipers could not understand. Carried to an extreme, this view meant that mystery had little place in worship. Baptism was not an act of God. If it was infant baptism, it was a symbol of God's love for us, and of our commitment to raise this child as a Christian. If it was an adult baptism, it was a witness that the person gave to his or her faith. Something similar happened with Communion, whose value was in the thoughts and feelings it provoked in believers.

All this was justified by means of a return to early Christian worship, now interpreted in modern, rationalistic ways. Early Christian worship was indeed highly didactic, for teaching was one of the main purposes of the "service of the Word." But on this frail principle was built much of the worship we experienced growing up. Since we stressed the importance of people understanding all that was done in worship, we were told and were convinced that ours was simply a restoration of the earliest Christian worship.

While teaching is an important element in worship, the worship of Judeo-Christianity also reminds us of another important dimension that must not be forgotten. It is now time to rediscover and reassert the inherently mysterious nature of worship. We must still find ways to enhance the didactic dimension of worship, and yet at the same time to stress and experience its inherent mystery. In both of these endeavors the worship of Judeo-Christianity may be helpful. Particularly, we would be greatly helped were we to rediscover and to experience anew that our present worship is joined by the worship of all creation and of the heavenly host.

THE SECOND PERIOD: FROM 100 TO 313 CE

We turn now to the second period, when the church became mostly Gentile in origin. It was a time when the church was harshly persecuted by imperial authorities and at the same time threatened by a series of doctrines that had to be refuted and rejected. This led to the development of an entire catechetical system whose purpose was to make certain that converts from paganism truly understood Christian life and doctrines, and that they were ready to follow them. At the same time, the new situation led to an emphasis on the study of Scripture—which had always been important in the life of the synagogues, but now became urgent in the face of the need to educate new converts so that they would be able to recognize and reject the many false teachings that were circulating. The first Christian generations, practically all Jews or at least God-fearers, had known the essential elements of the faith of Israel. Even before their conversion to Christianity they had worshiped in the temple and the synagogue, and knew much of the faith and traditions of Israel. What they had learned in such worship they brought into the church—while also leaving behind some other practices as the breach grew between church and synagogue. Before they became Christians, they had learned that Israel, as the people of God, found its identity in the history of the great actions of God—creation, the exodus, the return from exile, and so on. Therefore, the church also, as the people of God, was to find its identity in the same history, interpreting it now as preparation for what God had done in Christ.

Most of us who live in what was once called Christendom grew up within a context in which a Christian background was taken for granted. People did not have to be taught in church that there is only one God, that this God is Creator of all things, that God requires a certain behavior. Nor did they need to be taught that there is a Bible through which God speaks, or the stories of the exodus, the years in the desert, and so forth. This meant that when someone decided to join the church all that they needed was some general instruction on the particular form of government and theological emphases of the denomination or congregation they were joining, and they were considered ready for baptism. Something similar happened when Protestantism arrived in the traditionally Catholic countries of Latin America. People already knew that there was a Bible—although many had never seen one—that there is one God, that this God is triune, that there are certain moral principles to Christian life, and so forth. All that was needed was for them to accept the specific tenets of Protestantism, and they were considered ready for baptism. Thus, the catechetical system was neglected. Many churches and denominations had "membership classes" lasting a few weeks where what was taught was not the essentials of Christianity but rather the particular characteristics of the community of faith that the person was preparing to join. What was called "evangelism" was not really telling the good news to people who had not heard it, but rather reviving in them an apparently dormant faith.

Today Christendom is gone. The traditionally Christian countries of the West have become increasingly secularized, and as a consequence a growing number of people have very little idea of the basic tenets of Christianity, except the distorted views that are often expressed in popular media and in politics. Thus, in the current more secularized lands of former Christendom we are rediscovering the need for restoring some form of the catechetical system. We can no longer take for granted that people know what Christianity is all about. Together with a recovery of the catechetical system, we need to recover the didactic dimension that the service of the Word had in the early church. The sermon can no longer be simply a moral exhortation, nor an inspiring experience, but must help a congregation understand more deeply the meaning of Scripture and of the gospel. In this, the church outside the former lands of Christendom may have much to teach us. They have had to develop systems for helping people proceeding from all sorts of religious and cultural backgrounds to understand the relevance of the gospel for their situation. This means that now, with the demise of Christendom, they find themselves ahead of the older churches of Christendom, which must turn to them for guidance in the restoration of the catechetical system in a modern and postmodern world. The same is true of evangelism: it is less and less a matter of a revival of a dormant faith, and more and more a telling of a frequently misunderstood narrative.

Unfortunately, today there are churches and places where believers do not seem to be aware of these new circumstances, and still take for granted that those who seek to join the church know the essentials of Christian faith. The result is that church members are often carried away by every wind of doctrine, by numerological calculations based on the books of Daniel and Revelation, by the gospel of prosperity, by various forms of "Christian" nationalism, by doctrines of racial supremacy, and by other similar modern heresies. The only solution is some form of restoration of the old catechetical system. Many churches are moving in this direction. Notably, the Roman Catholic Church has instituted the Rite of Christian Initiation of Adults (RCIA)—which is more than a rite, for it involves a restoration of the catechumenate. Several other churches throughout the world are following suit. In the process, churches in what used to be Christendom are finding guidance in the practices of churches that were never part of Christendom. The same is true of the task of communicating the gospel to unbelievers: what we used to call the "younger churches" are much more adept at this task that are the older churches of Christendom.

In brief, when we consider this second period in our narrative, we find that the church at that time was able to respond to its new circumstances when its membership no longer came mostly from a Jewish background. Its response was essentially an emphasis on the theological education of the people that could well serve as a model for us today. Thankfully, in many churches throughout the world today we find a growing interest in the study of Scripture and theology. This includes more careful study of Scripture, not in order to learn it by heart, or to be able to quote a particularly relevant verse in various situations, but rather to understand what it means to be part of the people of God, to join, to live, and to continue the biblical narrative.

THE THIRD PERIOD: FROM CONSTANTINE TO THE INVASIONS

As so often happens in history, this third period in Christian history caught the church unawares. Persecution had been raging for some time, and suddenly through a series of unexpected edicts the church found itself not only tolerated, but also favored and eventually even courted by the authorities. This was the beginning of what is usually called the "Constantinian era," whose main feature was a close relationship among church, culture, and state. Collaboration among these, while opening new paths for the proclamation of the gospel and for impacting society, also had negative consequences, many of which lasted for centuries. One such result was the growing distance between clergy and laity, between believers at large and monastics, men as well as women, who still shared goods, devoted time to the careful study of Scripture, and considered themselves a priestly community whose task was to pray for the rest of the world. While this made it possible for monastics to lead what they considered a profound Christian life, it allowed the rest of believers to place much of their Christian vocation on the shoulders of monastics, and therefore to feel relatively free from it.

Reflection on this period of our narrative brings into focus another set of opportunities and challenges. Suddenly, a church that up to that moment had been persecuted and belittled found itself respected and powerful. Many of its leaders discovered ways to use this new respect and power in order to oppose injustice, to promote justice, and to defend the unprotected. But in general a good part of the church was so surprised by its new prestige that it simply accepted the mantle of power without reflecting upon the dangers that this might entail. The consequence was that the church found itself wielding a power that it did not know how to administer in the light of the gospel.

Something similar happens today in churches that until recently were marginalized in society and now find themselves in positions of increasing power. In Latin America, Protestants who a few decades ago were a minuscule part of the population now find themselves growing at an explosive rate, and therefore courted by politicians, marketers, and others. The result is that churches that had long insisted on the need for both church and state to be protected from mutual interference now have changed their tune. This has come to a point where a church rejoiced because one of its members had become a dictator! Something similar is happening in other places. In the United States, some evangelical groups that were traditionally considered marginal to society, and even boasted of not being part of the mainstream culture, when they had the opportunity joined the centers of power and bowed before the powerful.

All of this also affects worship. One of the consequences of that third period for Christian worship was the growing distance between worship leaders and the body of believers. As the congregations grew enormously, and ceremonies became more ostentatious, it became necessary to make clear who held positions of authority and who did not. Therefore worship, which should have shown a different set of values, generally imitated the unequal structures of society. Unfortunately, something similar is happening today in many churches, whose worship becomes increasingly hierarchical, centering no longer on the believers, but rather on their supposed leaders, and thus reflecting the values and ordering of society at large. This has come to the point that in some churches worship leaders are called "worshipers," as if only they, and not all the people, were worshiping. And the role models for such leaders are often music idols and television shows.

There is, however, a positive side. This third period of our narrative was also the golden age both of preaching and of worship. The preaching of John Chrysostom, Ambrose, Basil, and Augustine has never been equaled. Their genius was that they knew how to use the best of the surrounding culture—of the Greek and Latin cultures that they had inherited from their ancestors—for preaching that was clear, elegant, and profound, but also simple and certainly based on the Word of God. They did not use the Bible to avoid difficult questions. Rather, the Bible forced them to face such questions, and to do this in faithful obedience, not to the emperor or to any earthly authority, but to the Word of God. In worship itself, that fourth century has left an imprint that can still be seen in much contemporary worship, from the simplest to the most elaborate. Those leaders knew that the best way to make certain that the people held to true doctrine and good theology is to have that doctrine and theology firmly expressed and supported in worship—not only in preaching, but also and in everything else that was said and done: songs, prayers, gestures, and so on. When it was necessary to present some theological point in such a way that it would take roots among the people, some of the great figures of the fourth century wrote hymns that shaped the faith of the people. Something similar is happening today in some of what we used to call the "younger churches," where there is great creativity particularly in music and singing.

This leads to another important aspect in which much of today's worship may be similar to the worship of that ancient church: worship as celebratory. The reason that Christians met the first day of the week was not to obey a law that God had issued, but rather to celebrate the resurrection of Jesus; to celebrate the first day of creation, which now also had become the first day of the new creation; and to celebrate the last day, when the new creation will come to full fruition. There certainly was a place for the confession of sins—which too often today our celebratory emphases seem to set aside. But even above that confession was a strong affirmation of God's saving grace. Furthermore, when confession is deep and painful, the joy is greater and more profoundly felt. Today we often see churches whose worship includes fewer expressions of joy, and another sort of worship where all seems to be a superficial joy. True Christian joy is based on the confession of sin and the experience of grace, and we cannot have one without the other. The recovery of joy in worship is one of the notes of contemporary worship. This is particularly noticeable in Communion services, which originally were a celebration of the resurrection, but for centuries became funereal. Today, as that celebratory nature of Communion is being restored, also the frequency of Communion is being restored among Protestants.

THE FOURTH PERIOD: AFTER THE INVASIONS

Finally, we turn briefly to the fourth period in our narrative—of which we have offered only a quick outline. This fourth period was a time of chaos that lasted for centuries. As part of a society in crisis, the church in the West was also shaken by disorder and the destruction of most of its physical and intellectual inheritance. Even so, the church served to bring a certain measure of order into society and to continue its ancient function as a priestly people whose task was to represent the world before the heavenly throne. In difficult times, people knew that there were some people praying constantly for them. When it became necessary to secure food for cities where hunger struck as a consequence of social and economic disorder, the church organized delivery of food and the rebirth of trade. In brief, the church was able to fulfill two functions: that of a priestly people and that of meeting various human needs.

Once again today we are living in a time of chaos, angst, and destruction. As we write the last lines of this book, the entire world suffers the consequences of a deadly pandemic. Partly as a result of that pandemic, chaos reigns in various parts of the globe. Elsewhere are increasingly oppressive governments and economic systems. The global economic crisis has led to surging unemployment, homelessness, and hunger. The injustice that was always there has been laid bare.

Within this context the church continues to gather for worship—frequently, due to the pandemic, not physically, but virtually. At this juncture, if we have learned something important from all the pages leading to this one, it is that when we worship we do not do so only on our own account. We are the priestly people whom God has raised to bring before the heavenly throne the pains, anguish, needs, and hopes of this suffering humanity. Therefore, we do not gather for the mere joy of gathering, nor even primarily for our own spiritual edification, but rather in order to raise our plaintive cry to the Lord of all creation, asking for the well-being not just of this body of Christ that is the church, but also for all of creation, which also rests in the eternal hands of God.

However, we must care lest we become satisfied with nice words and self-justification. We must confess that, as we look at the entire church, the topic of worship, which should be joining all of us in a single praise to the one and only God, instead of doing so has divided us and continues dividing us. Some want a certain kind of music; others, another. Some prefer calm and quiet worship; others would rather raise a joyful noise. Some prefer to pray in silence; others seem to believe that the louder the prayer, the better it is. And so on. In the midst of all this that some have named "worship wars," the love that is to be the light of believers flickers, faith becomes rancor, and witness is eclipsed.

To all this is added another negative consequence: deceiving ourselves into thinking that the answer to the challenges of this day lies in one of these many solutions proposed in our worship wars. Rather than truly delving into the heart of the matter, we deal only with issues that in the last analysis are superficial.

TOWARD A RADICAL TRANSFORMATION OF OUR WORSHIP

Perhaps the first step for the reformation of our worship is to leave aside for the moment the so-called worship wars and, in a sort of armistice of faith, consider what the practices and experiences of the ancient church may teach us. In the Introduction to this study we have suggested some possible paths along those lines. In suggesting those paths, we are in no way calling the church today to imitate what was done centuries ago. Such an imitation would be another easy, superficial, and therefore not very useful response to the needs of today. What we are suggesting is not that we ask how the church worshiped or prayed in ancient times, or what words they said, or what kind of music they sang, but rather what was the basic vision they had of worship and its function.

In the face of this question, we must begin by affirming that the ancient church teaches us that true worship is always bidirectional. In worship we speak to God, and God responds. God not only speaks but also awaits our response. Any worship that is only praise, in which we shout and sing about how good and great God is, is only half of what it ought to be. Worship is a dialogue between God and God's people. In worship God speaks to us and we respond. In worship also we speak to God and God responds. If in this dialogue the Word of God promises us a kingdom of peace, justice, and love, our worship requires that we live in peace, justice, and love. If we praise God for the liberality with which we receive gifts from on high—life, church, goods, all of creation—we must also be ready to listen to what God tells us regarding the proper use of such gifts. It is not enough to say, "Lord, we thank you for giving us life." We also have to say, "Lord, our lives are yours, use them as you wish." If God's Word shows how sinful we are, that Word also demands a response of confession and repentance. Such a response allows us truly to hear words of grace and forgiveness. On the basis of that grace and forgiveness, God calls us to a newness of life. If through God's Word we are promised a kingdom of peace, justice, and love, our worship requires that we respond with decisions and actions of peace, justice, and love.

This takes us to the second great learning of this study, which we must stress. The present church's worship is part of a much vaster worship, glorious and overwhelming, that takes place in heaven in the presence of the throne of the most high. The worship that Revelation describes in incomparable metaphors and images is the true and eternal worship to God. What the church does meanwhile is to participate in that worship, to enjoy a foretaste of it, to prepare for the glory of day when it too will sing with angels and archangels and all the heavenly host that no one can count.

Another important lesson that we draw from our present study is that worship is not about the praise of the individual believer to God, and God's answer to that individual, but it is also and above all the praise that the entire people of God addresses to God, and God's answer to that people. Part of the purpose of worship is to form us, to shape us as disciples of Christ. But that formation is not primarily individual, for what it does is to shape all of us into members of the body of Christ, to graft us into this people that God is creating for Godself. It is as fellow citizens that we prepare for the final kingdom where our true citizenship already is. In a word, a fundamental purpose of worship that must always be remembered is the forming and strengthening of the people of God—not only or primarily of its individual members, but of all of them jointly as a single people.

Here we find the main and most tragic difference between ancient Christian worship and much of our worship today. At this point the ancient church has much to teach us. The individualism of our time and culture makes it difficult for us to see the importance of the church for Christian life. Each of us goes to church to offer God our own praise. In ancient times one went to church to join the enormous choir that in various parts of the world and even among the heavenly host sings the praise of God. Today we go to church to learn more about God—and that is good. But rarely do we think that we go to church in order to learn and to practice what it means to be the people of God. Today we even hear that we go to church to fill the gas tank and thereby be able to face the hazards of one more week of life. Certainly, worship gives us strength to face the joys and difficulties of life, but that is not the main function of the church.

The main function of the church, as we see it in the New Testament, is to be the people of God, just as in the Old Testament the main function of Israel is to be the people of God. The worship life of the church must be the anvil on which this people is shaped. Worship must be such that it helps us be truly the people of God and the body of Christ. This is true of each local church, and is also true of the church as a whole. Today it is common to think that I go to church in order to strengthen "my faith"—or perhaps the faith of "my family" or of "my children." Certainly, the church does that. But what is important is not my faith, or my obedience, or my holiness, but rather the faith, obedience, and holiness of this people, of this body that we call "church."

In conclusion, ancient Christian worship can serve as a guide, not so that we may imitate it, but so that we may rediscover the deep roots of its undeniable power. If we study it carefully, if we go to the same sources from which that worship drank, we may be able to leave to future generations a legacy similar to what our ancient ancestors in faith left us.

Meanwhile, to God be the glory, and let us continue rejoicing as we sing with angels and archangels, "Holy, Holy, Holy, Lord God of hosts, full are heaven and earth of your glory: Glory be to you, O Lord most high."

Index

CPSIA information can be obtained
at www.ICGtesting.com
Printed in the USA
BVHW032148301122
652718BV00033B/491